Internet-based Distance Learning

Internet -based Distance Learning

Indira Madhukar

AUTHORSPRESS

Worldwide Circulation through Authorspress Global Network
First Published 2002
Reprinted 2004, 2006
Reprinted 2007
by Authorspress

E-35/103, Jawahar Park
Laxmi Nagar, Delhi-110092

e-mail: authorspress@yahoo.com

Typeset in NewCenturySchlbk by Chitra Computers

Internet-based Distance Learning
ISBN 81-7273-086-1

Printed in India at Tarun Offset, Delhi.

Preface

The rapid changes taking place in the field of education is the consequences of various types of internet-based information handling technologies. The history of educational technology is littered with the high hopes and limited success of radio, film, TV, video, teaching machines, stand-alone computers and CD-ROM. If the facilities offered by computer networking and the still developing WWW are to fare better in the educational context than its predecessors, it must be closely integrated with tried and tested conventional teaching methods, and viewed neither as a panacea nor as a bolt-on extra. This point is clearly articulated for internet-based distance learning. The most important factor in the successful implementation and student uptake of online eduction is thorough, planned and supported integration with more traditional teaching media.

The internet technology deployed in education can help remove inequities between the schools of developed and developing nations, between inner cities and suburbs, between urban and rural areas. Internet can become the force that equalises the educational opportunities of a children regardless of location and social and economic circumstances. It will have an increasingly positive impact on the student's creativity. By placing a human face on the academic topics, web-based access to primary source materials can make learning come alive for many students. Educators are also great beneficiaries of the telematic revolution. It opens up new opportunities for casual dialogues on a wide range of topics, and helps overcome the sense of isolation sometimes felt by educators whose areas of interest have few local enthusiasts. In addition to conversing with peers, communication with learners, their parents, the community at large is facilitated with the same tools.

Though internet promises the panacea to better learning, sales hungry decision-makers have exploited it. Now it is faced with the challenge of maintaining the delicate balance between quality and quantity. Society has been credited with creating internet technology, but it is simultaneously creating society. Maintaining quality presupposes building a code of ethics into the internet infrastructure, just as science without responsibility is like a sword without a sheath; so too, internet-based distance learning without ethics will lead to gross debasement of human energies. The ethical values to bear in mind cannot be isolated from human values and responsibilities.

The use of internet in education is highly positive but the caveat is to avoid falling through the looking glass. The true challenge is for education to freeze a model that captures quality and computer technology into an integrated communication system. Such a blend will zoom educational goals to dizzy heights of sublimity. If we bear the key idea in our mind that the true power of educational technology comes not from replicating things that can be done in other ways but when required, do things that could not be done without it, we realise that most of our concerns are resolved.

The present book is devoted to analysing the impact of internet revolution on the educational world and discussing the relevance of the changes against the context of time and space, and the concerns that have emerged in consequence. It will an essential reference tool for academics, students, teachers, educators and to the public who are in search of alternative methods learning in response to the globalisation of education.

Indira Madhukar

Contents

1

Introduction

The internet has become one of the most important tools for educators and trainer of the 21st century. Internet-based distance learning (IDL) has become common in almost all the countries. Materials and courses of IDL, ranging from a simple syllabus to highly structured courses, are available in every nook and core of the world. Internet-based distance learning is a form of distance education in which the course contents are delivered and the interactions are provided by the technologies and methodologies of the internet. It is known as a media-rich, online environment that allows people to interact with others asynchronously or synchronously in collaborative environments; to gain access to remote multimedia databases for active, resource-based learning; and to manage self-paced, individual learning in a flexible way.

The transactional distance theory describes the pedagogical relationships existing in distance education environments that have the special characteristic of separation of one from another, and a consequent set of special teaching and learning behaviours. According to this theory, there are three key constituent elements of distance education: dialogue, structure, and learner autonomy. Dialogue refers to the extent to which teachers and learners can interact with each other, and structure refers to the responsiveness of an educational programme to learners. Learner autonomy is the extent to which learners make decisions regarding their own learning and construct their own knowledge based on their own experience.

The internet and the web help overcome the barriers of time and space in teaching and learning. Educators can play a role in the development of a vital form of literacy: the transformation of information into knowledge. The choices they make can also help determine which of these possibilities come to pass:

i) distance technologies as an add-on to existing institutions;
ii) 'knowledge in a box', impersonal, individualised, and socially isolating; or
iii) a networked learning society that keeps human relationships at the centre of learning.

Distance learning on the internet usually takes one of the following forms:

i) electronic mail (delivery of course materials, sending in assignments, getting/giving feedback, electronic discussion group);
ii) bulletin boards/newsgroups for discussion of special topics;
iii) downloading of course materials or tutorials;
iv) interactive tutorials on the web;
v) real-time, interactive conferencing using Multi-user Object Oriented (MOO) systems or Internet Relay Chat;
vi) intranets, corporate websites protected from outside access that distribute training for employees; and
vii) informatics, the use of online databases, library catalogues, and gopher and websites to acquire information and pursue research related to study.

The hypermedia contexts such as the web support constructivist approaches to learning, which are based on the belief that individuals construct their own understanding of the world as they acquire knowledge and reflect on experiences.

Learning at a distance can be both isolating and highly interactive, and electronic connectedness is a different kind of interaction than what takes place in traditional classrooms; some learners are not comfortable with it. Lack of non-verbal cues can create misunderstanding, but communications protocols can be established and relationships among learners developed.

Since humans are involved, social norms do develop in cyberspace, but they require new communications competencies. Online courses often feature consensus building and group projects, through which learners can develop skills in collaborating with distant colleagues and cooperating with diverse individuals. Such skills are increasingly needed in the global workplace.

If community is defined as shared interests, not geographic space, electronic communities are possible. Building a learning community is of critical importance to the creation of a successful virtual classroom. To succeed, distributed learning must balance virtual and direct interaction in sustaining communion among people.

Distance learning on the internet can be cheaper, faster, and usually more efficient than other learning modes, but not necessarily more effective. Access to data does not automatically expand students' knowledge; the availability of information does not intrinsically create an internal framework of ideas. To help learners make effective use of distance learning methods, skilled facilitation is essential.

The ways to overcome the challenges of the electronic classroom are given below:

i) establish the tone early in the course;
ii) to overcome the text-based nature of online discussion and to build group rapport and cohesion, introduce

participants to each other, match them with partners, and assign group projects;

iii) offer training and guidelines to help learners acquire technical competence and manage discussions;

iv) provide a variety of activities, such as debates, polling, reflection, and critique; and

v) use learning contracts to establish goals for participation.

The following strategies are intended to make distance learning more effective:

i) Understand the technology's strengths and weaknesses.

ii) Provide technical training and orientation.

iii) Plan for technical failures and ensure access to technical support.

iv) Foster learning-to-learn, self-directed learning, and critical reflection skills.

v) Develop information management skills to assist learners in selection and critical assessment.

vi) Mix modes—e.g., combine e-mail discussion with audio/video methods to enhance the social aspect.

vii) Structure learner-centred activities for both independent and group work that foster interaction.

Advantages of delivering distance learning on the internet include the following:

i) time and place flexibility;

ii) potential to reach a global audience;

iii) no concern about compatibility of computer equipment and operating systems;

iv) quick development time, compared to videos and CD-ROMs;

v) easy updating of content, as well as archival capabilities; and
vi) usually lower development and operating costs.

Carefully designed internet courses can enhance interactivity between instructors and learners and among learners, which is a serious limitation of some distance learning formats. Equity is often mentioned as a benefit of online learning; the relative anonymity of computer communication has the potential to give voice to those reluctant to speak in face-to-face situations and to allow learner contributions to be judged on their own merit, unaffected by any obvious visual cultural markers. The medium also supports self-directed learning—computer conferencing requires learner motivation, self-discipline, and responsibility.

Disadvantages of distance learning are described below.

i) At present, limited bandwidth and slow modems hamper the delivery of sound, video, and graphics, although the technology is improving all the time.
ii) Reliance on learner initiative can be a drawback for those who prefer more structure. Learner success also depends on technical skills in computer operation and internet navigation, as well as the ability to cope with technical difficulties.
iii) Information overload is also an issue; the volume of e-mail messages to read, reflect on, and respond to can be overwhelming, and the proliferation of databases and websites demands information management skills.
iv) Access to the internet is still a problem for some rural areas and people with disabilities.
v) Social isolation can be a drawback, and the lack of nonverbal cues can hinder communication. Although the internet can promote active learning, some contend that, like television, it can breed passivity.

In traditional academic institutions, web-based learning systems are generally housed administratively in a distance education department alongside other at-distance delivery methods such as correspondence, satellite broadcast, two way videoconferencing, videotape and CD-ROM/DVD delivery systems. All such systems seek to serve learners at some distance from their learning facilitator. Many such systems attempt to serve learners interacting with the learning source at different chronological times.

Distance education, then, is often referred to as those delivery modalities that seek to reduce the barriers of time and space to learning, thus the frequently used phrase anytime, anywhere learning. However, with that euphemism as not all topics or learning goals lend themselves to anytime as a delivery method. Learner audience has frequent opportunities to meet face-to-face with the instructor supplement traditional face-to-face classes. May replace materials previously delivered to student through Shrink-wrap course kits, packets or copy centres. Typically includes online syllabi, bibliographies faculty and class backgrounds. Instructor-led sessions are live, face-to-face in traditional classrooms. Typically asynchronous, implemented through either a web editor or an asynchronous course management system.

Generally common people are having confusion about the term 'online courses'. The term seems to be used in radically and confusingly different ways by different people. To help clarify these discussions the definitional dichotomy is given here:

Technology-enhanced learning: Learner audience has frequent opportunities to meet face-to-face with the instructor supplement traditional face-to-face classes. May replace materials previously delivered to student through Shrink-wrap course kits, packets or copy centres. Typically includes online syllabi, bibliographies, often hyperlinked, faculty and class backgrounds. Instructor-led sessions are live, face-to-face in traditional classrooms, typically asynchronous, implemented through either a web editor or an asynchronous course management system.

Technology-delivered learning: Learner audience is never or very rarely in physical proximity to the instructor also known as distance education, distributed education or distance learning. Instructor-led traditional classroom sessions are either eliminated, adjusted for some different form of non-real time interaction, or replaced with real-time virtual classrooms. May be delivered via blend of asynchronous and synchronous technologies. This category might also be broken down into two important sub-categories:

i) *Course sharing*: Using technology to share a scarce resource instructor among geographically disbursed learners in order to create economic economies of scale. Typically, the learner audience will comprise multiple groups of traditional on-campus learners gathered together in an electronically-facilitated group setting and may often involve a proctor/site coordinator that may enhance the group educational content with local customisation.

ii) *Non-traditional audiences*: Uses technology to deliver courses or programmes to learning constituencies that would not typically attend a traditional bricks-and-mortar campus. The focus of this sub-category is creation or sustaining of new, non-typical or underserved audiences for instance: working adults, homebound caregivers, homeschoolers, military, special education, etc.

These categories are important to appreciate because faculty and learner needs, pedagogical issues, and infrastructure designs may differ dramatically between these two subcategories. Neither delivery format may be appropriate for kinesthetic learners who focus best by doing it themselves instead of listening or watching or reading. Kinesthetic learners remember and grasp things better if they engage in physical activity as they learn. In fact, a definitional protocol categorising learner styles and types of content and prescribing appropriate tools is called for.

Combinations of various delivery methods may be the most appropriate vehicle for learning. By extracting the best of the classroom model and digital environment to create an integrated learning programme, we touch on an area referred to blended learning.

There are at least three general formats in which students learn. They are:

i) Directed study
ii) Instructor-led events
iii) Instructor-led or instructor-moderated communication.

Directed study: Directed study learning experiences rely on some structured plan that directs the learner through learning experiences without real-time interaction from an instructor. CD-ROM based tutorials, paper-based correspondence and 'click-to-learn' web-based systems are examples of this learning format.

Directed study may be supplemented by asynchronous interaction with the instructor, for instance through e-mail, voice mail, comments from threaded discussions. Traditional homework assignments also meet this criteria; thus requiring accredited academic institutions to think about what activities constitute accreditation-based contact hours and which activities constitute homework not considered to be part of contact hours.

Probably well over 90 per cent of today's online learning is in the directed study format. Learning experiences based solely upon directed study require the learner to have a highly developed internal self-motivation characteristic. Failure to have such internal drive tends to result in high attrition rates for self-study; this higher attrition rate can be seen in the historically higher dropout rate of correspondence student compared to traditional residential students on most campuses.

Instructor-led events: Instructor-led learning events are distinguished from directed study in that some commonly shared experience or event is led by the instructor. Instructor-led events have the capability to dynamically react to real-time environments and change the plan of study or flow of learning to meet the needs of learners at that particular time. This engagement style helps sustain learner interest and probably contributes to reduction of attrition rates. Traditional seminar-style classrooms and field trips are classic examples of instructor-led events. Instructor-led events have traditionally been the differentiating characteristic of accredited higher-education institutions. The for-profit correspondence school formats often maligned by higher education as diploma mills for their purported lack of rigour, either limit or fail to include instructor-led events as part of their curriculums.

Successful uses of instructor-led events often capstone material presented in previous self-directed learning or small group collaborative formats or create a catalyst for future learning presented in those formats. Additionally, instructor-led events are often used to assess and supplement cognitive application of abstract learning. Instructor led events over the web have some or all of the following capabilities:

i) *Awareness*: means a learner is aware of when other members are present online.

iii) *Shared objects capabilities*: Shared objects capabilities enable instructors and learners to view learning content simultaneously.

Instructor-led or instructor-moderated communication: Allow selective interaction between learners and/or instructor, but allows the instructor to control and guide the flow of interaction. Two delivery models are commonly seen:

i) *Broadcast model*: Sage on the stage, seminar/lecture style: Instructor delivers a monologue with little, if any, interaction from the audience. Since this model scales easily to accommodate large numbers of learners, it is probably most frequently implemented at this point.

ii) *Dialogue model*: Small group setting with an instructor creating a learning experience and dynamically monitoring and adjusting the flow of dialogue/learning.

The location of your training server is crucial. If the server is in an area with high line-use rates, the server may respond more slowly. Routers and other load-balancing hardware and software help direct requests to available servers. Proxy servers can both help and hinder. Proxies sit between the main server and your learner. Some proxies are set up to cache content, so that learners accessing the same page need not both go to the main server.

A number of software vendors provide consulting and outsourcing services regarding their products. A more trendy term for this is Application Service Provider (ASP). Additionally, several organisations provide independent consulting on one or more software tools. Services range from instructor training to turnkey course development to facilitated hosting services (Application Service Providers or ASPs). Inclusion in this list should not be construed as an endorsement of these services by the author; this listing is provided simply as a convenient, but incomplete, reference.

American Telecommunications Alliance links education and telecommunications to provide schools, colleges, state agencies, libraries, and other non-profit groups with several benefits in telecommunications services. The Alliance has been formed by an agreement among a national non-profit telecommunications association and the nation's four educational compacts—representing all areas of the country. The Alliance's mission is to provide low-cost access to top-quality telecommunications programmes and to give education an organised way to exert leadership in building technology policies and standards.

Persons developing websites or information for the web must be sensitive as to how a browser, machine, web, TV, or mobile device interprets or handles information. Recently, issues of compatibility and compliance to the Americans with Disabilities Act (ADA) as well as new international standards have also come to the forefront of accessibility issues. Concerns regarding compliance to ADA requirements and new international standards have encouraged groups to work on standards and guidelines that make web page accessibility easier for everyone. These guidelines have also improved accessibility with devices other than the typical browser.

With the growth worldwide of teaching and learning on the internet, attention is being paid to the nature and quality of online higher education. The US National Education Association (NEA) and Blackboard Inc. had unveiled an important, research-driven list of quality benchmarks for distance learning in higher education. The list of 24 quality measures is the centrepiece of Quality On the Line—an Institute for Higher Education Policy study commissioned by NEA and Blackboard Inc. The list is as follows:

The categories and benchmarks include:

i) *Institutional support benchmarks*

a) A documented technology plan that includes electronic security measures to ensure both quality standards and the integrity and validity of information.

b) The reliability of the technology delivery system is as fail-safe as possible.

c) A centralised system provides support for building and maintaining the distance education infrastructure.

ii) *Course development benchmarks*

d) Guidelines regarding minimum standards are used for course development, design, and delivery, while learning outcomes—not the availability of existing technology—determine the technology being used to deliver course content.

e) Instructional materials are reviewed periodically to ensure they meet programme standards.

f) Courses are designed to require students to engage themselves in analysis, synthesis, and evaluation as part of their course and programme requirements.

iii) *Teaching/learning benchmarks*

g) Student interaction with faculty and other students is an essential characteristic and is facilitated through a variety of ways, including voice-mail and/or e-mail.

h) Feedback to student assignments and questions is constructive and provided in a timely manner.

i) Students are instructed in the proper methods of effective research, including assessment of the validity of resources.

iv) *Course structure benchmarks*

j) Before starting an online programme, students are advised about the programme to determine if they possess the self-motivation and commitment to learn at a distance and if they have access to the minimal technology required by the course design.

k) Students are provided with supplemental course information that outlines course objectives, concepts, and ideas, and learning outcomes for each course are summarised in a clearly written, straight-forward statement.

l) Students have access to sufficient library resources that may include a "virtual library" accessible through the World Wide Web.

m) Faculty and students agree upon expectations regarding times for student assignment completion and faculty response.

v) *Student support benchmarks*

n) Students receive information about programmes, including admission requirements, tuition and fees, books and supplies, technical requirements, and student support services.

o) Students are provided with hands-on training and information to aid them in securing material through electronic databases, inter-library loans, government archives, news services, and other sources.

p) Throughout the duration of the course/programme, students have access to technical assistance, including detailed instructions regarding the electronic media used, practice sessions prior to the beginning of the course, and convenient access to technical support staff.

q) Questions directed to student service personnel are answered accurately and quickly, with a structured system in place to address student complaints.

vi) *Faculty support benchmarks*

r) Technical assistance in course development is available to faculty, who are encouraged to use it.

s) Faculty members are assisted in the transition from classroom teaching to online instruction and are assessed during the process.

t) Instructor training and assistance, including peer monitoring, continues through the progression of the online course.

u) Faculty members are provided with written resources to deal with issues arising from student use of electronically-accessed data.

vii) *Evaluation and assessment benchmarks*

v) The programme's educational effectiveness and teaching/learning process is assessed through an evaluation process that uses several methods and applies specific standards.

w) Data on enrolment, costs, and successful/innovative uses of technology are used to evaluate programme effectiveness.

x) Intended learning outcomes are reviewed regularly to ensure clarity, utility, and appropriateness.

Though internet promises the panacea to better learning, sales hungry decision-makers have exploited it. Now it is faced with the challenge of maintaining the delicate balance between quality and quantity. Society has been credited with creating internet technology, but it is simultaneously creating society. Maintaining quality presupposes building a code of ethics into the internet infrastructure, just as science without responsibility is like a sword without a sheath; so too, internet-based distance learning without ethics will lead to gross debasement of human energies.

2

Internet and Distance Learning Strategies

The education system is challenged with providing increased educational opportunities, within a context of rapid technological change and shifting market conditions, without increased budgets. Many educational institutions are answering this challenge by developing distance education programmes.

Distance education takes place when a teacher and students are separated by physical distance, and technology, i.e., voice, video, data, and print, often in concert with face-to-face communication, is used to bridge the instructional gap. These types of programmes can provide adults with a second chance at a college education, reach those disadvantaged by limited time, distance or physical disability, and update the knowledge base of workers at their places of employment.

Research comparing distance education to traditional face-to-face instruction indicates that teaching and studying at a distance can be as effective as traditional instruction, when the method and technologies used are appropriate to the instructional tasks, there is student-to-student interaction, and when there is timely teacher-to-student feedback.

A wide range of technological options are available to the distance educator. They fall into four major categories:

i) *Voice:* Instructional audio tools include the interactive technologies of telephone, audioconferencing, and short-wave radio. Passive (i.e., one-way) audio tools include tapes and radio.

ii) *Video:* Instructional video tools include still images such as slides, pre-produced moving images (e.g., film, videotape), and real-time moving images combined with audioconferencing (one-way or two-way video with two-way audio).

iii) *Data*: Computers send and receive information electronically. For this reason, the term "data" is used to describe this broad category of instructional tools. Computer applications for distance education are varied and include:

   a) *Computer-assisted instruction (CAI)*: Uses the computer as a self-contained teaching machine to present individual lessons.

   b) *Computer-managed instruction (CMI)*: Uses the computer to organise instruction and track student records and progress. The instruction itself need not be delivered via a computer, although CAI is often combined with CMI.

   c) *Computer-mediated education (CME)*: Describes computer applications that facilitate the delivery of instruction. Examples include electronic mail, fax, real-time computer conferencing, and World Wide Web applications.

iv) *Print*: Print is a foundational element of distance education programmes and the basis from which all other delivery systems have evolved. Various print formats are available including: textbooks, study guides, workbooks, course syllabi, and case studies.

The key to effective distance education is focusing on the needs of the learners, the requirements of the content, and the constraints faced by the teacher, before selecting a delivery system. Typically, this systematic approach will result in a mix of media, each serving a specific purpose. For example:

a) A strong print component can provide much of the basic instructional content in the form of a course text, as well as readings, the syllabus, and day-to-day schedule.
b) Interactive audio or video conferencing can provide real time face-to-face voice-to-voice) interaction. This is also an excellent and cost-effective way to incorporate guest speakers and content experts.
c) Computer conferencing or electronic mail can be used to send messages, assignment feedback, and other targeted communication to one or more class members. It can also be used to increase interaction among students.
d) Pre-recorded video tapes can be used to present class lectures and visually-oriented content.
e) Fax can be used to distribute assignments, last minute announcements, to receive student assignments, and to provide timely feedback.

Effective distance education programmes begin with careful planning and a focused understanding of course requirements and student needs. Appropriate technology can only be selected once these elements are understood in detail. There is no mystery to the way effective distance education programmes develop. They do not happen spontaneously; they evolve through the hard work and dedicated efforts of many individuals and organisations.

Successful distance education programmes rely on the consistent and integrated efforts of students, faculty, facilitators, support staff, and administrators. The following briefly describes the roles of these key players in the distance education enterprise and the challenges they face.

i) *Students*: Meeting the instructional needs of students is the cornerstone of every effective distance education programme, and the test by which all efforts in the field are judged. Regardless of the educational context, the primary role of the student is to learn. This is a daunting task under the best of circumstances, requiring motivation, planning, and an ability to analyse and apply the instructional content being taught. When instruction is delivered at a distance, additional challenges result because students are often separated from others sharing their backgrounds and interests, have few if any opportunities to interact with teachers outside of class, and must rely on technical linkages to bridge the gap separating class participants.

ii) *Faculty:* The success of any distance education effort rests squarely on the shoulders of the faculty. In a traditional classroom setting, the instructor's responsibility includes assembling course content and developing an understanding of student needs. Special challenges confront those teaching at a distance. For example, the instructor must:

a) Develop an understanding of the characteristics and needs of distant students with little first-hand experience and limited, if any, face-to-face contact.

b) Adapt teaching styles taking into consideration the needs and expectations of multiple, often diverse, audiences.

c) Develop a working understanding of delivery technology, while remaining focused on their teaching role.

d) Function effectively as a skilled facilitator as well as content provider.

iii) *Facilitators:* The instructor often finds it beneficial to rely on a site facilitator to act as a bridge between the students and the instructor. To be effective, a facilitator must understand the students being served and the instructor's expectations. Most importantly, the facilitator must be willing to follow the directive established by the teacher. Where budget and logistics permit, the role of on-site facilitators has increased even in classes in which they have little, if any, content expertise. At a minimum, they set up equipment, collect assignments, proctor tests, and act as the instructor's on-site eyes and ears.

vi) *Support staff*: These individuals are the silent heroes of the distance education enterprise and ensure that the myriad details required for programme success are dealt with effectively. Most successful distance education programmes consolidate support service functions to include student registration, materials duplication and distribution, textbook ordering, securing of copyright clearances, facilities scheduling, processing grade reports, managing technical resources, etc.

v) *Administrators*: Although administrators are typically influential in planning an institution's distance education programme, they often lose contact or relinquish control to technical managers once the programme is operational. Effective distance education administrators are more than idea people. They are consensus builders, decision makers, and referees. They work closely with technical and support service personnel, ensuring that technological resources are effectively deployed to further the institution's academic mission. They maintain an academic focus, realising that meeting the instructional needs of distant students is their ultimate responsibility.

Print is the foundation of distance education and the basis from which all other delivery systems have evolved. The first distance-delivered courses were offered by correspondence study, with print materials sent and returned to students by mail. While technological developments have added to the repertoire of tools available to the distance educator, print continues to be a significant component of all distance education programmes.

Various print formats available today include:

a) *Textbooks*: As in traditionally delivered courses, textbooks are the basis and primary source of content for the majority of distance-delivered courses. While textbooks should always be critically reviewed before adoption, this is especially critical when the learner and the instructor are not in daily contact.

b) *Study guides*: Distance educators use study guides to reinforce points made during class and through the use of other delivery systems. They will often include exercises, related readings and additional resources available to the student.

c) *Workbooks*: In a distance education context workbooks are often used to provide course content in an interactive manner. A typical format might contain an overview, the content to be covered, one or more exercises or case studies to elaborate the points being made, and a quiz or test for self-assessment. In addition, there is typically some form of feedback, remediation, or "branching" loop to recycle students through the instruction as needed.

d) *Course syllabus*: A comprehensive and well-planned course syllabus is the foundation of many distance-delivered courses. It provides course goals and objectives, performance expectations, descriptions of assignments, related readings, grading criteria, and a day-by-day overview of the material to be covered. The syllabus must be as complete as possible in order to guide the students through the course in the absence of daily contact with the instructor.

e) *Case studies*: If written imaginatively, case studies are an extremely effective instructional tool. In fact, case studies are often designed around the limitations of print and intended to spark the students' imaginations as they place themselves in the particular case under consideration. Many case studies present a content-based scenario. They raise questions, pose alternative solutions, and then branch students to different sections of the text. There, the consequences of the selected alternative are described.

Since print is largely a one-way communication medium, the challenge is to design instruction to maximise the amount of interaction in distance education print materials. Consider:

i) *Writing style*: Distance educators write instructional materials with language more like that used for speaking than for writing journal articles or books. His tips for writing instructional materials include:

   a) Use short sentences.
   b) Avoid compound sentences.
   c) Avoid excess information in a sentence.
   d) Use the active voice.
   e) Use personal pronouns.
   f) Keep equivalent items parallel.
   g) List conditions separately.
   h) Avoid multiple negatives.
   i) Use point form.
   j) Use familiar examples.
   k) Write as you would speak.
   l) Avoid unnecessary and difficult words.
   m) Avoid jargon; use technical terms only when necessary.
   n) Put sentences and paragraphs into a logical sequence: first things that affect many, then things that affect few; first the general, then the specific; first permanent provisions, then temporary ones.
   o) Avoid cultural and gender stereotyping.
   p) Focusing on content organisation before developing content. Prior to content development, create an outline of the material to be covered. Print materials

are often too wordy because the author is planning, organising and writing at the same time. Instead, organise content based on the identified goals and objectives. At first, focus on systematically and creatively ordering the flow of topics, not polishing a finished product. The end result will be a well-organised content outline from which the written content will easily flow.

ii) *Developing a course introduction*: Misanchuk suggests developing a written course introduction that will be the very first thing a distant student sees. The course introduction can include biographical background information about the instructor, a course overview, course goals and aims, a listing of any textbooks or ancillary learning materials that will be needed, and information about assignments, examinations, and grading.

iii) *Staying with a consistent format*: Learner anxiety with the unknown can be reduced through consistency in instructional presentation. Develop an effective format and organisational scheme and stick with it. Use adequate headings and subheadings to visually guide the reader through the material.

iv) *Using advance organisers*: Advance organisers are a means to connect new material with a learner's prior knowledge and cognitive structure. They should be of a more general and abstract character than the learning matter that follows and help the learner to relate different parts and concepts of teaching material to each other. Place the most general and comprehensive ideas at the beginning of a lesson and progress to more structured and detailed information.

v) *Using examples and analogies*: In a traditional classroom, teachers spontaneously provide examples and analogies to illustrate a point that students are having difficulty understanding. Since distant students and their teachers may not have this type of interaction, include lots of good examples and analogies in print-based materials. Be sure, however, that these examples address the various cultural groups, ages and experiences of the students.

vi) *Including questions*: Questions in print material can stimulate the learner to be more active and to deal more intensively with the learning matter. Use questions that aim at understanding rather than merely reproduction and memorisation of facts.

vii) *Adding a table of contents*: A detailed table of contents can help the learner to quickly refer to the appropriate section.

viii) *Incorporating a glossary of terms*. A glossary summarises all the new, often technical terminology encountered in a document. It may be helpful to delineate glossary entries in the instructional material by putting them in boldface type.

The major advantages of print materials are given below.

i) *Spontaneous*: Print materials can be used in any setting without the need for sophisticated presentation equipment.

ii) *Instructionally transparent*: The medium of delivery should enhance, not compete with, the content for the learner's attention. If the student reads well, the print medium is the most transparent instructional medium of all.

iii) *Non-threatening:* Reading is second nature to most students. As a result, they are easily able to focus on the content, without becoming mesmerised or frustrated by the process of reading itself.

iv) *Easy to use*: Given adequate light, print materials can be used any time and any place without the aid of supplemental resources such as electricity, viewing screen, and specially designed electronic classrooms. The portability of print is especially important for rural learners with limited access to advanced technology.

v) *Easily reviewed and referenced*: Print materials are typically learner-controlled. As a result, the student rapidly moves through redundant sections, while focusing on areas demanding additional attention.

vi) *Cost-effective*: No instructional tool is less expensive to produce than print. In addition, facilities abound for the inexpensive duplication of these materials.

vii) *Easily edited and revised*: In comparison to technically sophisticated electronic software, print is both easy and inexpensive to edit and revise.

viii) *Time-effective*: When instructional print materials are created, the developer's primary focus remains on content concerns, not the technical requirements of the delivery system.

The major limitations of print include:

i) *Limited view of reality*: Print, by its reliance on the written word, offers a vicarious view of reality. Despite the use of excellent sequential illustrations or photos, for example, it is impossible to adequately recreate motion in print.

ii) *Passive and self-directed*: Numerous studies have shown that higher learner motivation is required to successfully complete print-based courses. To a certain extent, the passive nature of print can be offset by systematic instructional design that seeks to stimulate the passive learner. Still, it takes more motivation to read a book or work through a written exercise than it does to watch a television programme or participate in an audio-conference with an instructor encouraging student participation and response.

iii) *Feedback and interaction*: Without feedback and interaction, instruction suffers, regardless of the delivery system in use. By nature, print materials are passive and self-directed. Even with print materials incorporating feedback mechanisms and interactive exercises, it is easy for learners to skip to the answer section.

iv) *Dependent on reading skills*: Most students have developed fairly good viewing skills by age four. These same children, however, often fail to develop adequate reading skills by age 12. Reading skills must often be improved. Lack of ability in this area cripples the effectiveness of even the most instructionally sound print material and must be overcome if print is to be used effectively.

Interactive Videoconferencing (IV) can be integrated into the distance education programme with minimal adaptation to the curriculum and course and is designed to support two-way video and audio communication between multiple locations. Most IV systems utilise compressed digital video for the transmission of motion images over data networks such as high capacity Integrated Services Digital Networks (ISDN).

The video compression process decreases the amount of data transmitted over the lines by transmitting only the changes in the picture. By minimising the bandwidth required to transmit the images, video compression also reduces the transmission cost. Interactive videoconferences are often transmitted on dedicated T-1 phone lines. These high speed lines are very effective for videoconferencing, but they are typically leased circuits with an expensive monthly cost. The fixed monthly charge is usually based on distance, not usage. Therefore, the cost effectiveness of IV systems increases with use. Interactive videoconferencing systems can operate at different data rates, at various fractions of T-1 capacity, enabling the transmission of multiple simultaneous videoconferences over the same T-1 circuit. An IV system can also share a T-1 circuit with other digital data uses such as internet transmissions or file transfers.

The core of IV is the codec (coder/decoder). This is the electronic device that transmits and receives the video signals that the class members will see on their television monitors. It may be easier to think of the codec as an extremely sophisticated modem. A modem takes digital data and transmits it over regular phone lines. The codec takes analog signals, compresses and digitises them, and transmits the signals over digital phone lines. Other types of equipment, such as television monitors, are needed to make IV successful. In addition, various forms of instructional technology can be incorporated into IV, including video cassette recorders/ players, microphones, cameras, and computers.

Some systems are also capable of simultaneously connecting more than two sites through the use of a multi-point control unit, or MCU. Multi-point conferencing can be effective although the scheduling, technical, and logistical dimensions of MCU conferences can be imposing. A relatively new "dial out" feature, allows the use of multiple telephone lines to connect two or more sites in the same conference. Simultaneously accessing multiple lines may be difficult in small areas. In addition, the cost of the telephone line usage may be prohibitive since the cost of the call would be multiplied by the number of lines utilised in the conference.

The major categories of videoconferencing systems are:

i) *Small room videoconferencing*: This system is designed primarily for small groups at all sites seated around a conference table.

ii) *Classroom videoconferencing*: This type of system usually uses high quality IV components, codecs, and an interface that allows all participants to be seen on the monitors.

iii) *Desktop videoconferencing*: This system utilises a personal computer and videoconferencing software. These systems are less expensive, but offer limited resolution. They are most effective for individual and small group use.

While designing instruction to be delivered over IV, the instructor should focus attention on all students, not just those at the "home" site. Lessons should incorporate a variety of activities for all students at the various sites. Use small group activities, student presentations, and an occasional break to add variety to the lesson. As a rule of thumb, instructors should change instruction methods every 10-15 minutes. In other words, switch from lecture to question-answer to small group activity on a regular basis. It is often helpful to bring guest lecturers into the classroom. It may also be helpful to have guest speakers at one or more of the distant sites. This will encourage involvement of the distant students, as well as allowing the students at the origination site to see what it is like to have the teacher at another location. When preparing class visuals, keep in mind that small fonts and light colours do not show up well over the monitors. A variety of formatting will also assist in maintaining student interest and attention. When formatting visuals, be sure that they will fit on the television monitor.

Instructional strategies for videoconferencing systems include:

i) *Establish class expectations*: In the distance education classroom, some students may adopt the TV attitude, expecting the course to be entertaining, not educational. Address this attitude through well planned and focused presentations with emphasis on teacher-student interaction.

ii) *Reduce distractions*: Students should also be forewarned to minimise extraneous noise and activity. Both detract from the quality of the course.

iii) *Use variety and interaction*: The instructor should begin the course by preparing the learners for an active experience. Interactive videoconferencing is interactive, unlike regular television, and students can make the class much more interesting by being actively involved.

iv) *Encourage dialogue*: By asking questions and noting body language, instructors can ascertain the interest and comprehension of the students at both all sites. This kind of attention will make all students feel more comfortable.

vi) Training for Instructors and Students: An instructor be taught how to use all features of the equipment. A short session (30 minutes) should be sufficient to give the instructor a hands-on overview of the equipment features. It would also be helpful to provide the instructor with a quick reference sheet outlining major functions.

Some of the critical operations that an instructor should be capable of performing are:

i) Turning on the codec and the monitors.
ii) Dialling the distant site(s) to establish a link.
iii) Controlling camera focus and field at the origination site and at the distant site(s).
iv) Adjusting the volume to an acceptable level.
v) Dialling out to a remote location.
vi) Selecting the appropriate data rate.
vii) Resetting echo cancelling capability.
viii) Switching to and from the document camera.
ix) Switching to and from the computer output.
x) Utilising a computer to generate and display multimedia presentations.
xi) Using the VCR to broadcast a video for all locations.
xii) Terminating the link with the distant site(s).
xiii) Shutting down the equipment.

Some institutions have technicians who will assist the instructor in setting up or monitoring the videoconference. However, the instructor should still be aware of the process because the technician may not always be available. Student training may also be critical since they may be called upon to operate the equipment if the instructor is at another site, is unavailable, or if a guest speaker needs assistance.

Interactive videoconferencing can be an effective instructional tool for the distance educator. As with other technologies, its usefulness is directly related to the instructor's understanding of its benefits, limitations, and utilisation strategies.

Interactive video has the following advantages:

i) Allows real time visual contact between students and the instructor or among students at different sites.
ii) Supports the use of diverse media. Blackboards, handwritten documents, and videos may be incorporated at all sites.
iii) Enables connection with experts in other geographical locations.
iv) Can provide access to at-risk or special needs students.
v) Provides additional access to students at remote sites.

As with any technology, interactive video has its limitations:

i) The initial cost of the equipment and leasing the lines to transmit conferences may be prohibitive.
ii) Companies which produce codecs have each developed unique methods of compression which are incompatible, although protocols have been established to allow communication among brand names. However, this universal standard compromises resolution and quality to a certain degree.
iii) Unless a strong effort is made by the instructor, students not located with the instructor may remain uninvolved in the course.
iv) If visuals, like handwritten or copied materials, are not properly prepared, students may have a difficult time reading them.

v) If the pipe that carries the transmission among sites is not large enough, the students may observe ghost images when rapid movement occurs in real time.

vi) If the system is not properly configured, class members may observe an audio echo effect. The result is audio interference that detracts from the learning environment.

Educators have witnessed the rapid development of computer networks, dramatic improvements in the processing power of personal computers, and striking advances in magnetic storage technology. These developments have made the computer a dynamic force in distance education, providing a new and interactive means of overcoming time and distance to reach learners.

The applications of computer for distance education fall into four broad categories:

i) *Computer Assisted Instruction (CAI)*: Uses the computer as a self-contained teaching machine to present discrete lessons to achieve specific but limited educational objectives. There are several CAI modes, including: drill and practice, tutorial, simulations and games, and problem-solving.

ii) *Computer Managed Instruction (CMI)*: Uses the computer's branching, storage, and retrieval capabilities to organise instruction and track student records and progress. The instruction need not be delivered via computer, although often CAI (the instructional component) is combined with CMI.

iii) *Computer Mediated Communication (CMC)*: Describes computer applications that facilitate communication. Examples include electronic mail, computer conferencing, and electronic bulletin boards.

iv) *Computer-Based Multimedia*: HyperCard, hypermedia, and a still-developing generation of powerful, sophisticated, and flexible computing tools have gained the attention of distance educators in recent years. The goal of computer-based multimedia is to integrate various voice, video, and computer technologies into a single, easily accessible delivery system.

The major advantages of computers are:

i) *Computers can facilitate self-paced learning:* In the CAI mode, for example, computers individualise learning, while giving immediate reinforcement and feedback.

ii) *Computers are a multimedia tool:* With integrated graphic, print, audio, and video capabilities, computers can effectively link various technologies. Interactive video and CD-ROM technologies can be incorporated into computer-based instructional units, lessons, and learning environments.

iii) *Computers are interactive:* Microcomputer systems incorporating various software packages are extremely flexible and maximise learner control.

iv) *Computer technology is rapidly advancing:* Innovations are constantly emerging, while related costs drop. By understanding their present needs and future technical requirements, the cost-conscious educator can effectively navigate the volatile computer hardware and software market.

v) *Computers increase access:* Local, regional, and national networks link resources and individuals, wherever they might be. In fact, many institutions now offer complete undergraduate and graduate programmes relying almost exclusively on computer-based resources.

The major limitations include:

i) Computer networks are costly to develop. Although individual computers are relatively inexpensive and the computer hardware and software market is very competitive, it is still costly to develop instructional networks and purchase the system software to run them.

ii) The technology is changing rapidly. Computer technology evolves so quickly that the distant educator focused solely on innovation not meeting tangible needs will constantly change equipment in an effort to keep pace with the latest technical advancements.

iii) Widespread computer illiteracy still exists. While computers have been widely used since the 1960s, there are many who do not have access to computers or computer networks.

iv) Students must be highly motivated and proficient in computer operation before they can successfully function in a computer-based distance learning environment.

The internet is the most powerful computer network in the world. It encompasses 1.3 million computers with internet addresses that are used by up to 30 million people in more than fifty countries. As more and more colleges, universities, schools, companies, and private citizens connect to the internet either through affiliations with regional not-for-profit networks or by subscribing to information services provided by for-profit companies, more possibilities are opened for distance educators to overcome time and distance to reach students.

The internet continues to grow rapidly. The mix of internet services and the relative traffic associated with each service continue to change as well. The services representing the majority of the traffic are FTP and WWW. The internet is a network infrastructure that was originally sponsored by a variety of federal agencies, including the NSF and the Advanced Research Project (ARPA). The internet was intended to be a network that would facilitate communication and collaboration among researchers and educators in universities, government agencies, and industry. That, however, is no longer the exclusive role of the internet. Two growing roles of the internet are supporting electronic commerce and providing distance learning solutions to schools.

The internet supports an increasing number of services, some of which are described below.

i) *Logon services*: Logon services are offered by internet providers through two types of TCP/IP-based protocols: Telnet and Rlogin. The Telnet command has the advantage of being available on any host that allows remote login capability.

ii) *E-mail*: E-mail is the most commonly used application on the internet. It is used by researchers in universities, government agencies, and corporations as part of their collaborative research process. It is supported by a wide range of delivery agents and delivery mechanisms.

ii) *Bulletin boards*: Many bulletin boards can be accessed through the internet. Two common public bulletin boards on the internet are USENET and LISTSERVE. USENET is a collection of thousands of topically organised newsgroups, covering everything from supercomputer design to bungee cord jumping, and ranging in distribution from the whole world to single institutions. LISTSERVE also provides discussion forums on a variety of topics broken out by topic or area of special interest.

iii) *File trânsfer*: File transfer services is used to transfer files between internet hosts. Researchers at universities, corporations, and government agencies can use FTP to download as well as upload files to supercomputer centres. Anonymous FTP is a simple extension to the basic FTP protocol that enables students and researchers to create and share public archives with others on the internet.

iv) *World Wide Web*: The WWW is a system that links information stored anywhere on the internet in a mesh of hyperlinks. These hyperlinks enable an educator or a student equipped with a suitable client to navigate through a distributed information resource by simply following pointers from one hypermedia document to another. The hypermedia document may include text, sound, still images, and video. The WWW makes information resources on the internet accessible to users who are not experienced in UNIX-based commands.

v) *Electronic whiteboards*: Electronic whiteboards allow a speaker's notes to be shared in real time with viewers over a wide area. This tool makes the dialogue among researchers, educators, and students more interactive and more effective, enhancing the collaborative research and learning process.

vi) *Videoconferencing*: Videoconferencing is an emerging internet service that enables students to establish low-end two-way video and audio connections with teachers and other students around the globe. This service originated as part of the Global Schoolhouse project. When available on a large scale, will provide a measurable benefit to students, because it provides them with international exposure.

vii) *Directory services*: Directory services provide users with the ability to locate information about other users, services, or service providers. Directory services are often divided into "white pages" and "yellow pages" services. The white pages service provides information about individual users, while the yellow pages service provides information about services and their providers.

VIII *Gopher services*: Gopher services allow students and researchers to browse through information across the internet without having to log in or know in advance where to look for information.

The WWW provides internet users with a uniform and convenient means of accessing the wide variety of resources (pictures, text, data, sound, video) available on the internet. Popular software interfaces, such as Mosaic and Netscape, facilitate navigation and use of the WWW. The central organising feature of the WWW is the home page. Every organisation and even every individual user of the WWW can create a home page that contains whatever information they want to present. The hypertext capabilities of the WWW facilitate linking of information within your own home page and with all other home pages on the WWW.

Distance educators can use the internet and WWW to help students gain a basic understanding of how to navigate and take full advantage of the networked world into which they will be graduating. Some instructional possibilities of the internet include:

i) Using e-mail for informal one-to-one correspondence. Feedback from the instructor can be received more quickly than messages sent by mail. Students can read messages at their convenience and easily store them for later reference.

ii) Establishing a classroom bulletin board. Distant students often work in isolation without the assistance and support of fellow students. Setting up a class bulletin board can encourage student-to-student interaction. With a class computer conference, individual students can post their comments or questions to the class, and every other individual is free to respond. The conference can also be used to post all modifications to the class schedule or curriculum, assignments/tests, and answers to assignments/tests.

iii) Engaging students in dialogue with other students, faculty, and researchers by encouraging them to join a bulletin board(s) on topic(s) related to the class.

iv) Developing a classroom home page. The home page can cover information about the class including the syllabus, exercises, literature references, and the instructor's biography. The instructor can also provide links to information on the WWW that would be useful to students in the class.

When incorporating the internet into a distance delivered course, remember that:

i) All students in a course must have internet and WWW access to ensure equal opportunities for computer interaction and feedback. Also, convenient access to a computer at home or work may influence student success.

ii) Students may face the concurrent challenges of learning basic computer skills, new software, and appropriate online communication skills. Troubleshooting student computer problems will probably become a part of normal instructional responsibilities. Setting up a specific classroom conference for ongoing discussions of specific hardware and software problems may help students to work through these problems on their own.

iii) Some students might hesitate to contribute to computer conferences or to send e-mail because of a lack of familiarity with the proper protocols. Encourage students to use e-mail, classroom conferences, electronic bulletin boards, and the WWW early in the course so they overcome inhibitions. Specifying a minimum number of e-mail communications per week will encourage active participation.

iv) Using e-mail can help the instructor provide feedback more quickly than surface mail or telephone. Prompt response generally increases student motivation and performance.

v) Prompt responses might not always be appropriate. Computer conferences can foster student-to-student interaction. To ensure that this interaction is sustained, work towards a facilitative role. It might be appropriate to delay response to a query in a classroom conference in order to allow students to respond to the issue and to each other.

vi) Becoming familiar with the resources available on the internet and the most effective ways to use them will be part of the instructional challenge. A number of helpful guides to the internet and WWW are available.

Internet connections are predominantly based on the TCP/IP stack of protocols. The IP layer is implemented on end systems as well as intermediary nodes. As a protocol IP is responsible for internet working multiple networks. These underlying networks may include LANs or WANs. TCP and user datagram protocol (UDP) are transport, protocols that are implemented on end systems to packetise all application-layer exchanges into appropriate protocol data units (PDUs) and to provide transport services suitable for the applications.

The application-level solutions are available to users in accessing the internet at the logical level which are the following:

i) *Time-sharing host solution*: The time-sharing host solution is more appropriate for the home and the networking environments. Through this solution, students and researchers can access the internet by obtaining an account on a time-sharing host that is located at the service provider's premises. In this case, the TCP/IP protocol stack resides on the time-sharing host. To access the time-sharing host, the user needs to have a workstation and a modem. To establish a connection with the time-sharing host, the researcher or educator needs to establish a dialup connection to the terminal server attached to the internet access provider's host. The dialup connection operates at speeds ranging from 2.4 Kbps to 14.4 Kbps. This dialup connection enables the user to dial into a terminal server that establishes a session with the time-sharing host. The host in turn establishes a connection across the internet with the target host. A file transfer then occurs from the target host to the time-sharing host; the file is downloaded to the user's workstation through a serial file transfer protocol such as Kermit or Xmodem.

ii) *Full TCP/IP connection*: The establishment of a full TCP/IP connection can be implemented in one of two ways:

a) a full TCP/IP suite may actually reside on the user's computer, or

b) a corporation may decide to establish an internet node on the corporate side.

The first full TCP/IP connection option enables the user to run the TCP/IP protocol applications on a PC, including e-mail, bulletin board (USENET), news programmes, Telnet, FTP, and possibly Gopher. In that case, the user's workstation acts as a peer with other hosts on the internet, which enables the user to move files directly from and to a hard disc, instead of going through the two step process associated with accessing a time-sharing host. This approach also enables the user to access remote file servers, via network file systems (NFS) as apparent extensions to the file disk. The full TCP/IP interconnection option requires establishment of an internet node on the corporate site.

The internet speed access methods can be divided into two categories: (i) low-speed access methods and (ii) high-speed access methods.

i) *Low-speed access methods* include dialup connections, X.25 dialup, toll-free dialup, and ISDN. Dialup connections are offered by the major internet service providers. The connections range in speed from 9. 6 Kbps to 28.8 Kbps. Toll-free dialup is offered by the major internet service providers. These connections also range in speed from 9.6 Kbps to 28.8 Kbps.

ii) *High-speed access methods* include two categories: fast packet services, such as SMDS, ATM, and FRS, and cable TV solutions, such as data/cable modems. The fast packet access solutions are offered by an increasing number of access service providers, while the data/cable solutions are offered by cable TV providers, such as TCI.

Internet services are offered by a number of providers, which can be categorised as national internet providers and regional/local internet providers.

i) *National internet service* providers operate in multiple cities across the United States. These providers provide participating members with access (gateways) to other domestic and international networks. They include the Advanced Network and Services, Inc. (ANS), California Education and Research Federation Network (Cerfnet), Performance Systems International, UUNet Technologies, Inc., and Sprint Corporation.

ii) *Regional internet providers* include the San Francisco Bay Area Research Network (BARRNet), Committee on Institutional Cooperation Network (CICNet), and Southwestern States Network (WestNet), all of which operate in the western region of the United States.

The Internet Engineering Task Force (IETF) standards are aimed at improving support for networked multimedia through bandwidth reservation and more effective use of multicast capabilities. Sending duplicate messages or setting up broadcast video-data collaboration conferences to multiple remote locations requires multicasting. The IETF standard, distance vector multicast routing protocol (DVMRP) is a multicast routing algorithm used in the internet multicast backbone network to connectivity (e.g., video) to workstations that support IP multicast.

DVMRP protocol operates by flooding all available routes. Protocols now under development are more efficient. Protocol-independent multicast (PIM) uses "rendezvous points" for registration of the senders and receivers of multimedia multicast traffic. Being protocol independent, it works with any unicast routing protocol. A standard also under development is real-time transport protocol, which uses time stamps and content identification labels on multimedia data units to ensure reassembly at the receiving end. Streaming II (ST-II) lets the originator control the bandwidth and latency in a multicast videoconference. A revised version, called ST-II+, allows for faster connection set-up and the ability of allowing receivers as well as senders to join a multicast group without needing a central administrative point; it was under development at press time.

The Reservation protocol (RSVP) offers a way to support bandwidth allocation on connectionless networks. It decentralises control over bandwidth allocations, letting each end system decide how much bandwidth is required to participate in a multimedia conference. The NII will comprise a collection of infrastructures from various industry segments. Some observers view the internet as lithe "true" NIL. They attribute their belief to the following strengths of the internet:

i) *Support by network service providers*: Access to the internet is increasingly supported by not only the traditional internet providers but also the LECs and the IXCs.
ii) *Number of people reached*: Estimates of the number of people interconnected by the internet vary from 15 million to 20 million.
iii) *High-performance backbone*: The NSF backbone is migrating from a DS3 platform to a higher-performance network, based on ATM and SONET.
iv) *Expanding range of applications*: The internet has supported data networks, which serve the research and collaboration needs of researchers and educators employed by universities, corporations, and government agencies.
v) *Affordability*: The internet remains one of the least costly approaches to provide interconnection, delivering on the NII promise of an affordable networking solution.

vi) *Extensive information resources*: This represents a source of strength of the internet as an application solution to distance learners.

vii) *Ease of use*: New services, such as WWW, make the internet easy to access and to use.

All these factors make the internet an important component of the NII, but it cannot be considered a complete substitute for the NII for the following reasons:

i) *Lack of support for rural communities*: While it is widely available, the internet has not yet reached 'rural communities' with local access nodes.

ii) *Lack of information filters*: A range of information resources on the internet are not of the highest educational, social, or moral value.

iii) *The internet as a public forum*: Like talk radio, the internet has become a public forum, where ideas are generated, discussed, and debated.

iv) *No guaranteed performance*: The distance learning community needs to consider that it neither be guaranteed a certain throughput across the internet nor a consistent reliability level.

v) *Lack of antiviral software*: Internet e-mail or downloaded files have been known to contain viruses, which cannot be eliminated without antiviral software on every machine in the network.

vi) *Junk e-mail*: Institutions connected to the internet can be flooded with useless and unwanted e-mail.

vii) *Security issues*: The security weaknesses of the internet limit its usefulness to interorganisational communications, including those associated with distance learning solutions.

Several solutions are becoming available to corporations that want to improve the security of internet access:

i) *Screening router firewall*: This solution involves using routers configured using native access rules to filter packets at the IP port level. The benefit of this solution is that it may not require additional investment on the part of the corporation since the router may be a part of the installed base.

ii) *Application-level firewalls*: This solution provides a higher degree of security than a router firewall. The implementation of this method is accomplished by forcing users to access the system only via application-level prompts.

DISTANCE LEARNING ENVIRONMENT

Increased precision of electronics in view of the development of digital circuitry and mass production of integrated circuit chips resulted in many new functions, lower prices, and better quality and reliability for communications systems. The educational community, however, has been relatively slow in adopting the potential, power of the new telecommunications systems.

The use of computers as a tool for delivering education was implemented and experimented with in the late 1970s and early 1980s. Politicians and government-allocated money for computer education, and educational software packages proliferated. Those packages followed, for the most part, a programmed learning paradigm that emphasised drill and practice. Boring and unimaginative software was largely to blame for the failure of the computer as a learning tool.

By the end of the 1980s, when better software became available, publishers were uninterested, and teachers were dubious and afraid of the high cost of computer technology. It was only in the early 1990s that telecommunications-based education started to realise its potential, especially with the advent of high-power personal computers (PCs), broadband communications, and digital video.

IDL is one of the technological tools that contributes to the solution of the educational problems that society faces. IDL refers to a portfolio of application and networking solutions that can be (and are being) implemented by universities, schools, corporations, and government agencies to enable them to enhance education and research processes.

IDL solutions establish telecommunication links between education receivers and various sources of knowledge over geographic areas that may span a metropolitan segment, a whole state, or the entire country. These sources of knowledge are not limited to distance learning providers, such as universities and corporate training centres they also encompass information and processing resources, such as libraries, supercomputer centres, and museums. The required links may involve voice communications, video communications, data communications, or a combination of these medias.

The quality of the distance learning programmes is a function of the selected type of solution and the particular needs of the distance learners. IDL solutions can address many of the challenges facing education and training institutions. Some of them are given below.

i) IDL can reduce the isolation of schools and colleges, and it can address anticipated shortage of teachers in those communities by linking them with education providers.

ii) IDL can eliminate the electronic isolation of the traditional classroom by linking classrooms with external sources of learning, such as museums, libraries and universities.

iii) IDL can enhance the quality of education by speeding the process of information transfer between education providers and education receivers.

iv) IDL offers the promise of instant sharing of information among members of the R&D community, speeding the research process and consequently, the development of new products and services.

v) IDL can resolve some of the financial problems facing universities by providing them with economics of scale. Through distance learning, a greater number of remote classes can be created, giving education providers the opportunity to generate more revenues per teacher or to reduce the tuition per student.

vi) By implementing distance learning solutions, a university can differentiate itself from other universities by being at the leading edge of technology.

vii) Through distance learning, government agencies can reduce the cost of retraining the structurally unemployed and welfare recipients.

viii) IDL enables corporations to upgrade the skills of their workforces to effectively compete in skill-intensive industries.

ix) IDL can reduce the training budgets of corporations by reducing costs of travel for educational purposes.

Today, educators are investing school capital and operating funds in IDL technology; in many schools and colleges, telecommunications has become a line item in the operating budget. Many distance learning communication solutions are in the market today to satisfy the needs of distance learning providers and receivers.

These application solutions can be divided into two categories:

i) video solutions and

ii) data solutions.

Video solutions: Video solutions can be further classified into four categories:

i) One-way video/one-way audio;

ii) One-way video/two-way audio;

iii) Two-way video/two-way audio; and

iv) N-way video/N-way audio with continuous presence.

Despite the drive toward digital technology and fibreoptics, a major portion of distance learning programming is still carried by analog satellite links, microwave links over-the-air and cable analog TV, and instructional television fixed service (ITFS). Once such recognition is made, one can then focus on an assessment of the advantages of a migration to digital. Schools can access educational TV programmes by subscribing to basic cable TV services or obtain them over an ITFS network.

The one-way video/two-way audio solutions enable distance learning providers to establish a one-way video/two-way audio with the recipients. While the video programme originates at one site, the distance learning receivers can be located at multiple sites. Transmission is either analog or digital. Traditional analog TV requires 6 MHz; digital transmission rates range from 3 to 6 Mbps.

The one-way video/two-way audio solution provides university students with the ability to ask questions and interact with other students in other locations. The one-way video/two-way audio solution is beneficial not only to university students but also to telecom/datacom administrators of universities for the following reasons:

i) A large number of satellite-based providers are currently available.

ii) Satellite and fibre systems deliver high quality pictures.

iii) The cost of one-way transmission is much less than the cost of hiring a teacher.

iv) There is support for inter-university and intra-university networking solutions.

v) The satellite-based one-way video solutions has a regional or national geographic coverage.

However, the one-way video/two-way audio solutions have their limitations:

i) The major problem with one-way videoconferencing systems to students is the accessibility of teachers.
ii) The relationship that develops between the student and the teacher through face-to-face interactions cannot be duplicated through the one-way video solution.
iii) Another problem is scheduling complexities, because in many cases, the daily transmission hours are often at odds with a school's own class schedules.

Video broadcasting systems can be classified into two:

i) *Private-business TV-based programming*: These systems are used by corporations internally, for example, to provide corporate training.
ii) *Shared institutional distance learning systems*: These systems are shared by multiple distance learning receivers and are managed by a single distance learning provider.

The two-way videoconferencing solution offers a potential improvement over the one-way video/two-way audio solution: interactivity. With this solution, all the participants can see each other, enhancing the collaborative learning process. However, its effectiveness depends on picture quality. The quality of the two-way videoconferencing picture, its affordability, and its geographic presence depend on the coding method and the networking solution provided.

Despite the benefits of this solution, it cannot on its own support all the IDL needs of universities. Data-oriented solutions, such as groupware and the internet, can complement the two-way video/audio solution in addressing the IDL needs of universities.

An example of a growing two-way videoconferencing solution is the Collaboration for Interactive Distance Visual

Learning (CIDVL). This is a multi-institutional effort, which was formally launched in 1993. CIDVL consists of 11 universities and corporations seeking to create a "virtual university" environment, providing courses and lectures to one another in the field of engineering. Initial members of CIDVL were Boston University, MIT, Penn State, Rensselaer Polytechnic Institute, 3M Corp., AT&T, United Technologies, and PictureTel Corp.

Other universities and corporations are entitled to join CIDVL as members by paying $10,000 for a three-year membership term. New members are also expected to offer their own intellectual contributions. Students enrol in a CIDVL course through either their individual university or corporation. University students pay per-credit fees to the remote institution offering the programme. Credit-transfer policies are arranged between the native university at which the student is enrolled and the remote university offering the course. The two-way video/two-way audio systems provide participants with simultaneous interactive image and voice communications, enabling individuals in different locations to communicate with each other as if they were in the same room. Users may be students communicating with their teachers over a long distance or executives communicating with their employees.

Videoconferencing systems involve the transmission of two-way video and two-way audio from one location to multiple locations. To reduce the amount of bandwidth required for transmission, digitisation and compression of audio and video signals are implemented. Custom or site-built rooms, including classrooms, are equipped with fixed systems to support video communication. Equipment is often built into walls or tabletops. The number of participants accommodated by this design is usually a function of room size and layout. This system represents the high range of video/videoconferencing systems and is appropriate for corporations that have made a major commitment to videoconferencing. High-end systems can support executive level videoconferencing usage, and complex applications that require significant peripheral equipment. These rooms are used by both educational institutions and corporations, although the venue, the design, and the audio/visual systems tend to be different.

Education institutions particularly need the following:

i) simple control systems;
ii) monitors and projectors ranging in size from 27 inches to 53 inches (or more);
iii) three or more cameras per system (one for the student, one for the instructor, and one for graphics capture);
iv) a high-quality audio system, including quality microphones and speakers; and
v) direct computer peripheral input to the audio/visual system.

Cabinet-mounted units contain the major equipment required for video/videoconferencing. Standalone systems accommodate the same types of applications and the same participants as custom-built rooms. Standalone units, however, offer a less costly and less permanent solution. These systems can be used by both educational institutions and corporations. Rollabouts are configured on carts with staging rooms for storing peripherals.

These systems, which represent the midrange of video/videoconferencing systems, have two advantages:

i) they are convenient because of their transportability and flexibility, and
ii) they are more affordable than high-end systems.

These advantages make rollabouts appropriate for companies with limited space, moderate budget and video/videoconferencing needs which may be dispersed throughout a specific location. These systems can be used by both educational institutions and corporations.

PC-based video/videoconferencing systems can be created by connecting PCs to local area networks (LANs), which are extended to wide area networks (WANs) through services such as switched, digital services. PCs can also be connected directly to WANs.

Although classrooms tend to have multiple monitors, many (corporate) video/videoconferencing systems rely on one monitor to display both the incoming and the outgoing video images. This is accomplished through windowing, whereby a small window displaying one image (usually outgoing video) is superimposed on the main window (usually displaying incoming video).

Alternatively, dual windows can display incoming and outgoing video or incoming video and graphics simultaneously. The number and set-up of monitors depends on the application, the room characteristics, and the type of videoconferencing installation (e.g., desktop, rollabout, custom-built). Large monitors tend to be more effective.

The number and the arrangement of cameras depends largely on the number of conference participants, students, or teachers; the application requirements; the room characteristics; and the type of videoconferencing installation (e.g., desktop, rollabout, custom-built). Cameras range from low-end systems, to on-charged-couple-device (1-CCD) systems with 470 lines of horizontal resolution, to 3-CCD cameras with 750 lines of resolution. Cameras can be positioned in one of three ways: with a joystick or control panel buttons, automatically to focus on the participant who is speaking, or manually.

Audio systems, including speakers and microphones must provide clear, simultaneous two-way communication. One desirable feature of an audio system is automatic echo cancellation, which adjusts the incoming and outgoing audio signals according to the acoustics of a particular room. A codec performs two functions: video digitisation and compression. Digitisation is the ability of the codec to convert analog video and audio signals into a digital bit stream for transmission over digital lines. When receiving the coded signal, the remote codec reconverts the digital signal back into analog video and voice signals, which are then sent to the video monitor and speakers. The codec also compresses the signal to provide efficient and cost-effective transmission. Typically the compression ratio is 100:1. The level of picture resolution provided by the codec depends on the sophistication of the digitisation and compression algorithms.

Video compression algorithms are based on the International Telecommunication Union-Telecommunication (ITU-T) or International Organisation for Standardisation (ISO, after the French) standards. ITU-T's standard H.261 covers transmission of video at rates ranging from 56/64 Kbps to 2.048 Mbps. ISO's Motion Picture Expert Group 1 (MPEG-1) supports entertainment-level video at 1.544 Mbps; MPEG-2 supports even better quality at 6 Mbps. The Motion joint Photographic Export Group (M-JPEG) supports quality video at 10-20 Mbps.

Video signals contain a substantial amount of intrinsic redundancy, so that compression can be undertaken prior to storage or transmission. Compression schemes that are able to reduce the raw bits by a factor of 100 or 200 are usually employed. There have been claims of compression ratios of 1:2,500 through the use of fractal methods. Audio/visual distance learning systems are not inexpensive and may typically require a system integrator to assemble and test.

Data solutions: Data solutions can be classified into two categories:

i) groupware
ii) Internet.

The groupware is an emerging alternative solution to the internet in meeting the needs of universities for intra-university IDL applications. The key intra-university applications supported by groupware are the following:

i) *Collaborative learning and research:* Groupware enables students to collaborate in real time on projects. Through groupware massaging applications, university students can submit their homework to teachers via e-mail, leave messages, or inquire about specific problems they are encountering in solving a specific homework assignment.

ii) *Access to databases:* Via groupware, the students can access public databases, private databases, fax, paging, voice mail, etc.

iii) *Remote classroom:* Groupware can complement desktop videoconferencing in conducting small classrooms. Through a small window on desktop workstations, university students are able to establish video-conferencing sessions with remote teachers.

iv) *Student/teacher and student/student interactions after hours:* Students residing in dormitories can exchange messages with teachers and other students, through groupware.

The major benefits offered by groupware includes the following:

1) *Low cost*: In implementing groupware, telecom/datacom managers incur a non-recurring cost.
2) *Multiple applications*: Groupware supports multiple IDL applications.
3) *Ease of use*: Multi-functional groupware solutions are based on GUIs, which makes them easy to use.
4) *Secure*: Groupware provides a secure solution for intra-company communications.
5) *Training and consulting*: The leading providers of multifunctional groupware provide their buyers with training or consulting.

Groupware which allows remote training through PCs connected to the training site by a switched or permanent network, usually employing computer-supported cooperative work (CSCW) software. Groupware refers to software that can support at least one of the following applications: electronic messaging, data conferencing, or messaging gateways. Groupware solutions link distance learning providers and receivers that are separated by a WAN. An increasing number of vendors offer groupware. Providers of groupware solutions extend beyond software providers to encompass network providers.

The internet supplies ad hoc access to information and databases. It has been growing rapidly in the last few years. Through the internet a user can receive a number of services, including logon services, e-mail, file transfer, host-to-host communications, and directory services. Universities have been using the internet for over a decade. The major uses are:

i) *Access to libraries and databases:* University students can access hundreds of libraries around the world, as well as library catalogue and full text-service delivery services, through the internet. The internet also enables university students and researchers to access a wide range of government agency information, such as space shuttle updates.

ii) *Collaborative learning:* University students can rely on a number of internet services in collaborating with each other. These services include e-mail, logon services, file transfer, host-to-host communications, and directory services. These applications enable university students to establish a dialogue with other researchers and scientists around the globe. It also enables them to transfer large files. In addition, through electronic whiteboards university students can share in real-time notes about specific technical topics.

iii) *Remote learning:* One of the growing capabilities of the internet is videoconferencing. The internet has demonstrated the ability to link multiple sites though entry-level two-way videoconferencing links.

iv) *Access to supercomputers:* The internet enables university students and researchers to access major supercomputer centres throughout the country.

Due to its low cost, support for a wide range of applications, and ability to provide university students and researchers with access to a range of information resources, the internet will continue to be a key networking and communications solution for universities. The internet solution provides students, researchers, and teachers with freedom from the constraints of time and space, interactivity, and instructional feedback. It has one major limitation, however, that universities need to take into account in selecting the applications supported by the internet security. Violations result from unauthorised password use, particularly given the emergence of programmes collecting names and passwords on the network.

Networking Solutions

To support the application solutions a number of key networking solutions are available. They include ATM-based solutions, fast-packet services, and ISDN primary rate interface.

i) *ATM solutions*: ATM solutions can provide universities with high transmission speeds and the ability to integrate data, voice, video, and multimedia communications. One university that has implemented an ATM-based networking solution is Duke Medical Centre in North Carolina. Administrators selected ATM as both a LAN and a WAN solution to replace an Ethernet-based LAN infrastructure.

ii) *SMDS*: SMDS can support the data-oriented IDL application solutions, including access to the internet and groupware communications. SMDS provides universities with several benefits, including cost reduction, support for high-bandwidth bursty data applications, flexibility, and security.

a) *Cost reduction*: SMDS could be more economical than ATM PVC solutions, particularly when there are many sites to be interconnected. SMDS can also reduce university administrative cost if network connections of a university cannot be predicted in advance, or if these connections are constantly changing.

b) *Extensive bandwidth capabilities*: SMDS provides telecom/datacom managers with a choice of various access classes, enabling them to start at a lower bandwidth level and than migrate the network to a higher access class as the communications needs warrant the upgrade.

c) *Flexibility*: SMDS is flexible because it enables telecom/datacom managers to include corporations in their networks that do not justify the expense of a dedicated line.

Besides the benefits, SMDS has several shortcomings. It is defined to support packet data traffic. It cannot support a number of IDL solutions, including one-way video/two-way audio and two-way video/two-way audio solutions.

iii) *Frame relay solutions*: Frame Relay Solutions (FRS) is emerging as a distance learning networking solution that can complement or substitute for other networking solutions, such as SMDS, NMLIS, and ATM CRS. As already noted, FRS is a data-only, connection-oriented frame-transport service that uses virtual connections. Statistical multiplexing techniques are used to support PVCs and, in the future, SVCs.

FRS on the market tends to be PVC-based. A PVC connection is usually established when the service is provisioned at subscription time, eliminating the need for user-to network signalling. PAS supports access speeds of 56 Kbps, n × 64 Kbps, and 1.544 Mbps. Frame relay provides universities with several benefits, including the following:

a) *Economic benefits:* FRS offers higher transmission speeds, simplified network design, and low operating costs compared to earlier packet services.

b) *Availability*: FRS is widely available and is currently supported by IXCs, LECs, and RBOCs.

iv) ISDN: It provides universities with another data and video communications alternative. This interconnection approach involves the use of switched digital facilities to link a student with a training site located across the city or the country. ISDN provides n´64 Kbps end-to-end digital connectivity with access to voice and data services for the same digital transmission and switching facilities. The more well-known interfaces are 2B+D, which provides two switched 64-Kbps channels, plus a 16-Kbps packet/signalling channel, and 23B+D, which provides universities with DS1 speeds. ISDN is now seeing a renewed push toward deployment. It can support the following IDL applications:

a) *Access to Internet*: RBOCs are increasingly addressing the needs of universities for access to the internet through ISDN solutions.

b) *Access to groupware*: ISDN can support both public and private groupware solutions.

c) *Two-way compressed videoconferencing solution*: The RBOCs are developing this capability to meet the needs of universities.

ISDN provides universities with the following benefits:

a) *"Wideband" bandwidth:* A group of ISDN solutions are available that can support the bandwidth needs of universities for lower-end videoconferencing solutions.

b) *Availability*: The RBOCs have been actively deploying ISDN to support the networking needs of universities, as well as other applications.

Networking solutions needed by education providers and receivers are not uniformly available, nor are they uniformly affordable. The affordability and ubiquity of these services cannot be improved without the creation of a National Information Infrastructure (NII). In US, this is a topic of intense debate and interest to the federal government as well as to state governments, universities, and network services providers. A number of initiatives are currently being carried out by these players.

The federal government and the state governments play vital indirect roles in speeding the process of creating an NII as well as in education reform. These roles include financial role, regulatory role, user role and educator role. The financial role of the federal and state governments refers to their efforts to finance and build statewide networks. The regulatory role of the state governments refers to the efforts of the public utility commissions of the individual states as well as to those of the FCC to remove barriers to competition and to provide incentives to the expansion of the distance learning programmes.

The telecommunications reform legislation of 1996 opens the telecommunications marketplace to greater competition, which, many expect, will increase the quality of and reduce the cost of service. The state and federal governments are large consumers of information technology. The state and federal governments play an important role as advocates of distance learning. They also play a direct role in resolving education problems. To play these roles effectively, the federal and state governments need to introduce regulatory and legislative reforms. They can also provide financial incentives to education providers and receivers. In addition, they can get directly involved in the distance learning industry by introducing new distance learning technologies. These technologies can address many problems such as the education of welfare recipients and the structurally unemployed. Carriers and telephone companies play an active role in building the NII and in delivering a number of services that ride on the NII. The telephone companies view the as a tool to face these challenges and to differentiate themselves from their existing and emerging competitors. Two closely related groups, the cable TV companies and the AAPs, are the main competitors of the traditional telephone companies in the creation of the NII and in the delivery of distance learning services. Their roles include building joint regional cable TV-AAP networks to provide an increasing number of services, including data over coaxial cable and access to educational TV programming.

AAPs are now receiving equal status to the LECs in a number of states. While many AAPs are allied with the cable TV companies, a few companies are not. These independent AAPs are building MANs and offering services, primarily to business users, that include private-line services, LAN interconnection services, and, increasingly, switched data services. Most AAPs are evolving along two parallel tracks: the traditional AAP—a fibre network providing private lines and special access in a downtown central business district—is becoming an endangered species in the view of some observers. AAPs are becoming either national AAPs or what have been called competitive LECs (CompLECs, also known as CLECs). National AAPs will continue to do what AAPs have done over the years: serve telecommunications-dependent businesses, which need the operational and strategic security that is accrued from having a diverse source of supply for critical local telecommunications services.

The distance education arrived on the scene, first as correspondence provision and later as an open and distance university-based offering provided an alternative pathway to pursue higher education not only for basic degree courses but also for professional courses in management, teacher education etc. By this time the conventional university system had consolidated its structure and stabilised its approach to what was called "good quality" higher education through the policies and action of University Grants Commission. These revolved around five broad thrusts:

i) Laying down minimum and essential qualifications and experience for various academic and other staff in college and universities.

ii) Developing norms and standards for academic provisions through model curricula, teaching plans and examination systems.

ii) Fixing of minimum necessary infrastructure in terms of land, buildings, classrooms, labs, library, etc.

iv) Providing funds and grants for developing new thrust areas such as computers, bio-technology, etc.

v) Establishing new postgraduate departments and centres of excellence as well as providing audio visual support through "countrywide classroom" broadcasts.

Without any statutory constraints and infrastructure restrictions on the number of students to be admitted, the distance education wings of the conventional universities came to be looked upon as cash cows. "Partly because distance education institutions launched courses without any reasonable understanding of the distance education system, very often without sufficiently preparing for effective distance education transactions."

The initial reaction of distance educators in India manifested in their building a defence mechanism for distance education systems and not for the conventional system. The perceived effectiveness of conventional education was used as a standard measure for the effectiveness of conventional education. The University Grants Commission has realised as well that they play a recommendatory and funding role and that, if an institution can mobilise funds independently, it will not bother about UGC recommendations and guidelines. Hence the ISO 9000 culture requiring not only profession of quality of products but a demonstrable proof of the quality culture in the operations from the inspection of incoming raw materials range of successive manufacturing operation, internal quality assurance mechanism at all intermediate stages as well as predespatch testing, were required to be documented and demonstrated to the outside trained and certified inspectors and lead assessors.

This, in turn, had its parallel effect on the other sectors including education which was rated as "service" which well defined the objective of taking in a raw students as an input and to transform him/her into a graduate fit for assisting in the wealth creation activities of the socio-economic system. The almost simultaneous establishment of the National Assessment and Accreditation Council (NAAC) by UGC and the National Board of Accreditation (NBA) by AICTE for the technical education sector bear out these common concerns and felt needs. Both these bodies have evolved specific criteria and techniques assessment of the relevant quality parameters. The NBA had, in addition, gone in for a system of grading of the programmes of institution based on the score it achieved on a designated scale.

Distance education system in this country has eight open universities and 58 distance (mainly correspondence) institutes/directorates attached to the conventional universities. The Indira Gandhi National Open University (IGNOU) is the flagship of this distance education system and under its Act, the Distance Education Council (DEC) was established to promote, coordinate and maintain standards. IGNOU has already established itself as a leader amongst distance education institutes. At IGNOU, quality assurance activities focus on all the major and critical processes in distance education quite similar to those at the open universities, but the measures taken to achieve the desired quality differ considerably. Existing built-in quality assurance mechanisms are as follows:

i) planning the course or programme;

ii) developing the course or programme;

iii) producing the learning materials;
iv) implementing the course or programme;
v) reviewing the courses and follow up activities; and
vi) developing human resources.

New technologies, namely satellite communication, fibre optic cable and computers have dramatically enhanced educational capabilities. By providing communication links, telecommunications can overcome distance barriers that hamper development. Thus through the use of new communication technologies, access to good educational programmes can be greatly extended to large audiences in rural and remote areas with tremendous flexibility in subject matter content and in locations served. Corollary to these technological expansions, the area of education which is considered to be fastest growing today is that of distance education. Distance education, based on the use of modern communications and multimedia materials, has proved to be the major new movement in human resource development in the current decade. The ability to cope with rapid changes in the higher education system will become the primary measure of success, of both micro and macro levels, as we approach the 21st century.

Change is occurring faster everyday. Many societies have shifted from industrial era to information era, and others are fast moving in that direction. The volume of information that becomes available, doubles every four to five years. Stating it another way, the total of all human knowledge that was available to an undergraduate in 1997 will be less than one per cent of what will be available to his/her counterpart in the year 2050. Teachers have to become experts in helping learners navigate through this sea of information rather than pretending to be effective transformers of that information into knowledge. Students must be trained to bring about that information. Those who survive this information explosion will be able to deal with it effectively and even more importantly, acquire knowledge. These changes have a major impact on education and training. In fact, education and training are also undergoing a major change. The focus has shifted to learning rather than teaching. Some of the major changes are:

i) From institutional-based learning to far learning organisations with just in time knowledged provisions;
ii) From fixed curricula to personalised curricula;
iii) From front ended education to lifelong education;
iv) From teaching to learning.

Distance education is going to be number one amongst the great world industries, within which will flourish an educational machine technology that will provide tools such as the individually selected and articulated two-way TV and an inter-continentally networked documentary call up system operative on any home two-way set. Bates has outlined the developments in communication and information technologies with implications for learning which are the following:

i) Integration of television, telecommunication and computers, through digitisation and compression techniques;
ii) Reduced costs, and more flexible user applications of telecommunications, through developments such as ISDN/fibre optics/cellular radios;
iii) Miniaturisation (tiny cameras, microphones, small high resolution display screens);
iv) Increased portability, through use of radio communication and miniaturisation;
v) Increased processing power, through new microchip development and advanced software techniques;
vi) More powerful and user-friendly commands and software tools, making it much easier for users to create and communicate their own materials.

In India distance education has emerged as a formidable system of higher education. There are at present eight open universities in India and about 50 distance education divisions attached to conventional universities. There is also a National Open School in the country. While one must admit that the conventional education system has played an important role in expanding education, particularly in the urban areas, over the last 50 years or so, one must accept its limitations as a means of mass education and especially quality education in the rural areas. The costs of infrastructure necessary for the traditional type of education have gone up tremendously, but most of the state governments are suffering from resource crunch. There are competing demands for public resources from various other non-educational sectors.

On the other hand, the population of the country is growing steadily, outstripping the growth of schooling facilities, with the exception of some areas. This fact coupled with the high dropout ratio has resulted in net additions of illiterate people from decade to decade. The conventional system of education has proved inadequate in the face of rapidly increasing population. The emergence of the information technology including the satellite-based telecommunication system has generated a potential of a sea-change in the education system all over the world.

Print, radio, television, audio-video cassettes, tape-recorders, overhead/slide projectors, filmstrips, etc., which permit only one-way communication have become old educational-technologies and have lost novelty in the developed world. The last one decade has seen emergence of a series of new, electronic-based innovations in the field of higher education, which permit vision, sound, data with inter-activity. Information highways are high speed data networks used to transport information and link people who want to be connected with others.

Teletext and Video-text are the two new information age services that will soon be widespread among home and business users. Teletext is a one-way service in which pages of information from a central database are broadcast on a regular television signal. Video-text is a more sophisticated two-way service using telephone lines.

E-mail, teleconferencing (audio and video) and computer conferencing are common activities on the internet and other electronic networks. The words information highway reflect speed, volume, powers, and efficiency. With the information highways becoming a reality in many countries, Conferencing Technologies (CT) have come to be used in a large way in collaborative distance and open learning. The success of CTs will depend on the extent to which learning tasks, such as attentiveness, idea generation, concept elaboration, feedback, etc., are fulfilled.

The CTs reduce the teachers' teaching functions without reducing the academic rigour. Since generally the adults are the participants of CTs, a collaborative type of learning is necessary. When integrated into the whole learning context, CTs offer sufficient flexibility to the learners and the educators. Thus, a virtual classroom can be created in which the class is taught using the satellite, microwave or cable linkages between them. The electronically linking of students and teachers at various locations by cable, microwave or satellite has made it possible to create this face-to-face teaching at a distance. There is no doubt that an extensive emergence of electronic-based technology in the field of education is in the offing.

However, one must not forget limitations in its use, especially in the developing countries. The advocates of the modern technologies in education presuppose that the learners have access to a wide range of high specification information and communication technologies; that these technologies can be used at time and in circumstances that are convenient for learners and optimal for effective study; and the learners have sufficient familiarity or experience of using them. Unfortunately all these presumptions are far from true so far as learners in developing countries are concerned. Though there may be television in the house, there is certainly a claim of all members of the family for using TV for entertainment purposes. Not many students have access to VCRs because of the costs. Even those who have VCRs may not always be able to use them in view of the competing demand for TV time by others. PC and modems are absent in most of the learner houses in the developing countries. Flexibility is also a limiting factor.

Multiplicity of languages used in the same country, as in India, also poses severe problems in reaching distance education to different parts through the broadcasting/networking systems. Thus, there are severe limitations in the use of high specification information and communication technology in the developing countries. It may take two to three decades to reduce these limitations to an insignificant level. It will be difficult to protect national, state or provincial boundaries from distance education. Governments will have to deal with the question, sooner or later, whether they would like to be net exporters or net importers of education. The answer of course is quality. The distance teaching institutions, in particular, will have to demonstrate superior quality of education that will override the public's preconceptions of the status of better-known, more conventional institutions as they enter into the distance teaching world via the internet.

Electronic-based technologies will dominate the education scenario in the developed countries. The 21st century will give rise to electronic educational institutions which will provide information on education and training needs and opportunities; quality control; accreditation; coherent curricula and other concomitant services. Many of the instructors or tutors may not belong to the educational institutions but will be independent contractors. Nor would it be necessary for learners to be registered with an educational institution. The educational institutions may only collect and deliver payments for fees and royalties to the owners of the software or the telecom companies. Unless the less developed countries are able to create an appropriate technological infrastructure to support the kind of learning needed in the 21st century, they would be left far behind. Building up of information highways are the *sine quo non* of the modern system. The need of the century is to exploit the information highway to the fullest possible extent.

However, Interactive Distance Learning (IDL) is one the technological tools that can contribute to the solution of educational problems and challenges which universities are facing. The IDL links enable universities to establish closer ties with their corporate and government clients by enabling them to rapidly share information among members of the R&D community, speeding up the process of R&D and the development of new products and services. The IDL can also resolve some of the financial problems facing universities by providing them with economies of scale. Through IDL, universities can create a greater number of remote classes. This creates education providers with the opportunity to generate more revenues per teacher or to reduce the tuition per student.

A university can differentiate itself from other universities by being at the leading edge of IDL technology. However, universities cannot hope to maximise the benefits of automation without attacking those problems through specific IDL applications, identifying the communication applications that are solving the problems, and implementing innovative solutions that can address the problems. Various university buildings need to establish intra-university and interuniversity communications links with university branches, other colleges, dormitories, and external sources of information.

The following IDL applications drive universities needs for the establishment of these links:

i) *Collaborative learning*: Collaboration is important to university students so they can share and analyse scientific data, have extended discussions with other peers, and work together to produce papers and journals. Traditionally the sharing of information relied on text-based e-mail and on face-to-face meetings. Increasingly, university students and researchers are seeking computer graphics and animation-generation systems with text.

Collaborative learning encompasses the establishment of communication links among students, teachers, and researchers. Collaboration is not limited to the formal hours of schools, nor is it limited to a university campus. Students can benefit from getting in touch with their professors after class hours for several reasons:

a) to inquire about a specific project or report assignment,

b) to deliver the work to their instructors electronically, and

c) to receive comments back from their professors.

ii) *Access to databases*: Students, instructors, and researchers need to have access to a large number of databases. The nature and locations of the databases are shaped by the type of research that an individual is performing. These databases have two common characteristics:

a) They are accepted standards in their respective research communities, and

b) They are large. The large size of the databases and the impracticality of duplicating them in every research lab across the nation necessitate the availability of broad-band networks to researchers to maximise the speed of scientific research and development.

iii) *Access to supercomputers*: University needs for access to supercomputers are shaped by the needs of the various groups of researchers operating in an university environment. For collaborative learning to be effective, educational experts believe that schools have to change in the following ways:

a) Effective collaboration becomes more useful as the number of teachers and students participating in a specific collaborative effort decrease.

b) Effective collaboration among students and teachers belonging to the same team requires more effective scheduling for groupwork.

iv) *Access to libraries*: In preparation for their assignments, students need to access digital libraries as a substitute for physical access to libraries. This will provide them with access to a wider range of information resources that may be available in their university library. They need connectivity to these libraries to access electronic books, periodicals, and other publications.

v) *Remote learning*: Universities need to create remote classes to support the educational needs of their smaller branches as well as those of smaller universities. Remote classes provide universities with the following benefits:

a) they increase the number of teachers per student, and

b) they reduce the costs associated with building new classes and expanding campuses.

To create a successful remote education solution, universities need to consider the following needs of students:

a) *Interactivity*: This is a key element of any successful IDL programme. The more the IDL solution selected by the university involves interactivity, the more it will be successful in getting students involved, enabling them ask questions and be stimulated while taking the course.

b) *Instructional feedback*: This extends beyond the provision of grades by instructors to students on specific assignments, and it encompasses providing answers to questions after university hours.

c) *Elimination of time constraints*: Through IDL solutions, students and instructors can, to some extent, free themselves from the constraints of time. This means that an effective IDL solution should enable students to maximise the time of their interactions beyond classroom hours.

d) *Motivation*: An effective IDL solution should enable students to have fun as they interact with other students and teachers.

In selecting the IDL applications, telecom/datacom managers of universities need to take into account a number of factors, some of which are specific to the university telecom/datacom environment. The telecom/datacom infrastructure of a university is shaped by several factors:

a) whether the university or college is public or private,
b) the founder of the university,
c) the size of the university,
d) the specialisation of the university, and
e) the physical location of the university.

The telecom/datacom environments of large universities resemble those of large industrial parks. The university telecom/datacom infrastructure may include some or all of the following elements:

i) *A voice networking environment*: This is supported by a PBX or centrex and extended over a metropolitan area through either private lines or a public switched network system.

ii) *Legacy systems*: This include older minicomputers, administrative mainframes, and even Ethernets and token rings.

iii) *A client/server environment*: Clients and servers, which may be spread around the campus and interconnected across LANs, such as ethernet, token ring, and FDDI.

iv) *Satellite-based networks:* It used by universities both to originate and to receive IDL programming.

Universities are innovators and are willing to explore new technologies, even if those technologies are not well proven. In contrast, corporations would consider only a proven technology before committing their resources to the adoption of a technology.

i) *Geographic coverage*: Telecom/datacom managers of universities seek application solutions that support the geographic range of universities.

ii) *Ease of use and administration*: Telecom/datacom managers value application solutions that are easy to administer and to use by IDL receivers and providers.

iii) *Intra enterprise versus inter-enterprise communications*: The appropriateness of the application solution to a university may depend on the extent of the needs of telecom/datacom managers for interuniversity versus intrauniversity communications.

iv) *Inter-operability and compatibility*: Telecom/datacom managers are seeking solutions that are not proprietary but based on open standards. This would enable them to not have to rely on a single vendor.

v) *Support for installed base*: Telecom/datacom managers value solutions that can build on their installed base of information systems.

vi) *Access methods and speeds*: Telecom/datacom managers have needs for different access methods and speeds in support of applications solutions.

REMOTE DISTANCE PROGRAMME

The traditional model of learning is based on principles of an instructor-directed environment. Learners have been required to do what the instructor tells them to do. This model is experiencing a shift to a learner-directed environment as learner requirements within the workforce increase due to a variety of factors, including constant technological change.

The key element necessary for any learning to take place is communication. In order for concepts, procedures, principles, etc., to be fully understood, the learner must communicate them to others. In addition, the learner must be able to demonstrate his or her ability to complete the learned task. Today we still send staff to a training facility, away from their physical workspace. This follows the traditional model of instructor-directed learning. However, from this scenario learners only retain approximately 20 per cent of what they were taught. The other 80 per cent of what they were taught may be necessary to their job function, but not necessarily applicable on day one of their return to the workplace.

Self-paced learning tools have been implemented at many companies to replace rather than augment instructor-led learning. Given the growing mass of products to choose from in this genre, learners can select the product that best fits their learning style. In this case, learning new skills or reviewing previously learned skills is directed by the learner with respect to learning style, learning capability, and learning time. Skills learned in this manner are applied immediately.

Accelerating need for knowledge throughout modern society is driving the expansion of alternative online learning technology. Increasingly, students of every stripe, whether in universities, corporate cubicles, or at home, are being asked to learn online. A mushrooming variety of courseware is now available over internal networks, wide area networks, and the internet/ intranet. The advantages of round-the-clock access to learning at any location are apparent. In many cases, however, students are expected to work on their own, often with no guidance from an instructor. A great deal of discussion is taking place among educators concerning the effectiveness of this shift to asynchronous or on-demand learning. Every online learning educator is challenged to find the proper mix of asynchronous and synchronous learning to maximise their instruction.

In the traditional classrooms, some students are able to complete assignments with little help from the teacher, while other students require individual instruction. The challenge for traditional teachers has always been to engage the students through interaction with them and the rest of the class. A live instructor, interacting with students, is an essential part of the successful traditional classroom. Over the last decade, multimedia learning has become a vital part of many learning systems, on CD-ROM, CBT, and now online. The lessons of CD-ROM have been clear concerning asynchronous learning. In those cases where the CDs were delivered to the student without any intervention on the part of an instructor, the percentage of students completing such courses was lower than expected. When a live instructor was made available via phone, video, or in person, the completion rates increased.

Facilitated learning motivates more students to achieve the desired results. There have always been cases of mission critical learning, where the knowledge transfer must be verified by definable results. Facilitated learning has been the most effective method for training in industrial methods, technical fields, software skills, aviation, and many other areas requiring a high level of retention by students. Even such mundane tasks as computerised order entry can be a mission critical skill if it is vital to the success of a business.

The role of the instructor in online learning depends on the type of training, technology employed, and as noted above, the expected results. The combination of facilitated and on-demand learning can take many forms:

i) *Help desk model*: Roughly half of the calls that are made to the corporate help desk are training related. At some corporations, staff instructors are required to spend a certain amount of time on the help desk. In the help desk model of learning, the instructor is an on-call resource, available to answer questions and provide training over the phone to facilitate learning which is predominantly self-paced.

ii) *The 80-20 rule*: In these last two sections we have described a traditional model of learning where only 20 per cent of the learning provided is retained and 80 per cent is re-learned later. In the learner-directed model, 80 per cent of learning takes place asynchronously and 20 per cent takes place through facilitated communication. This new 80-20 model takes place over a different length of time and with a larger toolbox than the traditional model. As we add more asynchronous learning tools to the learner's desktop or workspace, we still need to ensure that effective learning is taking place. This amplifies the critical role of an instructor or facilitator. For many types of training, the 20 per cent of online learning facilitated by an instructor is essential to make the 80 per cent self-paced learning successful.

iii) *Assigned homework model*: In this model, learning is primarily instructor-directed with a portion of work done asynchronously. Homework is a specific task assigned to the learners by the instructor. The homework must be completed by a specific date. In a following class, homework is shared and discussed among the students. In this sharing of information, learning is reinforced.

iv) *Instructor dependent model*: In this case, the instructor directs all of the formal learning. No formal asynchronous study is assigned. The learners work on their own only as needed. Each of these instructor-directed models is appropriate for given learning applications. The key to the success of each model is the individual instructor's ability to engage the learners in interactive exercises and meaningful discussions that enhance overall learning.

Instructor/student communications may be integrated with online learning using currently available technologies:

i) *Audio conferencing*: telephone conferences connecting participants around the world are routinely used for business meetings. The same technology can be used in parallel with online data sharing to complete the facilitated learning paradigm.

ii) *Internet audio*: Recent advances in compress techniques have made internet/intranet audio practical to integrate with online learning systems.

iii) *Videoconferencing-desktop*: Videoconferencing is increasingly available as the technology of choice for facilitated online learning, especially in mission critical training situations.

Technology has been able to help today's training industry produce faster and more portable ways to deliver learning. In fact it has created the online learning industry. The internet and the corporate intranet are the new media for training delivery. Of all the online learning technologies currently available, few offer the capability to provide instructor-directed learning.

The facilitated or instructor-led model is still critical to learning. Combined with online technology, this is fast becoming the most powerful learning media for mission critical or results oriented training. Facilitated online learning allows for maximum reach to remote learners. It is an efficient media for distributing information quickly. It has the capability to leverage technolcgy and subject matter expert resources. Whatever paradigm shattering technologies await us in the future, the role of the instructor is sure to be recognised as vital to ensure results-oriented online learning.

Distance education can be defined as planned learning that normally occurs in a different place from teaching and as a result requires special techniques of course design, special instructional techniques, special methods of communication by electronic and other technology, as well as special organisational and administrative arrangements.

An instructional system is in continual interaction with its environment and achieves a 'steady state' or dynamic equilibrium while still retaining the capacity for work or energy transformation. Important words here are continual interaction and dynamic. Although the system is trying to maintain balance, it is still learning and developing. In organisations, a basic system has five implications:

i) it has an objective or purpose;

ii) the elements have an established arrangement, and each element has its own sub-objectives;

iii) a synergistic interrelationship must exist among the subsystems;

iv) the process of input to output is more important than the parts of the system; and

v) the objective or purpose of the whole outweighs the subordinate objectives of the subsystems.

The DEL model is designed to encompass lifelong learning within a distance education framework. The DEL system can be used to design, implement, and evaluate distance learning programmes. As a functional model for consortiums and individual distance education courses, it has wide applicability. The model is adapted from a food-service systems model developed at Kansas State University in the 1970's.

Outputs: The field of education has been oriented towards broadcast learning, where an expert who has information transmits or broadcasts it to students and the student simply regurgitates this material on a test. Achievement of content mastery and the development of well-rounded citizens who cooperate in the community, state, nation, and world are desired outputs of our newly developed DEL model. These outputs are interactive with their environment. Learning more about how effective distance education processes are accomplished is also an important goal. Satisfaction of the individuals or teams involved in making the process happen and the fiscal accountability of the system are also important outputs.

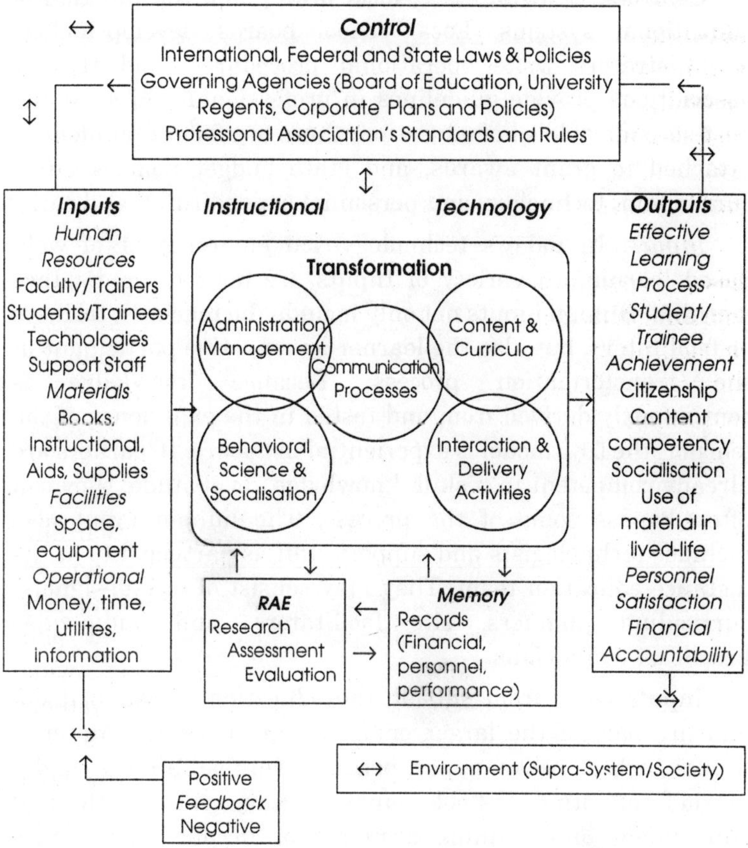

Figure 1: Distance education model

Whether in a profit or non-profit organisation, educational institution, corporate training setting, or global consortium, satisfied employees and fiscal bottom lines are important to the survival of the system as an entity. DEL system design must balance and prioritise these outputs, up front, before deciding how to develop the individualised learning strategies. Controls play an integral role in transforming system inputs into successful output.

Controls: Central, state, local laws guide the function of educational systems. Local school boards develop policy, administrators write operational procedures, and teacher associations provide guidelines in professional ethics. At the post-secondary level of education, there are federal guidelines attached to grant awards, and state budget policies affect curriculum, technology and personnel expenditures.

Inputs: In today's technology-rich environment of web-based learning, a variety of Inputs are needed for distance learning. Human inputs not only include the teachers, trainers or facilitators, but also the learner as an active participant in the transformation process. Because knowledge is continuously derived from and tested in the experience of the learner, the DEL model is experiential in nature. If learners are already competent in a skill, knowledge, or attitude, they can often bypass some of the process. The human input also includes technologists and support staff as participants in the distance education team. They may consist of web designers, curriculum planners, site facilitators, and audio-video broadcast technicians.

Inputs come from outside the educational system itself, and are part of the larger environment of society. Material inputs such as books, paper, pencils, overhead acetate, and a myriad of other school supplies have moved through educational and training systems for decades. Now, new supplies, such as software, multimedia CD-ROMS, laser paper, toner, internet browsers, and computer and video systems, are important parts of today's learning system. For some distance education operations, space is a pressing issue. As more students learn by distance both web and video-based-classroom space needs could shrink. However, space is needed to set up some distance teaching rooms, video equipment and computer infrastructure.

Operational inputs of money, time, utilities, and information flow are necessary to make distance learning happen. Telephones lines, satellite time, and electricity to run equipment all contribute to cost. Time is also a precious commodity. Distance education planners need to allow more time for preparation, coordination, and implementation of delivery than those involved in more traditional educational systems.

Transformation: The transformation element is designed with five subsystems interacting to produce the desired outcomes and reflects a team approach. Administration and management personnel interpret controls, staff the team, provide for the support and resources, and lend needed motivation and vision. They should be actively involved in knowing their market, their audience and their learners' needs. They also control the financial resources. Dates offers some strategies for administration and management. Content and curriculum specialists are involved in analysing and designing learning modules appropriate for learner focused, just-in-time, competency based training. Interaction and delivery have always been a part of the instructor's or trainer's implementation role.

In the DEL system, interaction and delivery require specialised attention. For both internet and video based education, facilitating and coaching are replacing the traditional, instructor lead approaches of the past. Planning for teacher-student, trainer-technician, learner-learner, and trainee-content interaction takes special attention.

Today, the net-generation are being socialised in a whole new world through e-mail and the internet. Planning interactive activities such as introductions, teamwork, cooperation, and required comments is an ongoing process. Each person is unique, his or her learning styles vary, and putting everyone in web-based classes most likely will not work. Communication is the linking process that interconnects management, content, delivery, and socialisation.

It is essential to the planning and delivery of knowledge and experience, and to the evaluation and continuous improvement of the process. Every organisation is faced with keeping track of its efforts, especially its history. Student and trainee records, accreditation history, communication files, personal data, performance criteria, benchmark data, testing, assessment and evaluation records, and financial reports are just some of the memory records kept in education systems. Technology greatly reduces the "file" size once required; much of today's historical data are found in corporation and school computer networks.

Closely related to the memory of an operation is what we have combined to call the Research, Assessment, and Evaluation (RAE) subsystem. Research based content, process evaluation, and learner assessments provide the needs on which to base competencies. RAE is important in the early stages of developing a DEL course or consortium (marketing, needs assessment, formative evaluation); through the operational phase (competency measurement); and on to the final-output (team satisfaction, budget analysis, learner performance, and summative evaluation).

Feedback: In an open social system, like the educational system, both positive and negative feedback support continuous improvement. In a closed system that does not interact with its environment, feedback is primarily negative, and focuses on corrective action. Output boundaries are essentially permeable. They interact with their suprasystem and help correct (negative feedback) or improve (positive feedback) controls, transformation functions and required inputs. Successful outputs create positive reinforcement and growth in the system, while negative feedback helps self-correct the system. Feedback lines are broken in places to indicate the give and take relation with the larger societal environment because society holds the system accountable.

Suprasystem: The Environment or Suprasystem in which lifelong learning operates can further be seen by observing the small arrows that penetrate the DEL system. Constant environmental changes impinge on the system, such as: a satellite going down during delivery, a fax failing to provide planned-for interaction, net-congestion occurring during video streaming, or a corporate headquarters cutting training dollars. Understanding this permutation should help planners visualise various contingency plans needed to minimise adverse environmental impacts-proper planning prevents poor performance.

Instructional technology: Instructional technology underpins and permeates the DEL system. It is the backdrop to this system. Without the foundation in instructional technology, the RAE, Memory, and Transformation subsystems fail to communicate; and the system will fail. "Instructional Technology is a delivery vehicle, a means of presenting information in ways that foster learning. In a distance education system, technology is Used not just in presenting, but as the linking process across time and space. The central ellipse in the DEL model is the information processing infrastructure of technology: satellites, voice-video streaming, interactive multimedia, hardware/software, white boards, and other digital information transfer devices. The equipment bridges the gap of time and distance between sender and receiver.

TEACHING STRATEGIES

The incentives for trying distance instruction are rarely commensurate with the investment of time and energy it requires. The various approaches that teachers take to tackling this tough assignment and each instructor may have his or her own unique contributions to the process. However there are categories that are common among many of the distance instructors. Some of them are discussed here.

The dive-in technique: This is one of the most common approach to teaching via distance technology. Teachers using this approach basically do little preparation other than adapting the print on their transparencies, practising with the technology controls and, possibly, trying a couple of dry runs before the actual delivery of the class. While this approach often leads to trauma, it amasingly can work sometime—over time. It usually means, however, a very difficult beginning for both students and teachers. When this method works, it is most often because the teachers:

i) have previous experience with media, be it audio-video, computers, or the internet;
ii) see some models they like;
iii) recognise the needs and potential that distance education can fulfil;
iv) have developed excellent skills in communication and adaptation;
v) nurture a positive, flexible approach to teaching; and
vi) use active involvement strategies in their teaching.

Many teachers have already developed their abilities to adapt to adverse teaching/learning conditions. Through trial and error, those with flexibility and patience will find a way to succeed. Even the most resilient divers, however, express surprise at the degree of preparation it takes to teach via technology and the aversion that local/originating site students feel when they have to forbear the difficulties cause by remote teachers who are learning on the job.

Chinking approach: Some instructors have the foresight to look at the major instructional elements or chunks in their teaching and consider how to transport each to the new technologies. For example, one faculty member used visitations to rehabilitation facilities as part of her behaviour-disorders class. When she realised that the remote students would be unable to visit the sites that she had always used, she first decided to have them visit sites in their own locations and report to the class. Later, she decided that having all students tape record or videotape their visits and share meaningful portions of their experiences would enrich the class for all.

The start-from-scratch approach: Confronting the challenge of teaching via distance technologies, some instructors have realised that their curricula and instruction as originally designed were limited by their assumptions about the traditional classroom. These insightful instructors perceived that their designs for the traditional setting had not been shaped in such a way as to maximise the power of distance technologies. Thus, they decided to start from the beginning and take a thorough look at the assumptions underlying the design of each objective and activity. This approach gives the designer the opportunity to approach the subject anew, unfettered by the restrictions we unconsciously inherit from the traditional classroom setting. It takes some wisdom to realise that, just as distance technologies impose barriers to learning and communicating, so does the traditional classroom.

The following steps should be followed to most thoroughly implement the start-from-scratch approach:

i) Extend the course objectives to define what student outcomes are desired. This means asking the question: What should students be able to do with the information or skills emphasised during the course?

ii) Make a list of the unique opportunities that the media being used can bring to the course. For example, two-way audio-video systems provide the opportunity for students to meet and work with colleagues from remote locations. Internet-based discussion groups can give students an opportunity for deeper analysis of content and issues.

Don't forget that activities can be done in the remote students' own community. Be determined to use these advantages in a course to compensate for the more personal touch of face-to-face learning.

iii) Research and observe many different distance courses to define models that could work for the distance class. There are others out there doing this, and using the best of what can be found will give one a jump-start on any course.

iv) Identify the larger chunks of instruction and substitute activities that actively involve students or engage them in authentic, practice and application of the material. For example, instead of reading about a problem online, have students go into the community and identify problems in the real world, bring them to class and work to solve them with classmates-better yet, have them go back and work with community members to solve them.

v) Structure lessons that consist of segments. Intersperse group activities, discussion, interactive multimedia, etc., with the traditional activities of reading or listening. If it is an AV-based classroom, go no longer than 15 minutes of presenting information before calling for meaningful feedback or application related to the material. If it is an online class, have students do projects or present material themselves.

vi) Involve students in the unfolding of the course. Student attitudes can change from negative to positive if they are involved in solving the unique problems presented by distance instruction. They can often think of suggestions that may not occur to the instructor. Remote students have knowledge of the local community that the instructor may be able to use in the course.

vii) Remain flexible until the course is satisfactory to all. Many instructors and students consider a course finalised once they have put together the syllabus. But if genuine assessment of learning is occurring from both vantage points, the course and subsequent designs of the course should cater to the reactions of the learners.

viii) Be aware that it may take some time for students to fully adjust to and appreciate distance education. Students and teachers alike have spent most of their lives learning in face-to-face situations and are predisposed to this form of learning. They are likely to see distance learning as impersonal and resent the extra effort it takes on the part of the learner. Over time, they may come to see the advantages of this form of learning.

There are a variety of ways to be successful in this new arena. Research is emphasising that it is not so important what technology is used, but how it is used. Effective learning cannot take place with poor instruction, no matter what medium is used. As with most first technology experiences, some teachers are overwhelmed by the constrictions of teaching via distance technologies. Because of their preconceived definitions of teaching and learning they may underestimate the adaptability of students who are also capable of developing their own approaches to distance education.

There are sophisticated distance learner in many remote places across the world. They often have the positive support of a local institution/agency and know others who have received courses/degrees by distance. Many of these students feel fortunate to have classes delivered to their communities so that they do not have to waste, so much time travelling. They develop flexibility in their learning as a result of this positive attitude. Once faculty are actually teaching remote students, they have little trouble seeing that they are reaching students who may not otherwise have been able to complete these courses/programmes. This revelation inspires many to create new approaches to serve the needs of their learners.

The increasing understanding of learning environments, intelligent systems, agent technologies, and other related educational platforms enables us to now have a better perspective of how technology should be used in the context of pedagogical and organisational design. As processes and work become increasingly complex, technology can assume the more mundane functions and free us for tasks that are more complex and fuzzy. Additionally, as society becomes more global, collaboration across borders through networks becomes increasingly necessary. More interaction and collaboration efforts are needed with other institutions, organisations, and societies.

To make an impact on developments in learning and instruction, it is necessary to identify the strategic areas for research that would make a contribution to knowledge and scientific advancements. Considering the emerging technologies from the educational, instructional, and learning perspectives, we can identify some fruitful areas of IIT in education research:

i) *Pedagogy of online environments*: Learning in online environments has received such hype that the business world is dictating the parameters for what e-learning should be. There is a need to consider what content dimensions should be online, learning styles of students, and facilitating dispositions of teachers. There is an important need for education to spearhead the pedagogical directions for e-learning.

ii) *Simulation, visualisation, and modelling*: With modern technology and complex algorithms, we now have the ability to synthesise and collate complex data and variables into views that are more easily handled cognitively. Students can benefit from simulations in order to understand and play with variables that would otherwise be perhaps costly and dangerous.

iii) *Mind-tools or cognitive tools*: There is currently an important emphasis on how epistemic tools can help students to structure knowledge. These structures can be incorporated into IIT-based environments. These epistemic structures could include lists, tables, concept-maps, tree-structures, etc. Technology could also facilitate the collaborative construction of knowledge using these structures.

iv) *Assessment tools*: Technology can track students' progress in situ, and such tools and models can assist teachers in understanding students' conceptual difficulties in tasks such as project work. These tools generally provide teachers and students with meta-knowledge of their work in progress.

v) *Wireless computing*: The widespread advancement of wireless technology such as the cell phone, is making headway into learning and educational domains.

vi) *Tools for learning communities*: Recent research literature has emphasised the social nature of learning, stressing the processes and social structures undergirding knowledge construction. Such a focus has resulted in a proliferation of networked environments, multi-user virtual collaborative environments, and agents that support collaborative work. The social practices that revolve around schooling are as important as the learning that occurs within the individual mind. A lot of implicit learning or incidental learning occurs as students and teachers interact in a social context.

vii) *Tools for project work and authentic tasks*: Tasks given for learning must be authentic and challenging. Issues of authenticity relate to how learning should be context-rich, where associations of meanings are made personal to students' perceptions. Additionally, it is necessary for learning to be designed for transfer and generalisations to other contextual and disciplinary domains.

viii) *Integration of media, tools, and strategies*: With the proliferation of different multimedia applications and tools, there is a need to develop sound pedagogical strategies for how these types of media would be appropriately used in learning and instruction.

ix) *Qualitative changes in learning*: Complementary with the use of tools, strategies, and media, there is a need to-measure the qualitative changes, e.g., conceptual and epistemological, in students' learning. Such a focus is at the forefront in current research.

x) *Multiple intelligences and learning styles*: Research must address the dimension of relating multiple intelligences learning and teaching styles with the appropriate use of media, tools, and strategies.

xi) *Knowledge states and types*: Depending on the kinds of knowledge that students acquire, different tools, strategies, and media should be used for learning and instruction. It is through the appropriation of such cultural-scientific artifacts that students can subsequently negotiate and construct further understanding.

xii) *Social-cultural issues*: Although social-cultural issues are not new, little is known of the implications for IIT-enriched environments. Contexts such as policies and societal norms have a profound impact on learning outcomes.

Basics of Internet

The term 'internet' literally means 'between or among networks'. It is a powerful communication tool, a giant Information superhighway system connecting computers and the local, regional, and global networks together. In other words, the internet is a large collection of networks that are linked together so that millions of users can share their vast resources. The internet began in 1968 when the United States Department of Defence research network linked seven different university computer science departments in response to a need for military institutions and universities to share their research. In the 1970s, university networks continued to grow as many organisations began building their private networks. In the 1980s, the National Science Foundation created five supercomputer centres at major universities. This special network is the foundation of the internet today. The most significant recent development in digital technology has been the phenomenal growth of the internet.

The phenomenon of today's internet technology has changed our daily life. Massive amounts of information can be reviewed through desktop computers. We are able to communicate with others through electronic mail, video-conferences, and chat lines without leaving our offices or homes. Compared to the web, limits of each technology, including videotape and CD-ROM, certainly restrain our creative abilities in the design and delivery of our learning materials.

The key is to remember that even as we use technology to shape our environment, technology is shaping us. Technology rearranges our perceptual world and subtly redefines our relationship with our environment. A study by internet commerce reports that there are 34.6 million web users. We see the fast growing trend of using the web as a vehicle to deliver online educational programmes. Educators should examine the approaches they choose for enhancing the learning process and make it as good, if not better, than conventional teaching methods in the classroom.

Web technology permits us to represent the learning materials in any combination of media format, such as text, image, graphics, and animation. This multimedia information environment can be accessed and displayed simultaneously. The high level of interactively inherent on the web gave the users dynamic control of information. Interaction with linked information was very structured in terms of proficiency level and direction.

The internet is constantly growing as more and more universities, schools, organisations, companies, institutions and individuals make available new resources. The internet makes these resources available to each and everyone of us, without distinction, through our computer networks.

Any commercial or institutional service that has internet access provides five basic services:

i) sending messages via electronic mail (e-mail),

ii) logging into distant places with Telnet,

iii) sending and retrieving files by FTP,

iii) reading and posting information to Usenet, and

iv) browsing for information using Gopher and the World Wide Web.

The major promising areas of emerging internet technology are:

i) audioconferencing,

ii) videoconferencing, and

iii) virtual reality.

Internet Relay Chat (IRC) lets other users or other internet computers see what is typed on our screen. However, the latest software like Net Phone are making two-way spoken communication possible over the internet. Video conferencing requires a very fast (384 kbps or faster) internet connection in order to be effective. Softwares like CU-SeeMe allow computers equipped with video cameras to communicate with each other using live video-audio. Each image appears in a small window on your computer. Visual Reality software gives the impression of three-dimensional interaction.

There are advantages as well as disadvantages to an internet technology. The advantages of the internet in the social studies instruction are the following:

i) Provides a classroom without walls. Provides virtual reality.

ii) Links social scientists and experts with students.

iii) Gets information instantly from a variety of sources. Helps active learning

iv) Promotes interactive learning.

v) Caters to the needs of students.

vi) Displays a greater range of perspectives.

vii) Receives current issues of national and international newspapers and journals.

viii) Receives electronically full texts of works of such authors as H.G. Wells and Shakespeare.

ix) Receives lesson plans from various websites and teachers around the world.

x) Creates high interest as students communicate with other distance classrooms on social studies projects.

xi) Sends and receives e-mail.

xii) Telnet logs on the libraries of the world.

xiii) Provides online discussion groups for teachers.

xiv) Provides information for research projects.

xv) Provides co-development projects with other classes (online). Helps monitor current events.

xvi) Provides opportunities for penpal activities.

xvii) Provides teacher education opportunities via the internet. Provides opportunities for electronic fieldtrips.

xvii) Provides data bases, pictures, maps, tables, charts, and sounds and other resources.

xix) Allows file transfer (FTP) to students and teachers from other computers.

xx) Provides video-audio conference capabilities.

The major disadvantages are:

i) The internet presents an environment that invites students to plagiarise and ignore the copyrights or intellectual property rights.

ii) The internet contains some material which may be considered inappropriate or even offensive.

iii) Information found on the internet lacks a standard or criterion. Needs a definitive criteria and process to evaluate the information.

iv) Lacks limits placed on what goes on the internet, what students can see and use if not strictly supervised.

v) There are many unseen effects on culture when we change the stuff of "culture into binary code".

vi) Misuse of the internet: Bad or ignorant behaviour of one student or teacher or user of the internet could Jeopardise the internet privileges of others.

vii) Exposure to an abundance of information presented by the internet is potentially dangerous.

viii) There are many unknowns: how the internet may affect us as individuals, citizens of a society and members of the global community.

ix) There are no gatekeepers for the internet information. Anyone can publish misinformation without much consequence.

x) The internet is open for the good, the bad, and the ugly. It is a place where hate groups, anarchists or even terrorist organisations may share information or solicit new members. Inflammatory claims and opinions, often disseminated under the veil of anonymity, could become pervasive on the internet.

xi) The internet does not yet provide places for deliberation though it provides places for faceless individuals to express anonymous views and places to examine a lot of material and background information.

xii) Finding relevant internet material is like separating the wheat from the chaff. It is, to say the least, a time consuming effort.

xiii) The internet material has not been subjected to any evaluation or assessment process. Research on what students learned form a particular website or material from the internet is lacking. This assessment issue must be addressed.

xiv) The internet which allows ready dissemination of information also allows ready dissemination of misinformation.

The instructional uses for the internet is growing as fast. A small sample of myriad activities and limitless possibilities are given below.

i) *Co-development projects*: Students get together online to plan and produce joint projects such as newsletters on current events, based on family interviews, or exchange of local cultures.

ii) *Research projects*: Students can locate information on the internet to answer specific questions on topics of interests. Students can present their findings in the class and follow by critical discussion.

iii) *Teacher discussion groups*: Some sites have set up for teachers to have online discussion groups in which teachers can exchange ideas, advice and information on a variety of topics.

iv) *In-service education opportunities*: Workshops, strategies session, tutorials and even full courses are becoming increasingly available via the internet.

v) *Electronic field trips and guided tows*: Virtual trips are designed to explore unique locations and interesting subjects.

vi) *Social action project*: Online communication provides students access to people in other parts of the world that can support social problem solving. In this type of participation, students are addressing important global, social, political, economic, human rights concerns or environmental conditions.

vii) *Electronic penpals*: Using e-mail, students can exchange messages across the country or around the world at little or no cost. Electronic penpals is the simplest activity. Each student is linked with a partner whom the student writes letters which has been shown to be very motivating.

The internet has the potential to provide teachers with a tool that can lead to significant changes in the nature of classroom instruction and learning. The student exploration of vast amount of information in a global scale raises many questions about what kind of information is being accessed, what is being done with it, how to examine critically and make sense out of it and when it becomes too much.

Internet is a vast resource for obtaining information available in the form of graphics, text, sound, and video. The information varies considerably in difficulty, accuracy, specificity, authenticity and quality. Also, unlike textbooks or encyclopedias, the content of the internet is, by and large, unedited and unrestricted. We do need a framework for evaluating the internet information. For evaluating the internet materials, teachers have to teach critical thinking skills and information processing skills. Through the study and careful examination of the internet material, students realise that errors exist because of biases and different frames of reference. Bias means a predisposition to a particular point of view.

Some internet-related guidelines for teachers are given below.

i) The acceptable use policy in the school with clear objectives, conditions, tales and consequences of breach of rules should be developed.
ii) Students and teachers should be impressed upon that the use of the internet is a privilege, not a right, and the misuse or inappropriate use will result in a cancellation of those privileges.
iii) Users of internet should be expected to abide by the generally accepted rules of network etiquette such as politeness, appropriate language and ethical use. Ethical

guidelines are needed not only for the users of the Intetnet but also for the publishers of those materials on the internet.

iv) Teachers should ensure that students have requisite skills so that students can focus on their research.

v) Teachers should ensure that students have critical skills to evaluate the credibility, accuracy, validity, and worthwhileness of the information from the internet. Abundance of information makes the teaching of critical thinking skills more vital than ever, given the accelerated rate of internet use by schools and individuals.

vi) Teachers should ensure that the internet-based teaching and learning help promote meaningful, Integrative, active and challenging social studies.

vii) Students should be made aware that the internet-generated information reflects the programmer's cultural, gender, and ethnic bias. They should be skilled to detect that bias.

viii) Teachers should be prepared to deal with plagiarism and cheating.

ix) Teachers should develop models of moral education and curriculum material for dealing with what their students encounter online.

x) More research is needed to determine if students have learned from spending time at a website or engaging.

Some commony used terms of the world of internet are given below:

Archie : A tool for searching for files on the internet

Primary file : The second transfer mode in which files are transferred identical in appearance to the original document.

Bookmarks	:	A Netscape feature to mark favourite pages for quick access.
Browser	:	A programme that interprets and displays HTML documents.
FTP	:	FTP (File Transfer Protocol) allows files to be transferred between computers on the internet.
Gopher	:	A way of retrieving files from another computer.
HTTP	:	HTTP (or Hyper Text Transfer Protocol) is used by the WWW to transfer information, web documents begin with http://
Hypertext	:	A document containing links to another document.
IRC	:	IRC (Internet Relay Chat) is live across the internet.
Etiquette	:	Internet etiquette, "the rules of the road".
Nescape	:	A popular internet browser.
Search engines	:	Software programmes designed for sending information on the internet.
Server	:	A computer runner software that allows another computer for exchanging information.
Telnet	:	Acts as a terminal on a remote computer.
Usenet	:	A cybercafe where people from everywhere in the world gather to discuss and share ideas.
URL	:	URL (Uniform Resource Locator or address) address of the file you are searching for.
Veronica	:	A programme that searches for files across gopher servers.
WWW	:	WWW (World Wide Web) connects sites through hypertext links.

PROBLEMS OF DISTANCE STUDENTS

In a distance education setting, the process of student learning is more complex for several reasons. Many distance-education students are older, have jobs, and families. They must coordinate the different areas of their lives which influence each other — their families, jobs, spare time, and studies. Distant students have a variety of reasons for taking courses. Some students are interested in obtaining a degree to qualify for a better job. Many take courses to broaden their education and are not really interested in completing a degree.

In distance education, the learner is usually isolated. The motivational factors arising from the contact or competition with other students is absent. The student also lacks the immediate support of a teacher who is present and able to motivate and, if necessary, give attention to actual needs and difficulties that crop up during study. Distant students and their teachers often have little in common in terms of background and day-to-day experiences and therefore, it takes longer for student-teacher rapport to develop. Without face-to-face contact distant students may feel ill at ease with their teacher as an individual and uncomfortable with their learning situation. In distance education settings, technology is typically the conduit through which information and communication flow.

In the beginning period students may have some difficulty determining what the demands of a course of academic study actually are because they do not have the support of an immediate peer group, ready access to the instructor, or familiarity with the technology being used for delivery of the distance-education course. They may be unsure of themselves and their learning.

Distant students who are not confident about their learning tend to concentrate on memorising facts and details in order to complete assignments and write exams. As a result, they end up with a poor understanding of course material.

Memorisation of facts and details is a surface approach to learning and cab be summarises as:

i) *Surface approach*

a) Focus on the signs.

b) Focus on discrete elements.

c) Memorise information and procedures for tests.

d) Unreflectively associate concepts and facts.

e) Fail to distinguish principles from evidence, new information from old.

f) Treat assignments as something imposed by the instructor.

g) External emphasis focusing on the demands of assignments and exams leading to a knowledge that is cut-off from everyday reality.

h) Distant students need to become more selective and focused in their learning in order to master new information. The focus of their learning needs to shift them from a surface approach to a deep approach.

ii) *Deep approach*

a) Focus on what is signified, e.g., the instructor's arguments.

b) Relate and distinguish new ideas and previous knowledge.

c) Relate concepts to everyday experience.

d) Relate and distinguish evidence and argument.

e) Organise and structure content.

f) Internal emphasis focusing on how instructional material relates to everyday reality.

Adult students and their instructors must face and overcome a number of challenges before learning takes place including: becoming and staying responsible for themselves; owning their strengths, desires, skills, and needs; maintaining and increasing self-esteem; relating to others; clarifying what is learned; redefining what legitimate knowledge is; and dealing with content.

i) *Becoming and staying responsible for themselves*: High motivation is required to complete distant courses because the day-to-day contact with teachers and other students is typically lacking. Instructors can help motivate distant students by providing consistent and timely feedback, encouraging discussion among students, being well prepared for class, and by encouraging and reinforcing effective student study habits.

ii) *Owning one's strengths, desires, skills, needs*: Students need to recognise their strengths and limitations. They also need to understand their learning goals and objectives. The instructor can help distant students to explore their strengths/limitations and their learning goals/objectives by assuming a facilitative role in the learning process. Providing opportunities for students to share their personal learning goals and objectives for a course helps to make learning more meaningful and increases motivation.

iii) *Maintaining and increasing self-esteem*: Distant students may be afraid of their ability to do well in a course. They are balancing many responsibilities including employment and raising children. Often their involvement in distance education is unknown to those they work with and ignored by family members. Student performance is enhanced if learners set aside time for their instructional activities and if they receive family support in their academic endeavours. The instructor can maintain student self-esteem by providing timely feedback. It is critical for teachers to respond to students' questions, assignments, and concerns in a personalised and pleasant manner, using appropriate technology such as fax, phone, or computer. Informative comments that elaborate on the individual student's performance and suggest areas for improvement are especially helpful.

vi) *Relating to others*: Students often learn most effectively when they have the opportunity to interact with other students. Interaction among students typically leads to group problem solving. When students are unable to meet together, appropriate interactive technology such as E-mail should be provided to encourage small group and individual communication. Assignments in which students work together and then report back or present to the class as a whole, encourage student-to-student interaction. Ensure clear directions and realistic goals for group assignments.

vii) *Clarifying what is learned*: Distant students need to reflect on what they are learning. They need to examine the existing knowledge frameworks in their heads and how these are being added to or changed by incoming information. Examinations, papers, and class presentations provide opportunities for student and teacher to evaluate learning. However, less formal methods of evaluation will also help the students and teacher to understand learning. For example, periodically during the course the instructor can ask students to write a brief reflection on what they have learned and then provide an opportunity for them to share their insights with other class members.

viii) *Redefining what legitimate knowledge is*: Adult learners may find it difficult to accept that their own experience and reflections are legitimate knowledge. If the instructor takes a facilitative rather than authoritative role, students will see—their own experience as valuable and important to their further learning. Having learners use first-person language to help them claim ownership of personal values, experiences, and insights.

ix) *Dealing with content*: Student learning is enhanced when content is related to examples. Instructors tend to teach using examples that were used when they received their training. For distance learning to be effective, however, instructors must discover examples that are relevant to their distant students. Encourage students to find or develop examples that are relevant to them or their community.

REFERENCES

Ackermann, E., 1996, *Tools for Teaching: The World Wide Web and a Web Browser*, (http://www.mwc.edu/ernie/facacad/WWW-Teaching.html)

Brundage, D., Keane, R., and Mackneson, R., 1993, "Application of Learning Theory to the Instruction of Adults", In Thelma Barer-Stein and James A. Draper (eds.), *The Craft of Teaching Adults*, Toronto, Ontario: Culture Concepts, pp. 131-144.

Burge, E., 1993, "Adult Distance Learning: Challenges for Contemporary Practice", In Thelma Barer-Stein and James A. Draper (eds.), *The Craft of Teaching Adults*, Toronto, Ontario: Culture Concepts, pp. 131-144.

Galbreath, J., 1995, "Compressed Digital Videoconferencing", *Educational Technology*, 35(1), pp. 31-38.

Huges, K., 1994, *Entering the World Wide Web: A Guide to Cyberspace*, Enterprise Integration Technologies.

Kochmer, J., 1995, *Internet Passport: Northwestnet's Guide to Our World Online*, Bellevue, WA: NorthWestNet and Northwest Academic Computing Consortium, Inc. (http://info.nwnet.net/passport).

Misanchuk, E.R., 1992, *Preparing Instructional Text: Document Design using Desktop Publishing*, Englewood Cliffs, NJ: Educational Technology Publications.

Misanchuk, E.R., 1994, "Print Tools in Distance Education", In B. Willis (ed.), *Distance Education: Strategies and Tools*, Englewood Cliffs, NJ: Educational Technology Publications, pp.109-129.

Moore, M.G., Thompson, M.M., with Quigley, A.B., Clark, G.C., and Goff, G.G., 1990, "The Effects of Distance Learning: A Summary of the Literature", *Research Monograph* no. 2. University Park, PA: The Pennsylvania State University, American Center for the Study of Distance Education.

Morgan, A., 1991, *Research into Student Learning in Distance Education*, Victoria, Australia: University of South Australia, Underdale.

Schuemer, R., 1993, *Some Psychological Aspects of Distance Education*, Hagen, Germany: Institute for Research into Distance Education.

Verduin, J.R., Clark, T.A., 1991, *Distance Education: The Foundations of Effective Practice*, San Francisco, CA: Jossey-Bass Publishers.

Willis, B., 1993, *Distance Education: A Practical Guide*, Englewood Cliffs, NJ: Educational Technology Publications.

3

E-Learning

The core purpose of education has been to ensure that our citizens had the skills they needed to actively participate in a democratic society. Today, the world is far different from the one, which existed alongside an emergent industrial economy, powered by muscle, water and steam. In the past where access was limited, information was treated as a scarce resource, and educators had the task of imparting this information for the benefit of learners. In that world content was abundant, and is therefore a poor basis for an educational system. What is scarce today is context and meaning. It used to be the mark of an educated person to have a vast reservoir of facts on which to rely.

The rapid changes of our era have ensured that work and learning will be closely aligned with each other throughout our lives. The educational system of today needs to impart to all learners three new foundational skills: to make learning a relevant and lifelong process—a process of continuous growth change and evolution and adaptation. The schools of the 20th century were clustered around the idea that time would be constant and learning would be variable. Today with computers taking over, jobs that can be done with minimum education are fast diminishing. Skilled jobs and the need for lifelong education are on the increase.

Schools of the future should therefore be institutions, which will provide whatever support is needed to achieve excellence. The idea of schools as a fixed time activity is being replaced by the concept of continuous learning built around a variety of tools and techniques.

The 21st century classroom will be wherever the learner is located—at school, on the bus ride home, in the park, at a museum, or in the playground. Traditional tools will co-exist with the hightech tools of the telematic era. The teacher's role in this distributed setting to be quite different from that of content presenter and test giver. A more productive role will be that of co-learner—an expert guide who helps students navigate the subjects being explored.

The teacher in this setting will operate in a system based on four components: campfires, watering holes, caves, and life. The campfire is the informational space associated with lectures and other methods of direct instruction. The watering hole is the conversational space occupied when learners converse among themselves or with their teachers about a particular topic. The cave is the conceptual space where ideas are developed in relative solitude and where student projects are designed and built. Life is the contextual space where the things have been learned are applied in the world outside of school. Learning has always taken place in these four spaces, yet 20th century schools often failed to provide the right balance and learning suffered as a result.

Through the telematic revolution, multimedia and telecommunication applications can be made to both the direct teaching method that emphasises individualised work and to the constructivist method that focuses on group learning. These four learning spaces provide a framework for the community at large that can envision educational opportunity. Flexibility is the key for the effective definition of the roles.

Modern technologies are space collapser's, time shifters and creative tools that extend our reach. Technology deployed in education can help remove inequities between the schools of developed and developing nations, between inner cities and suburbs, between urban and rural areas.

Technology can become the force that equalises the educational opportunities of a children regardless of location and social and economic circumstances. The internet eliminates geography as a limiting factor. A child in a remote hamlet can have the same access to the same reference materials as one located in the cosmopolitan city. Time is transcended by telematic tools. Technology will have an increasingly positive impact on the student's creativity. Access to multiple expressive modalities in important.

As Howard Gardener's theory of multiple intelligence has shown, each of us has multiple pathways to learning, only a few are valued in the schools. Resources like this not only help learners gain mastery of subject, but also help them develop a deeper relationship with the topic being studied. By placing a human face on the academic topics, web-based access to primary source materials can make learning come alive for many students. Educators are also great beneficiaries of the telematic revolution. It opens up new opportunities for casual dialogues on a wide range of topics, and helps overcome the sense of isolation sometimes felt by educators whose areas of interest have few local enthusiasts.

In addition to conversing with peers, communication with learners, their parents, the community at large is facilitated with the same tools. Parents who, for whatever reason, are unable to attend a student's study team meeting at school can take part through videoconferencing.

Though technology promises the panacea to better learning, sales hungry decision makers have exploited it. Now it is faced with the challenge of maintaining the delicate balance between quality and quantity. Society has been credited with creating technology, but technology is simultaneously creating society. These observations would also suggest that technology is beginning to exercise a benevolent tyranny over human kind.

People have become compulsive information consumers who favour the passive reaction of information as a form of entertainment over the more challenging act of thinking. Maintaining quality presupposes building a code of ethics into the telematic infrastructure, just as science without responsibility is like a sword without a sheath; so too, telematic education without ethics will lead to gross debasement of human energies.

The ethical values to bear in mind cannot be isolated from human values and responsibilities. It should also provide built in evaluative means that protect internal human ecological aspects. Primarily quality checks must respect human rights to privacy, to avoid intrusion and abuse of these rights, and to avoid placing all information on equal levels. Any e-learning programme needs an in-built quality check for it to function efficiently. At every phase it should be made and validated.

To achieve the above objective a number of specific safeguards must be undertaken. Each programme of study should result in learning outcomes appropriate to the rigour and breadth of the degree or certificate awarded. At every phase of the programme a check should be made and validated. The programme should be consistent with the institution's role and mission. The institution should provide for the assessment and documentation of student achievement in each course and award certificates at the completion of the programme.

The institution should demonstrate a commitment to ongoing support, both financial and technical, and to the continuation of the programme for a period sufficient to enable students to complete the degree/ certificate. The institution should evaluate the programme's educational effectiveness, including the assessments of student learning, and the outcomes, student retention and so on.

Use of technology in education is highly positive but the caveat is to avoid falling through the looking glass. The true challenge is for education to freeze a model that captures quality and computer technology into an integrated communication system.

E- LEARNING MODULES

The web-based learning modules promises to change how some students learn and how some faculty teach at the university. The decision to build a site involves a careful consideration of costs in terms of time and effort weighed against potential beneficial learning gains for students. Possible benefits for students using web modules include convenience for distance learning, expanded and easier access to digital materials, greater student control of learning, and enhanced online collaboration.

The modules can be used as homework for face-to-face classes, as the building blocks of distance education courses, and as stand-alone instructional units for public outreach. Web-based materials incorporate the latest in web design with interactive exercises, video, audio, and communication features and often meet high standards of instructional and graphic web design. The faculty who create such modules learn quickly that designing and assessing their value can be challenging, requiring skill in instructional and graphic design, programming, and assessment of learning outcomes. Understanding the benefits of the web can help instructors decide if producing web-based materials is worth the effort.

Remote access is the primary incentive driving web-based instruction. Web-based learning materials are a convenient alternative for students who cannot or do not want to take face-to-face classes, go to the lab during open hours, or attend a recitation in person. However, the realities of users' hardware can make assigning web-based materials problematic. Web sites with complex graphics or large video or audio files can cause painfully slow downloads on computers with 56K or slower modems. Research shows that web users are impatient, waiting ten seconds or less before they lose interest in a web-site. Before building a site, make sure that the end user will be able to easily access the site given your anticipated technical design.

Easy access to information is an integral part of web-based technology, as users are immediately linked to up to date digital libraries, online publications, and more. Access can also mean exposure to authentic, real-world information not easily available through other sources. For example, foreign language students can view the websites of real businesses, universities, online museums, or other websites in different countries. Some links to websites are an integral part of learning, as students find specific information, analyse documents, or evaluate the credibility of sources others, like dictionary or library links, are embedded throughout the site as resources.

The web can present video, audio, and animated materials as well as give programmed feedback for user-entered responses. The web-based materials can be regularly updated or revised. Java applets can be used to create complicated interactive learning materials; easy-to-use freeware for creating interactive assessments is available on the web. For example, instructors can automate tedious or time-consuming tutorial activities such as memorisation, the correction of mathematical problems, musical ear training, or foreign language production and comprehension.

For those deciding to use any of these capabilities, the cost of development, greater download times, and more complex hardware capability must weighed against the benefit for the student. The overarching concern about the use of more complicated programming is whether the outcome of using a particular type of software actually helps a student achieve the learning objective of a lesson.

Some web-based lessons allow students to choose which instruction they receive, making more individualised learning possible. For example, students may repeat or skip lessons, manipulate and rewind images or video, engage in simulations or visualisation, and practise skills. Student control is especially desirable for lessons that cover a wide range of difficulty so that students can enter and exit the lesson at an appropriate difficulty level, and is also important for skill building exercises so that students can repeat a lesson until it is learned.

While student control is often seen as desirable, it also means he instructor must relinquish some control of how students use materials. For example, students may access materials in an order different from that which the instructor considers to be the most helpful for learning the material.

E-mail and bulletin boards built into learning modules allow students to respond to each other and the instructor, giving people the opportunity to revise and reflect upon their work. E-mail can also enable collaboration among students from different schools, states, nationalities, and ethnic and socio-economic backgrounds.

Many web modules are now used in hybrid contexts, as students in face-to-face classrooms work and communicate with each other online, either during or outside of class. Bulletin boards can remove discussions from classrooms or extend them, allowing students to communicate with each other at their own convenience and in a safe environment. They also make course dialogue both visible and permanent, as threaded discussions are archived and referenced by both students and faculty. If managed well, online discussion can make possible more reflective discussion, as students have the chance to revise and think about written statements.

Yet online discussions must be monitored and sustained, and students must perceive that there is good reason for participation, especially if it means extra time. For the instructor, the amount of time and effort devoted to moderating online discussion is not trivial. The decision to build a complex, web-based learning module should not be taken lightly. The costs in terms of money, time, and effort that could be better used elsewhere can be formidable.

Instructors can reproduce the successful efforts of publishing companies by making conscious choices about lesson content and instructional design and by carefully assessing the value added to student learning.

Reviewing existing web sites can prevent reinventing the wheel. Hundreds of exemplary homegrown learning materials are found at the World Lecture Hall, Academic Info, the University of California at Riverside's Infomine, and the Maricopa Center for Learning and Instruction. A web search also provides familiarity with online resources such as databases, dictionaries, assessment tools, or other websites that can be linked to the site. Before linking to or borrowing from other sites, learn about the complexities of copyright.

All learning materials contain philosophical assumptions about now students learn, and these assumption, are implemented in an instructional design. It is important that philosophical and design choices are conscious choices, yet in many cases these decisions happen by default as designers unconsciously translate and reproduce existing instructional methods used in books, other media, or in their classroom practice directly to their online lessons. If resources are available, hire an instructional designer; if not, have a designer review the plan and make suggestions.

Some important considerations for designing the core of a lesson are the following:

i) *Intended use and audience*: Class-linked websites are usually either supplements to class work, or substitutes for existing class material. Supplementary materials may be optional, providing for a more comprehensive understanding of class content, or required, such as exercises that allow for extra skill development. If, on the other hand, the lesson is used as a substitute for class work and/or materials, web content should function as class material and equal or improve on the quality of existing materials and instruction. Outreach websites used by the general public face a different kind of scrutiny and planning than sites used by classes, departments, or campuses. These sites are meant to be used by a wide variety of people and are designed to motivate and entertain as well as educate. Outreach sites should have a professional appearance and should be easy and enjoyable to use. Large-scale curriculum efforts conduct surveys and interviews to learn if the planned lesson fit the needs of the projected users. For smaller scale projects, a needs assessment is a more informal effort: the instructor can talk with students, other instructors, and content experts about what they want from new lessons, how lessons fit with current class activities, and how projected lessons fit with recent trends or discoveries in a discipline.

ii) *Learning and performance objectives*: web-based learning materials are built around a learning goal, which can be as straightforward as students will learn the four bones of the knee or as complicated as students will have a comprehensive understanding of the factors leading to the great depression. In self-contained materials, the learning objective should be explicitly stated so that students will have a clear idea of what they will learn by the time they finish the lesson. Students also need to understand when they have achieved the learning objectives, so some way of letting them know when they are successful should also be built into the site. Stating the learning objective explicitly will also help outline the lesson and guide the development of assessments. Performance objectives are derived from learning objectives. These are clear statements about what students should know and be able to do at the end of a lesson stated in terms of empirical assessments or observations.

iii) *Instructional method/pedagogy*: Much of modern instructional design is grounded in pedagogical theories emphasising inquiry-based, active, or problem-based learning. Developing learning materials on the web that are personally meaningful and which engage students in the active analysis, synthesis, and evaluation of information is challenging. Interactive, hands-on exercises or simulations embedded in web sites are a step toward active learning. Active learning activities also include visiting websites with authentic contexts or sites that afford access to primary source documents. Electronic communication can also foster collaboration and distributed expertise by removing spatial and temporal barriers to collaboration, and by allowing access to common data sets. Some critics of the recent push for educational technology observe that many web-based lessons merely reproduce traditional instruction by emphasising the memorisation of content and its regurgitation on tests. "Gift-wrapping" is a common practice of professors who take written lecture material and post it on the web, but there is nothing about the web that forces instructors to present material in this manner.

iv) *Scaffolding*: While students are learning independently, it is essential to build ways to access help with subject matter. Hypertext can link students to terms, definitions, explanations, and images. Help can be in the form of text, supplementary links, illustrations, or video/ audio files and can be programmed so that they are always available, or delivered to students only after they make repeated attempts at an exercise.

v) *Assessment online*: Assessments are an excellent way to add interactivity to the site, keep students engaged and reinforce material through the movement of clicking typing, and dragging and dropping. When giving feedback, decide whether the students are told only "correct" or "try again" or if they are given more detailed responses. Feedback can include extended explanations of why specific answers are correct or incorrect, and assessment questions can also link back to the material in the lesson. Web-based assessments are an appropriate way to provide instructors with a valid picture of what their students know. The two related issues for assessing students online are item type/assessment method and communication with the instructor.

Computers are good at automating multiple-choice, matching, and short fill-in-the-blank test items, but are usually not set up to grade essays and performance assessments. There is a relationship between item type and the kind of knowledge that can be validly assessed. Multiple-choice, matching, and short answer items are more suited to recognition, memorisation, and problems with clearly defined answers, while essays, performance assessments, and portfolios better assess higher-order thinking skills such as analysis and problem solving. To use these latter types of assessment, a certain amount of personal interaction and communication are required. Essay questions can be submitted via e-mail or students may post a response to a threaded discussion question.

vi) *Clear instructions and navigation*: Instructors often counter that students could stop and read the instructions, but people tend to scan, rather than read, what they find on the web. Developers find a way to force users to read the instructions, such as presenting a page with instructions which the user cannot skip and asking that they click an "ok" or other button to continue into the lesson. Another suggestion for improving both instructional design and website design is to include a site map or "concept map", so that students always know where they are in a lesson. This allows students to move to various parts of the lesson with a click of the mouse, to visualise how different components of the lesson relate to each other, and to know when they are finished. Depending on the intended use of the lesson, time and money can be spent ensuring smooth usability.

Crucial planning phase is skipped in web development and design choices are made "on the fly", or by default. This can cause wasted effort as programmers must later go back and fix poorly executed designs. Weak planning can also mean that the content and the instructional design of the site are more heavily influenced by the programmer than by the content and instructional experts. Begin by creating an outline or map of the site. This can be easily done in a low-tech manner on a piece of butcher paper with movable "sticky notes" used to represent separate screens or even by tearing out pieces of notebook paper. Using this type of schematic, decisions can he made about what sections follow and/or link to each other. Next, draw a rough picture of each screen that will be included, indicating text and picture layout. Finally, attach to the storyboard an "asset list," including and describing all text, image, video, or sounds and links to be included on each screen include the computer file names for all elements of the site. After the storyboarding is complete, review all the features of each page to be sure they are essential for student learning and not merely included to enhance graphic design.

Working with experts will help in the development of easy-to-use, visually pleasing web-based materials with sound instructional design. Experts include:

i) instructional designers, usually specialists, professors, or graduate students found in education schools or on staff in learning centres who can review and make suggestions for improvements;
ii) technical experts, programmers or web designers who help avoid the steep learning curve by programming difficult parts of the site or by teaching the instructor the appropriate code;
iii) graphic designers, who can help implement a professional and pleasing visual design for the site; and
iv) evaluators, found in a wide variety of disciplines where learning materials are produced. Evaluators can provide valuable advice on data collection instruments used in pilot testing, can give an independent viewpoint on the quality of a site, act as intermediaries between those

using the site and its developers, and help design and monitor outcome assessment studies.

When the site is ready to pilot, show it to a small group of faculty, graduate students, or others who will try it out and look for technical problems, typos, or other obvious mistakes. Be sure to test with different browsers and on different operating systems. Ask testers to go out of their way to use all of the site's features or even to try to break it. Provide a simple survey form so they can record the location of technical glitches, poorly worded instructions, download times, or other design problems. After correcting the first wave of errors, ask a small group of students who are representative of target users to try the site.

This means if the web module is intended for students in the 1,000 level class, ask 1,000 level students who have not yet learned this content to try it out. Try to find students with different levels of computer proficiency and academic standing, not just students who show an interest in computers, the best students, or the students who benefit most from extra credit. Again, the computers and connections used should also be similar to those that will be used by the target users. At least two test-and-revise cycles will be needed to ready the site for use.

Observe how students use the site. Record what the students do and pay special attention to if, or how long, they stay on individual screens, if they use specific features of the programme, or if they get stuck at specific parts of the site. Common usability problems we have found during observation include screens skipped by students due to long text passages and places where students become frustrated and confused due to a lack of clear instructions.

Think-aloud interviews allow instructors to elicit suggestions for improving the site, unclear directions and content, overly difficult content, and student perceptions of learning. A feedback button can also be embedded in each screen so that students can make written comments while they are using the site.

A directed interview or survey can occur during or after use when student impressions of specific components or features of the site are wanted. Surveys can also be administered to students who try out the site at home. Usually, interviews ask for general impressions of the site, what students like and dislike about the site, and suggestions for improvement. During the later phases of usability review, interviews can be used to test changes made to the site by asking students directly about specific features of the site.

Now the site is ready to be piloted with real students in classes. This is necessary because students using materials which make up part of their grade may use the site differently than those who are just trying it out. Informal class discussion with students after they use the site is a good way to learn general impressions of the site, but again, better feedback is gained through an anonymous survey.

Instructors using web-based materials as a substitution for existing material want to be sure that students learn at least as much with the new materials as with the old. In collaboration with faculty, we often compare groups of students who have learned the materials with different teaching methods, assigning different materials and methods to two groups of students, then giving both groups the same test and checking to see if test scores between the groups are significantly different. Comparative studies should be conducted carefully and interpreted with caution.

Most comparative studies do not show differences between groups because of the technology used to convey material. While general equivalence between different types of material or teaching methods may be a desired outcome, care should be taken when drawing this kind of conclusion from a single comparison. It is possible to miss a difference due to small numbers of students in comparison groups, a shot and unreliable test, or because of a variety of other confounding influences and failings in a research design. It is also possible to make the opposite mistake and claim that there are differences when none really exist.

Selection bias is a serious issue because it is usually not possible to randomly assign students to comparison groups. Testing for selection bias is possible through the use of pretests and/or surveys to determine whether existing groups of students have about the same level of knowledge, computer skill, attitude, or any other variable at the beginning of a class. Statistical procedures can adjust for some differences in prior knowledge between groups, although these procedures do not remove this bias.

If the materials or the learning objectives are a new addition to a syllabus, an effort can be made to assess if students learned something by using the website, and if so, what exactly was learned. Pre- and post-tests are the traditional method of gauging if students have reached a pre-determined objective. Performance assessments often give a more valid understanding of what students know and can do than traditional written tests. A more subtle concern with any type of comparison involves changes to curriculum arising from the usc of technology. One reason instructors choose to use a multimedia environment, such as the web or CD-ROM, is because they think they can achieve a learning goal not possible using traditional methods.

When conducting a comparison, an instructor must be very confident that both the new and traditional methods are teaching the same material; if adaptation of the technology has changed what is taught, comparisons are complicated or rendered invalid. Some websites do not aim to teach academic subjects and are not easily testable. Obviously, a test will not provide good evidence that a student was quicker at overcoming culture shock, is more interested in science, or is more motivated to travel to a foreign country.

E-CLASSROOM

There is tremendous growth of internet use in schools. Meanwhile, the emphasis on the integration of the internet as an instructional tool and as a part of the curriculum has proceeded unabated without equal consideration for its viability. The focus of today's schools is on helping students become skilled and critical thinkers, participating actively in society's development. Such skills can more easily be nurtured by incorporating instructional styles where students are partners in the teaching-learning process, and by having a curriculum that promotes the development of these skills. Changing to this approach of learning from the traditional teacher-centred instruction has become increasingly common in many colleges and schools.

The internet provides students with confidence in learning. It is seen as an alternative to the teacher-directed learning environment by encouraging active learning. The internet gives simulation of real-world settings as it allows students to visit those places while in class. Use of the internet can save time for other activities in class because the instructor can post materials online so that students can have access to them, and thus time that would have been used going through those materials in class can be used for other activities.

Novice users often do not have an idea of how to use the internet, even with the help of search engines and directories. In citing Oliver, Kelch and Karr-Kidwell state: the internet may pose a challenge for some students in finding information needed for a certain topic, and not knowing the key search word can be a detrimental when using the World Wide Web. Although internet use in class has been to allow students access to information, quite often they get lost in the world of the internet only to end with irrelevant information.

The completion of the study found that the internet provided both positive and negative influences on the themes. The positive influences are:

i) source of information,
ii) independent and individualised learning,
iii) in-depth understanding and
iv) motivation.

Source of information: Internet provided a rich resource of materials, while it also became an alternative source of information for students. The students acquired materials and information from the internet for their projects. The internet gave students access to information on text, video, and audio, which they could not obtain from the teacher or textbook. The students also used the internet when the teacher was busy helping other students. For those who feared asking questions in class, the internet was a quiet, private replacement of the teacher. The internet also provided up to date information for students and the teacher.

Independent and individualised learning: Internet encouraged independent learning by students. It was a learning aid that made it possible for students to obtain online help for their projects by using tutorials found on the internet. As observed and pointed out both by the students and the teacher, the internet individualised students' learning. Although students in the class consisted of experienced and novice students in technology use, the teacher did not individualise instruction for the class.

In depth understanding: The teacher and the students agreed that the internet gave students an in depth understanding of what they learned. Due to time constraints in class, students are given skeletal information requiring the students to turn to other sources of instruction and reference such as the internet for supplemental materials. Students stated that the use of the internet to supplement instruction increased student understanding.

Motivation: The teacher and the students voiced the belief that the internet motivated students in their learning. Being an extraordinary source of information, with a combination of visual, graphic, sound and movies, the students found learning with such technology interesting and fun.

Internet also imposed negative influences on the learning of the students. The negative influences were focused around four themes:

i) interference with student concentration,
ii) time consuming,
iii) questionable resources, and
iv) dependence on the internet.

Interference: Internet interfered with students concentration on class work. The researcher's interviews and observations found that the internet 'dilutes' the academic environment of the class, and in effect removes students from the classroom. As students read e-mails, or were caught up with news on the CNN web site, followed sports on ESPN, accessed the Napster site for the latest music albums, and saw advertisements of leisure products, they often became distracted from the class environment.

Time consuming: In the class, students wasted time surfing the internet. Searching the internet does not mean using search engines or directories and simply getting information needed. It requires skills to get the right information with the least time possible. As observed in class, students moved from search engine to search engine and between directories looking for the same piece of information. Students' time was also wasted when the internet became slow because the networked system could not cope with many students online at the same time.

Questionable resources: Students' learning involves using resources that are credible. With the internet, there is no control. It is a free-for-all information source where anyone can publish online any time. This has the danger of having inappropriate and unreliable information posted. In using the internet, students copied materials whose reliability, and credibility was questionable.

Dependency: Students developed a dependency on the internet during the class. Students turned to the internet for information rather than using the knowledge they already had, and regarded the internet as indispensable to their learning even when inappropriate.

Internet has changed the instructional approach in the classroom. Traditionally, the teacher is supposed to teach with students listening. In this classroom, the students also contributed to the teaching. Students were updating the teacher on new innovations on some of the technologies they were using as the class progressed. Internet had reduced interaction in class. As evidenced in the class, there were few questions asked by the students, discussion between the students, and the teacher was rare, and students hardly responded to the teachers' questions and comments due to their focus on searching the internet during the class period.

Students' use of the internet has undermined the teachers' confidence, affecting the teacher's confidence in his own competency and skills. The teacher also feared that the students appeared to know what he was teaching, and hence his role was not significant. Thus, the teacher's authoritative control of the class, which is witnessed in traditional classrooms, was challenged.

Students who surf the web for long periods of time are not active participants in the class. Such students rarely finished their in-class assignments on time. The teacher complained that these students come to his office when he has other commitments to make-up their assignments, or bring them to the next class meeting. According to the teacher, this creates a backlog of work, and interferes with the orderly scheduling of class activities and assignments.

Internet affected the instructional styles of the teacher and the students. As an important tool for teaching and source of knowledge for students, it had realigned the teacher-student relations. Unlike the traditional class, where the teacher is the *de facto* head of the class as a source of knowledge, and controller of class activities, the internet had reduced the role and significance of the teacher in both perspectives mentioned. Students no longer felt that they had to rely entirely on the teacher when in class. The students and the teacher concurred that there is need to control internet use in class. The teacher indicated that the uncontrolled use of the internet would in the long run hurt the students instead of helping them.

Internet use in the class conducive for the classroom environment. The following guidelines should be taken into consideration with the ultimate aim of making the internet an effective resource:

i) Use of the internet in class needs to be monitored. As the internet has the potential to sway students from the academic-oriented environment of the classroom to the outside, non-academic world, monitoring will limit such unnecessary escapades by students.

ii) Teachers should identify beforehand lessons and/or activities that will necessitate use of the internet. This will instill disciplined use of the internet by the students.

iii) Teachers should provide internet search guidelines and skills at the beginning of the course and bookmark important sites for students.

iv) Teachers should diversify instructional strategies with textbooks, group discussions, CDs, and videos instead of focusing solely on the internet.

v) Teachers should discourage students from pirating on the internet.

E-BOOKS

Our society is increasingly driven by the interconnectedness of markets, economies, people, communication, and education. The internet is perhaps the greatest purveyor of cross-cultural communication and information transfer. However, satellites, wireline, and wireless networks, among others, are also tools leading the charge in developing borderless nations. But the last 20 years has also seen the networking of individuals within single locations.

The local area network (LAN) has pushed the envelope of computer networking to the extreme. New standards are allowing even computer and other information appliances in offices or homes to be networked via wireless connections. We are a connected society, and the use of technologies and protocols to connect all kinds of devices is likely to rise dramatically in the next several years and will prove vastly important to economies and the transference of education.

As the number of non-traditional and corporate professionals rise in education, mobility becomes an important factor in meeting the needs of this demographic group. While certainly mobile, the traditional book remains a frustrating nuisance, especially if one has to lug around several books while travelling on business. The book, in its traditional form, remains an isolated island of information, can be, at times, constraining, and clearly is unable to connect to any other electronic devices.

More and more of our educational technology is wired or connected in some fashion. From computers, to video-conferencing, to CD-ROMs, to distance learning systems and yes, to the internet, the demands to have a connected network of educational mediums is a major drive today to fulfil traditional, non-traditional, and corporate education needs. Many pundits claim we have entered the knowledge age, where information creation manipulation, and exchange, in the form of economic output, will be the growth engine of the 21st century.

While not a new concept altogether, the e-book, in its latest iteration, provides an interesting avenue in the quest for better education and better educational technology use. The e-book, in its raw form, is nothing more than electronic text. The e-book reader is the vehicle that is garnering the lion's share of attention in the industry today.

The development of HyperCard and hypertext technology provided the enabling software and tools to create electronic, interactive books. These books could be downloaded to a PC, where non-linear, random accessibility was possible. The problem was that since the electronic text was stored on the hard drive, the portability, unlike a hard or soft copy book, was very limited. Today, a variety of e-books are available, such as the Rocket eBook, the SoftBook, the Everybook, the Classbook Reader, the Librius Millennium Reader, and the RCA eBook

These first generation e-books are gathering attention, both from consumers and the computer and publishing industries. Trade publishers estimate that within a few years, 10 percent of all books will be sold to be read as e-books. Even others, namely software providers such as Microsoft, claim within 20 years, 90 percent of all books will be sold to be read as e-books. Some go as far as to suggest that eventually e-books will do the heavy work of conveying information and entertaining us while the traditional book will retreat to the status of a collectible.

E-books are a reality today and will certainly be a part of our future. The e-book itself is a relatively small, hand-held device, that is today primarily a storage-and-display unit. The device plugs into a cradle that attaches to a computer, or in some cases, when a modem is included, to a phone jack, where access and textbook download is accomplished. Prices are as low as $ 300.

E-books can hold about 10,000 pages of text, so the reader/student could carry multiple books, for multiple classes, without the physical strain of lugging around a heavy backpack throughout the day. But the e-book is more than just a lightweight, portable reading device. E-books offer a variety of features and functions that turn it from newfangled electronic reader into a useful, educational technology. Whether in a traditional classroom setting or distant, independent study, the book, or some form of printed instructional material, is almost always used. And more times than not, multiple printed textbooks and materials are required.

With e-books, not only can you store multiple texts, you also can electronically search and cross-reference within and outside of the text. This offers clear timesaving benefits for the student, particularly when coursework requires the analysis and synthesis of material from multiple textbooks. The e-book also offers features and functions that not only save time or open up a "virtual" book library, but also a means of personal creativity. For example, e-books offer variable font size.

Many e-books come with a stylus, allowing the reader to underline passages or scribble notes in the margin. This is ideal for the student who wants to capture key thoughts without having to "maim" a paper book. Furthermore, e-books offer the option of book marking pages by simply touching the page.

Higher-end e-books come with full-colour, high-resolution displays. So, high-impact graphics are available in addition to the text, creating a multimedia reading and learning experience. Additionally, many magazines and newspapers are also available in electronic format.

The book has been around significantly longer than any other medium used for education or training. Even today, the book is a dominant part of the educational landscape; this is not going to change anytime soon. The book has, for hundreds of years, influenced the way we reason, imagine, invent, and yes, learn. However, in a world of the 'wired', the book arguably has a big shortcoming: It is not connected to anything else. This shortcoming limits the book as an educational technology.

E-books can and do have the ability to connect to networks via built-in modem ports. The e-book can be docked to personal computers to further extend their networking capabilities. In the not-so-distant future, e-books will be able to directly connect to other e-books. Additionally, as libraries, for example, further extend the electronic access and networking of databases, card catalogues and books, newspapers, and magazines, the capability to 'plug' e-books into library networks for all sorts of access and downloading is inevitable.

The potential possibilities of e-books are limitless, only restricted by the imagination of the manufacturers and the users. In an increasingly networked society, the means and delivery of education will require more, not less connectivity, books included. The e-book offers not only the benefits of the book, but a whole host of features and functions that extend the traditional book into a true electronic, internet worked, multimedia-rich tool for educational use.

REFERENCES

Berge Z. L., 1999, "Interaction in Post-secondary Web-based Learning", *Educational Technology*, 39(1), pp. 5-11.

Brown, J. S., Duguid, P., 2000, *Learning-in Theory and in Practice*, In J. S. Brown, P. Duguid (eds.), *The Social Life of Information*, Cambridge, MA: Harvard Business School Press.

Duffy, T., Jonassen, D., (eds.), 1992, *Constructivism and the Technology of Instruction: A Conversation*, Hillsdale, N., Lawrence Erlbaum Associates.

Entwistle, A and Entwistle, N., 1992, *Experiences of Understanding in Revising for Degree Examinations Learning and Instruction*, 2, pp.1-22.

Forsyth, I., 1998, *Teaching and Learning Materials and the Internet* (2nd ed.), London: Kogan Page.

Galusha, J. M., 1998, *Barriers to Learning in Distance Education, Interpersonal Computing and Technology*, 5(3-4), pp. 6-14.

Roberts, L., 1996, *A Transformation of Learning: Use of the NII for Education and Lifelong Learning*, In D. P. Ely & B. B. Minor (eds.), *Educational Media and Technology Yearbook 1995/1996*, pp. 50-66, Englewood, CO: Libraries Unlimited.

von Glasersfeld, E., 1992, "Constructivism Reconstructed", *Science and Education*, 7, pp. 379-384.

4

Learning in Cyberspace

Information and communication technologies (ICT) may play a crucial role, offering the learner new opportunities to participate actively in the learning process via network-based activities. This prospect highlights the need to provide training based on new methodologies that exploit the potential of ICT, whether in the form of personalised courses or as learning paths within the context of virtual communities pursuing collaborative learning.

The spectrum of potential fields of application is extremely varied, including the likes of in-service training for school teachers, distance education and training within small- and medium-sized enterprises, open and distance learning, and so-called integrated (online/onsite) education offered by universities. In the face of such variety, in-depth study is required into the conditions determining the choice of the most effective methods and technologies. Separate mention should be made of the business world, in which innovation and constant market evolution are leading to the gradual abandonment of traditional, procedural-type education in favour of endogenous growth through the exchange of know-how.

Valuable support can be gained from ICT when combined with knowledge management methods, and hence with the organisation of communities of practice engaged in collaborative learning. Communities of practice are self-managing virtual learning groups in which professional growth is based not so much on delineated learning paths but rather on experience-sharing, the identification of best practices, and reciprocal support for tackling day-to-day problems in the workplace. This type of learning can be defined as mutual or reciprocal learning in order to distinguish it from other collaborative learning strategies that might be called directive learning, wherein someone manages or steers the learning process.

The constant market evolution being fuelled by innovations in technology, organisation, management, and marketing calls for constant effort on the part of companies in order to keep up. This gives rise to the need to train, update, and often retrain staff to ensure that the company does not fall behind in the race to modernise. However, these firms face a critical problem in that they have a low capacity for endogenous growth. This is a form of growth obtained in two ways:

i) by capitalising on and spreading throughout the firm the know-how and tactical knowledge that individual staff members have gained through direct experience; and
ii) by acquiring new expertise that the company lacks.

Large corporations often have internal divisions for instructing, training, and updating their own staff, while the same is not true of small corporate entities. Consequently, when facing a specific training need, the latter tend to opt for either or both of the following paths:

i) sending staff to training courses held outside the company by public training bodies, universities, specialised training centres, large corporations capable of passing on their expertise, etc.; and
ii) calling on outside experts and specialists to provide workplace training on company premises.

In both cases the course provider can decide whether to adopt a face-to-face approach, distance education, or a combined onsite/online strategy which mixes onsite activities with individual study and thus allows distance interaction among participants between one onsite event and another. Partial or total distance education, however, entails the adoption of specific instructional methodologies involving ICT use for multi-channel interaction typical of online education.

In order to satisfy the enterprise world's demands, distance courses need to:

i) feature some degree of onsite activity;
ii) emphasise group learning; and
iii) provide ongoing support from tutors and experts/specialists.

There are many obstacles to overcome, chief among them the lack of qualified trainers actually capable of designing and running distance courses. The result is that the professional training sector is still weighed down by tradition, and that technology, where it is used, is mainly employed for implementing learning paths based on delivery and individual exploitation of multimedia material (video recordings, courseware, print material, etc.); and as a vehicle for mass distribution of material (e.g., internet), tele-lessons held in videoconferences, etc. What is lacking is a quantum leap in methodology that would permit professional training to embrace fully-fledged online methods and regard network resources not just as a transmission channel but also as an environment for collaborative training activities.

Training bodies are not yet convinced there is market among small- and medium-sized businesses for online training courses, a belief borne out by the fact that a fair share of such firms in Italy, still lack the communication technology suitable for participating in such courses. But even supposing that infrastructure conditions were favourable, the right path for meeting business needs would not necessarily be to take processes that closely resemble those of so-called formal training an transfer them online. The stages that make up formal training are:

i) identification of training needs;
ii) educational design;
iii) production of learning material and a possible proposal for online activities based on online education strategies; and
iv) course delivery over a medium to long timespan.

No matter how rapidly these stages are conducted, the process from need identification to completion of formal training will inevitably be too lengthy for the modern company today, firms are forced to react practically in real time as training requirements arise, adopting very specific actions applied with almost surgical precision. The outcome is that the business world is calling ever more frequently for training targeted on a specific problem. This has given rise to what might be called dosed training.

Training providers are being asked more and more for something halfway between consultancy and training, between responding to a specific problem and developing skills and knowledge so that in the future the company is capable of handling similar problems by itself.

When speaking of formal training, we mentioned the problem of the lack of specialists for running online courses. The availability of people who are capable of acting as training mediators, of building a bridge between a company's training needs and the educational resources for meeting them. Those in the knowledge management field would speak of a facilitator, namely, someone who can provide the vital link between a learning community and the knowledge manager, who has the knowledge to meet learning needs.

In formal training, the provider or the learning material itself, plays a directive role with regard to the learners, and we have moved towards dosed training, in which the direction is indicated selectively and promptly by those seeking training. In both cases, however, we are dealing with an action managed by an external figure such as a trainer, a facilitator, a consultant, etc.

KNOWLEDGE MANAGEMENT (KM)

Knowledge management (KM) became a hot term late in the rise of dot.coms, but seems to have outlasted their crash. Typically used in large corporations, the application of the term varies widely, embracing both technical infrastructure and cultural/social paradigms. KM is relevant to web based learning in that software designed to capture and catalogue Knowledge must also recombine and provide back that information in a useful relevant way to someone who may be unfamiliar with the content sounds like web-based learning. It also strikes that the development of Learning Content Management Systems may be an early implementation of knowledge management systems with the focus on learning.

Knowledge management sector has inspired some companies, consortia, and even groups of individuals with common professional problems to initiate networked collaborative training approaches. These are based on a simple but powerful idea to create communities that ground their professional growth on mutual learning processes. This is a kind of peer learning that is already common in many professions and is a natural way of learning:

i) *Socialisation of the problem*: If a problem arises, help can be sought from someone who is likely to have already tackled that problem.

ii) *Socialisation of best practices*: If the suggested solution is understood, learning has taken place which will then increase knowhow.

iii) Even if no immediate solution is found, it is possible to seek allies in the search for one.

ICT offers the means to provide continuity and to optimise communication within groups of individuals who would otherwise find it far more difficult to distribute information, knowledge and best practises among members. Consider the obvious case of how a simple e-mail message can deliver a request for help to an enormous readership comprising people who perform the same professional role.

Network technology is a powerful ally where there is a need to stay in touch outside of face-to-face meetings or informal discussion. It is therefore an amplifier of the communication within a community of practice, namely, the circulation of information and material (explicit knowledge) or of opinions, suggestions, and knowledge based on personal experience (tacit knowledge) that have not been codified in a text/manual or other support/ information channel.

A community of practice must be above all a real community, one based on its members' physical/personal acquaintance with one another, on reciprocal esteem and trust, and most importantly, on willingness and capacity to identify oneself as a member of a single entity—the community of practice.

A community of practice will communicate solely via CMC. There are, however, a few exceptions, such as software programmers, one of the first virtual communities to be formed and to operate exclusively online. Such communities are made up of people used to working with ICT and capable of judging objectively whether a member's suggestion is sound or not; a programming solution either works or does not, so an immediate decision can be made on whether or not to adopt it. However, there are other areas like interpreting regulations or applying administrational procedures where one needs to take a colleague's word solely on trust. If we extend the approach to these areas, then the conditions mentioned earlier are the ones which really guarantee that a community of practice will work.

The KM sector offers tools and methods for acquiring knowledge and for sharing it with others. However, this covers a range of different cultural behaviours. Some see "knowledge creation" as the creation of databases, while others believe that it has nothing to do with data but is rather based on informal operative knowhow. Much of this knowhow is stored in the minds of middle management, the very people who have often been displaced by company re-engineering and the subsequent introduction of computers . This approach to knowledge, is typical of Japanese business culture, which differs from the Western variety in a number of ways, especially in:

i) how knowledge is viewed;
ii) what companies do with knowledge; and
iii) who the key players are.

From the Japanese point of view:

i) knowledge is not to be regarded merely as data or information that can be stored in a computer—it involves emotions, values, and intuition;
ii) companies should not merely manage knowledge but create it as well; and
iii) each member of the organisation needs to be involved in the creation of company knowledge, with middle management acting as the main organisers of knowledge.

According to the Japanese point of view in knowledge management there are two kinds of knowledge: explicit and tacit.

i) *Explicit knowledge*: It can be expressed in words and numbers, and can be distributed as data, scientific formulae, product descriptions, manuals, basic principles, and so on. This kind of knowledge is easy to transmit in definite and organised form and is the variety historically favoured in the West.
ii) *Tacit knowledge*: It is highly personal and difficult to define, which also makes it hard to communicate and

> share. It embraces subjective perception, intuition, and foresight, and is firmly rooted in personal experience, as are one's ideals, values, and emotions. There are two sides to tactic knowledge. The first is the technical dimension, comprising the kind of skills and tricks of the trade that are hard to define and are usually covered by the term knowhow. For example, craftsmen, sportsmen, chefs, and the like build up a wealth of practical skills developed through years of professional experience, but they often have difficulty expressing the technical and scientific principles that underpin their knowledge. Highly subjective perception, intuition, foresight, and inspiration gained through years of practical experience all fall into the technical category. The second is the cognitive dimension. This consists of the convictions, sensations, ideals, emotions, and mental models that are so deeply rooted as to lead us to take them for granted.

Explicit knowledge is easy to manage on a computer, communicate by network, and store in a database, but the subjective and intuitive nature of tacit knowledge makes it difficult to handle or transmit in a logical, systematic way. In order to spread this kind of knowledge within a company, it needs to be converted into words and numbers that everyone can understand. It is in this very act of conversion from tactic to explicit that company knowledge is created. The role of technology in this process differs greatly from the management of explicit knowledge using databases.

The main aim is to get people to communicate, and so effective support can be gained from technologies for interpersonal communication, especially those that facilitate group interaction. This leads to a new way of viewing network-based learning, one which is based on sharing experience, identifying best practices, and reciprocal support for tackling day-to-day problems that arise in one's work. We can define this type of collaborative learning as reciprocal learning, so as to distinguish it from directive learning based on a process driven by someone following a clear training programme.

According to Wenger:

> Communities of practice presents a theory of learning that starts with this assumption: engagement in social practice is the fundamental process by which we learn and so become who we are. The primary unit of analysis is neither the individual nor social institutions but rather the informal communities of practice that people form as they pursue shared enterprises over time. In order to give a social account of learning, the theory explores in a systematic way the intersection of issue of community, social practice, meaning, and identity. The result is a broad conceptual framework for thinking about learning as a process of social participation.

The concept of communities of practice has been pioneered by the Institute for Research on learning (IRL), a spin-off of the Xerox Corporation in Palo Alto, CA. In cooperation with the IRL, Xerox executives launched a study to observe how employees actually did their jobs. What evolved was the notion of communities of practice.

Communities of practice approach is based on the following assumptions:

i) Learning is fundamentally a social phenomenon. People organise their learning around the social communities of which they are members. Schools are powerful learning environments only for individuals whose social communities coincide with the school.
ii) Knowledge is integrated in the life of communities that share values, beliefs, languages, and ways of doing things. These are called 'communities of practice'. Real knowledge is integrated in the doing, the social relations, and the knowledge and expertise of these communities.

iii) The process of learning and the process of membership in a community of practice are inseparable. Learning is inseparably entwined with membership in a community. It is what allows us to be a member and adjust our status in the group.

iv) Knowledge is inseparable from practice. It is not possible to 'know' without 'doing.'

v) The ability to contribute to a community creates the potential for learning. Circumstances in which we are engaged in real action that has consequences for both us and the community of which we are a part create the most powerful learning environments.

There are at least two situations in which collaborative learning can gain from the establishment of a community of practice:

i) the need for follow-up to a course of whatever form through self-help among course alumni; and

ii) the need to create communities of professionals based on the concepts of knowledge sharing/knowledge management.

Training courses are not always long enough to guarantee the complete acquisition of the knowledge and skills dealt with. Indeed, in many cases it would be more accurate to speak of informative rather than formative training. Take residential courses, for example. In the space of a few days, it is difficult, if not impossible, to transfer the skills that participants need for autonomous application of their newly acquired knowledge within their particular professional field. And the more methodological the course content, the more unlikely the chances of success in this regard.

Distance courses are certainly no exception here. The most critical moment arrives following the conclusion of a course, when individual participants attempt to apply what they have learned, relying, totally on their own resources. Mastering the main course contents does not necessarily mean being able to put that knowledge into action.

When the first difficulties arise, the sense of isolation that is always lurking in the background can lead to demotivation, often resulting in the squandering of the educational and economic resources that have been invested in the student.

Hence the strong need for online support in order to provide continuity between training and transfer activities. This may either be a scheduled part of the course or activated spontaneously by the participants themselves. In the former case, it is the course provider who is responsible for offering online support during the transfer phase. In the second, support stems from self-help among the participants themselves. This means the creation of a community of course alumni who keep in touch after the conclusion of the course. In this way, when it comes to applying their new learning, they are able to help one another by socialising the problems faced.

One of the earliest experiences in the establishment of communities of practice supported by network technologies dates back to 1992 in Italy. In that period, the Ministry of Education was launching a national programme for the introduction of computers in schools, and to this purpose several hundred teachers were trained to become local tutors supporting colleagues in their respective schools.

On the basis of a similar experience undertaken in 1985, one of the first needs addressed was that of keeping the local tutors in touch with one another after residential training had concluded. To this end, ITD designed and implemented a computer conferencing system that the teachers could access via modem from their schools. The experience proved to be very fruitful and produced indications about the effectiveness of the approach adopted. However, the potential size of the community involved was limited by the high cost of communication at that time.

Internet use was then still confined to the scientific community and computer conferencing was mainly conducted via direct point to point calls, which, if made to destinations out of the local area, incurred considerable cost. Today, technology and communication costs are far more affordable and so the formation of communities of practice comprising training course alumni has become standard. Even while undergoing training trainees are already getting used to the idea of continuous learning supported by the sharing of problems/ solutions, experiences, and so on.

The establishment of a community of practice, in the case of course alumni, takes place after the course has concluded. By contrast, when it comes to online learning based on the concept of knowledge sharing, groups of professionals are formed in a spontaneous manner for the purpose of enriching skill, and/or knowledge through collaborative strategies. Hence, the formation of these two types of community differs greatly, as do the reasons that encourage members to take part in them. For course alumni, aggregation in communities of practice is encouraged by the resonance created by the common experience the participants have shared in during the course.

For professional groups, however, motivation comes from the realisation that sharing experience and knowledge offers an excellent opportunity for collective growth. In this case, the sole driving force for joining the community is interest in the topic under discussion: members may be spread over a wide geographical area and might not necessarily belong to the same organisation or sector. In order for community collaboration to be self-fuelled and long-lasting, individual members must do more than merely draw on the experience of others; they need to play an active and constructive role in contributing to the development of new and better professional practices.

The terms data, information, and knowledge are often used interchangeably in everyday use. Although they are related, semantically they we quite different. It is useful to distinguish among these terms as we use them before proceeding. Data are raw facts, usually the result of observations or measurements from some environment. Information is data that has been manipulated so that it is made meaningful for a particular context. This transformation is typically accomplished through organisation, aggregation, filtering, or some other manipulation that results in an appropriate interpretation of that data. Knowledge is more complex than information and more valuable too. It is the "knowhow" that lets a human actually use the information to solve a problem. Knowledge is an organised collection of facts, rules, and heuristics as well as how and when to apply them to solve-a problem.

Humans can acquire knowledge by being told, by seeing an example of how another human being solved a problem, by analogical transfer between unrelated domains, by reasoning from deep structures such as from books and formal education, or by observation, experimentation, and discovery. Acquiring knowledge begins early in human existence, is reinforced in traditional schooling and life experiences, and continues for most humans until their death.

The knowledge acquisition techniques of being told and example are learned early. Parents and teachers provide children a great deal of know how by telling them what they need to know and how to apply what they know to solve different types of problems. Parents and teachers also know that setting the appropriate example for children is very important because children imitate what they see being done.

If humans become comfortable with abstraction, they will be able to recognise patterns that can contribute to the acquisition of knowledge through analogy. Analogical reasoning assumes that if two situations are known to be similar in some respect, it is likely that they will be similar in others. For example, to grasp the behaviour of electricity, a teacher might use the analogy of water running through a pipe. The voltage corresponds to pressure, the amperage to the volume of flow, and the resistance to the capacity of the pipe. Analogy allows great flexibility in applying existing knowledge to new situations.

If humans care to, they can compile their knowledge into books that become the source from which other humans can reason to obtain the same knowledge or use it as information to derive new knowledge.

Obtaining knowledge by observation, experimentation, and discovery requires a human to have a level of curiosity about the problem domain and an ability to make an inference that can be tested. From in observation or the result of an experiment, a human can infer general rules or regularities that can lead to the discovery of new knowledge. When humans are very young, they are curious is about a great many things.

Humans often use these means of knowledge acquisition in combination, in general preferring being told and example to reasoning from deep structures. Each method has its limitations and drawbacks. Sometimes who is doing the telling contributes more to the value of the knowledge being articulated than what is being told. To many a first grade student, the teacher has profound knowledge and is an "expert" on just about everything. Adults know that this is not the case; however, adults too can be quick to give expert status to humans who just have a bit more knowledge than they do.

The knowledge being applied can range from common sense knowledge that many humans are expected to have, to expert knowledge that only a few humans have concerning a particular subject. Knowledge engineers are the humans who do knowledge engineering. They perform three major functions:

i) identify problem domains,
ii) select methods for knowledge acquisition, and
iii) construct intelligent systems.

Appropriate problem domains for knowledge engineering are domains in which humans solve problems that are unstructured, have a large number of variables, contain lots of uncertainty, and have multiple or conflicting goals. An ideal situation is to have available in the organisation a human who does the problem solving well, knows how to communicate or demonstrate that it takes to do the job well, and can do the job well repeatedly.

More difficult problems are typically those that cannot be captured in a limited knowledge base. These domains often require larger knowledge bases, including a great deal of common sense knowledge, used to relate knowledge from a wide range of domains and sources. Progress in this challenging area of research has been slow, but promising. The eventual maturation and use of large scale knowledge bases containing this sort of common sense knowledge will make intelligent systems easier to construct and maintain, due to knowledge reuse, and a great deal more effective, as they bring more knowledge to bear.

There are several methods that knowledge engineers might use to acquire the knowledge that will be automated. The classical method is being told. The method requires knowledge engineers to elicit knowledge from knowledge holders, analyse that knowledge, and represent it in a form that can be used by a computer. To be effective, knowledge engineers must be good listeners, have open minds, think clearly, and communicate well.

Knowledge engineers collect information by listening, interviewing, and observing human subjects who hold the desired knowledge. This can be time consuming and difficult if the knowledge holders are inarticulate, elusive, or uncooperative. Furthermore, if the knowledge holders are experts, it is common for them not to consciously know how they do what they do that makes them experts. This is to say they have compiled quite a bit of expertise and become more inarticulate about what makes their behaviour expert or effective.

They do not normally present their knowledge in well-formed pieces of logic; their knowledge is usually fragmented.

When they articulate it, they usually leave out chunks of pertinent information that drives the know how. Therefore, knowledge engineers must analyse the knowledge that has been articulated to make sure that gaps of knowledge do not exist. If the knowledge engineers do not understand the knowledge, then they will not be able to represent it. Representing the knowledge that has been extracted from a human knowledge holder is another challenge. AI provides several ways of expressing knowledge in a computer-tractable form, and knowledge engineers must decide which form is appropriate from the use of the knowledge in an intelligent system.

Today software tools exist that use autonomous algorithms for acquiring data and organising it into information for knowledge compilation. One such system is DISCIPLE—an apprenticeship, multistrategy learning approach for building intelligent agents. A human teaches DISCIPLE how to perform domain-specific tasks in a way that resembles the way that the human would teach an apprentice, by giving DISCIPLE examples and explanations as well as by supervising and correcting its behaviour.

In this type of environment, the knowledge engineer supports the human knowledge holder in the use of the software tool by preparing appropriate problem scenarios for the human to show the software how to solve or by guiding the human through any difficulties being encountered using the software tool. Closely related but sufficiently different are the software tools that develop knowledge by analogy. The basic idea behind this method is that if two things are known to be alike in some respects, then it is possible that they are alike in other respects. As with the previous method, an example is presented to the software system but this time there is no human to specify the class to which the example might belong.

Reasoning from deep structures usually means using knowledge available in an ontology. An ontology is a specification of a conceptualisation. It is a description of the concepts and relationships that exist with respect to some problem domain. An ontological commitment is an agreement to use a vocabulary in a manner consistent with respect to the theory specified by the ontology. So knowledge engineers develop ontologies for the purpose of enabling knowledge sharing and reuse.

During the first year of the High Performance Knowledge Bases (HPKB) initiative sponsored by the Defence Advanced Research Projects Agency (DARPA), an empirical study was performed on reusing prior knowledge in the formation of ontologies. The results indicated that reuse does help in the acquisition of new knowledge though many factors affect how much it helps. Participation in this HPKB study motivated knowledge engineers to develop a semi-automated system called PROMPT for ontology merging and alignment. Their results show the potential for leveraging previous knowledge engineering.

However, a great deal of human intervention is still necessary to effectively merge or align knowledge from disparate knowledge bases. The scientific method is typified by the observation, experimentation, and discovery cycle. Either a knowledge engineer or an intelligent system can guide this cycle. Regardless of who or what undertakes the effort, the Empirical Inquiry Hypothesis is at the centre of the investigation. This involves using observation to develop a hypotheses, transforming the hypothesis into a computer programme, and running the programme.

In the current terminology, data mining asks questions in a structured and precise way developing a hypothesis, and the formation and testing of the hypothesis is called knowledge discovery. For example, the Swedish Defence Research Establishment has developed a data mining and knowledge discovery system to help deal with the violation of Swedish marine territory by foreign submarine intruders. The submarine intrusion problem represents a class of problem in which observation is from a complex structure of known and unknown facts, experimentation uses genetic algorithms to find a category of sequence similar to the current sequence, and discovery is a short-term prediction and a confirmation of a submarine's future tactical movement.

The use of intelligent agents as cognitive tools—mental and computational devices that support, guide, and extend the thinking processes of students. Such tools can be used by educators in three ways:

i) intelligent agents can support the student's higher order thinking skills by reducing information overload;
ii) intelligent agents can help improve the performance of students, as each student becomes the cognitive apprentice of his or her own intelligent agent; and
iii) the student can create an intelligent agent as a learning experience.

Some applications of knowledge engineering are described below.

i) *Ontology development*: A formal ontology of subject, is an emerging information retrieval technology that seeks to organise large-scale digital libraries by constructing a workable ontology for searching by subject. The information on the internet cannot be as well understood as the contents of a library can. The internet also constantly grows and changes, leading users who are often unable to find needed information, and, probably more often, overload with information.

   None the less, the internet provides online computer access to a wealth of digitally stored information from documents and books to pictures, music, video, and audio. There is no limit to the number of places where these sources may be stored or the contexts in which they may be organised. To facilitate the construction of an intelligent agent that will help student with the information overload of the internet, knowledge engineers have been studying the concept of subject in order to determine a formal ontology of subject for a large-scale digital library card catalogue system. They have discovered a good deal of ambiguity regarding the usage of subjects in existing card catalogue systems. They have analysed a great deal of history of subject classification in philosophy and library science and are attempting to formalise the notions into a single framework for representing the concept of subjects. The current work presents a top-level ontology that not only is an accurate hierarchy of topic categories but also represents topic and subject at a deeper semantic level.

ii) *Cognitive apprentice*: The second is an application of a learning agent shell that assesses .the student's understanding of some historical events. The DISCIPLE approach has been used to implement a learning agent that generates history tests to assist in the assessment of students' understanding and use of higher-order thinking skills. Knowledge engineers working with a history teacher created a customised DISCIPLE agent by developing a specialised problem solver and two domain specific interfaces. The specialised problem solver is a test generator. One interface facilitates the communication between the teacher and the DISCIPLE Learning Agent Shell and the other facilitates the communication between the agent and the students. The teacher identifies a set of historical concepts that are appropriate and necessary for students to learn and the historical sources that can enhance the student's understanding of these concepts.

iii) *Intelligent agent construction*: Another application is learning agent technology whereby students will construct learning agents to impart their own expertise to others, while at the same time learning about the underlying AI concepts and techniques. DISCIPLE is currently being used at the United States Army War

College to construct learning agents for strategic decision-making, while at the same time educating students about AI. Students will create intelligent agents based on their accumulated expertise in the domain. At the same time, the students will learn the underlying AI concepts at work in the learning agent.

Knowledge Sharing in E-environment

To facilitate the transfer and sharing of knowledge, human beings have, for centuries, used a variety of communication aids. As time has passed these aids have had to evolve and adapt in order to support the ever growing and diverse types of knowledge that are continually being created.

There are four significant advances in communication technology to facilitate knowledge transfer:

i) various aids to facilitate reading and writing activities;
ii) printing/photocopying for the mass distribution of information;
iii) radio and TV broadcasting for the global dissemination of non-interactive, non-print material;
iv) the use of computers for the realisation of interactive information systems.

Presently there is a move towards the global sharing of electronic resources through the use of an information superhighway. Obviously, this represents a further important development with respect to the creation of technologies that support knowledge sharing. System builders and implementors must choose those technologies and techniques that are most appropriate to the situation in hand. Obviously the communication and information storage technologies that are employed will significantly influence the mechanisms that are used in order to store, retrieve, disseminate and present information to users.

Paper-based technologies have been the ones most extensively used for knowledge sharing applications. However, in the light of new developments in information technology it is important to consider whether or not paper is still the most efficient and effective way to record and disseminate information and knowledge. Within educational systems the issues of efficient and effective knowledge transfer are particularly important—especially, in an era of diminishing financial support. Naturally, there are many limitations associated with these traditional teaching methods.

Electronic course delivery (ECD) is a viable alternative delivery mechanism to facilitate the efficient and cost-effective presentation of learning and training resources within a university and/or college context. ECD is concerned with the use of electronic materials and delivery platforms to support and enhance teaching and learning experiences—either on an individual or a group basis. In order to realise the goals of ECD there are a number of underlying areas which need to be addressed. These include the use of electronic lectures; mechanisms to facilitate lectures-on-demand; the extensive use of tele-teaching, tele-tutoring and collaborative learning at a distance; and support facilities such as electronic libraries.

Obviously, the use of electronic libraries will be an important foundation for the successful use of ECD. It is through such facilities that users will gain access to electronic books, magazines, journals, newspapers, internet resources and various other artefacts that are published electronically using 'digital paper'. Of course, as well as ensuring that the necessary storage, communication and delivery technologies are in place to support ECD, it is also imperative that appropriate software and courseware resources are made available.

Naturally, the courseware products that are used must fully implement three important pedagogic activities.

i) they must provide methods and strategies which will ensure that students are adequately assessed;

ii) must embed appropriate remediation facilities; and

iii) they must make available suitable performance support tools which will facilitate effective and efficient skill development.

With the advent of information superhighway individuals are able to browse or search a vast distributed information resource and retrieve information in a wide range of media forms. What is often lacking, however, is any consideration of how such information is processed by the reader, thus becoming usable knowledge.

Some of the issues surrounding the facilitation of information can take place either with respect to the provision of working knowledge or to the provision of deep knowledge. Information can be enhanced through the introduction of performance tools and/or assessment and/or remediation strategies. In other words, access to information is not sufficient to allow knowledge sharing. It is the changes that occur in end-users which are the key to knowledge sharing.

To provide understanding in the longer term reflection or reflective observation need to be initiated in users. Reflection implies an interaction with information without which knowledge transfer could not take place. Often, individuals reflect on their learning experiences while not actively engaged with an information resource. This can either be a subconscious process—typified by the Gestalt notion of illumination or the conscious processes that learning materials are intended to foster. In other words, knowledge transfer implies processes that can be encouraged or facilitated and go beyond the simple viewing of information.

There are several issues involved in the transfer from information into deep knowledge.

i) it is important to develop mechanisms that can actually assist the conversion process,

ii) it is important for users to be able to assess their progress.

iii) any discrepancies that arise between information content and users' interpretations must be remediated.

One of the most important techniques that can be used in this regard is the use of assessment strategies. When people are engaged in learning they need to interact with the material. Unfortunately, for many people, information access can often be a relatively passive process unless targeted at undertaking specific tasks. Nevertheless, people often do access information to gain knowledge rather than to solve particular problems and it is under these circumstances that the provision of mechanisms for the application of information becomes crucial. Assessment has a number of useful characteristics that can be utilised. They are:

i) motivation;
ii) activity;
iii) completeness; and
iv) correctness.

For many people, assessment is inherently motivating. People actually want to know how much they know. It also links into basic competitive drives which cause individuals to strive for high performance. Of course, engaging learners in a practical activity allows them to apply what they have learnt. It takes students away from relatively passive information processing to an active style of interaction. Furthermore, the corollary of individuals having an indication of what they know is that they can also become aware of what they do not know. This includes information that has been misinterpreted and/or misunderstood. Assessment provides the mechanism by which the need for remedial action can be identified. This can be action initiated by the student as a result of computer-based feedback.

Assessment is a useful mechanism for monitoring progress and giving learners an indication of how well they are doing. If necessary, remediation can then be used to help those who are under-performing. In contrast, performance support techniques are intended to extend human ability beyond the levels that are normally accessible to them. The study of performance support is therefore concerned with the design and provision of mechanisms, techniques, technology and tools to facilitate and augment an individual skill and knowledge performance within a given task domain.

Computer technology is being used as a basis for the realisation of performance support systems. A system that is based upon some form of embedded computer facility is often referred to as an electronic performance support system (EPSS). An can be defined as a human-activity system that is able to manipulate large amounts of task related information in order to provide both a problem solving capability as well as learning opportunities to augment human performance in a job task by providing information and concepts in either a linear or a nonlinear way, as and when they are required by a user. Electronic performance support systems are now increasingly being used within educational settings.

When used within this area an EPSS can help support staff and students in two important ways.

i) by accelerating skill and knowledge acquisition.

ii) by enhancing the ability levels of both staff and students.

In order to accelerate skill acquisition, computer-based assessment tools can be used to provide assessment mechanisms that provide real-time monitoring and feedback. In addition, advanced knowledge-based tools can be used to deliver deep knowledge and remediation embedded within the context of original learning/training tasks.

Through the use of EPSS techniques, students and staff can thus be provided with more complete, varied, valid and stimulating knowledge. Numerous examples of the use of EPSS techniques within education are now starting to appear in the literature. Within a university context, Barker et al., have described the application of EPSS techniques for the operation of an electronic, open access student information service (OASIS). The electronic OASIS is a basic mechanism to support ECD based upon the use of electronic lectures and various forms of automated assessment of students.

MOTIVATIONS FOR EFFECTIVE LEARNING

Effective learning can not take place without motivation. Motivation is a characteristic of people, and it therefore elicits different courses of action, different emotions and different cognitive interpretations of events from learners. Ongoing motivation leads to lifelong learning. Researchers sought to identify whether particular elements of information technology (IT) design, increased or reduced motivation more than others, and this was achieved by paying careful attention to the following factors:

i) opportunity for responsive feedback and individual involvement;
ii) the presence of motivating instructors;
iii) learners being active—able to make their choice of pace and content;
iv) collaborative learning;
v) curiosity and self discovery.

There are identified as potential motivators for students in an IT environment.

Opportunity for responsive feedback and individual involvement: To provide students with responsive feedback and individual involvement, internet, e-mail and teleconferencing were therefore built into the site design. Students were offered internet e-mail access to lecturers, and a biweekly teleconferencing meeting was also available for their use, whereby students could participate in electronic chat sessions with staff and fellow students.

The presence of motivating instructors: A teacher who cannot motivate students in the conventional classroom is likely to face the same situation using computers. The multimedia and internet programs were therefore designed by motivating instructors, to encourage students to learn. The lecturing staff therefore encouraged students and demonstrated a passionate commitment to the internet site.

Learners being active—able to make their own choice of pace and content: The premise of this design element was the work done by Pintrich *et al.*, that "when the instructional focus is on practice, rote application of rules and adherence to teacher specified activities, students place little value on the tasks and display less motivation". The internet site design therefore followed Pintrich's premise that "learners are motivated when allowed to choose how they will act and how much effort they would expend on each task". It was felt that by giving students this choice, motivation, commitment, deep involvement and strategic thinking about tasks, would improve.

Collaborative learning: This feature was based on the conclusion reached by Weiner that "collaboration builds motivation". The internet site design therefore incorporated Class Home Pages, whereby students in each class would work on projects, and post the results of their work on to the Class Home Pages for review by their peers.

Curiosity and self discovery: Curiosity is an important element in attaining and keeping the learner's attention. The internet site design therefore enabled the introduction of many changing facets, unavailable with traditional course delivery methods, such as on-demand videos and graphics.

Instructionists advocate the traditional belief of education, whereby students learn better through improvement of teaching instruction. Teachers are active. Students are passive. Antithetically, constructionists, believe that students advance through discovery and participation—learning and remembering, by discovering the specific knowledge they require and not simply receiving it from others. To improve this learning process, constructionists maintain that minimal structured individual guidance from teachers is needed. In this context, IT resources, as an adjunct to human teachers, continue to confront educators with opportunities and challenges. Constructionists and instructionists continue to debate the relative merits or otherwise of IT in support of their respective points of view.

Teachers are extremely versatile and adaptive—their pedagogic ability greatly exceeds any computer learning packages. The concepts of 'teaching' and 'learning' are seen as separate elements of an education closed-loop model that is borrowed from control engineering theory. It contends that teaching is in the forward path of a closed-loop education system, and that learning is in the feedback path. In this model, teaching takes place using 'information' prescribed in a syllabus.

Teaching is seen fundamentally as a process in which a large amount of information is compressed and delivered by the teacher to the students in limited lecturing hours. Learning, on the other hand, is a slow process of digesting and converting information to knowledge and skills, both during and after lecture hours. Consequently, physical attendance at a lecture by a student does not necessarily mean that learning is taking place or taking place efficiently. Learning efficiency varies from student to student and is largely influenced by students' capability and motivation. Hence, motivation is represented in the feedback path as a switch. When student motivation drops to zero, the feedback path is switched off. The system becomes an open loop. Teachers receive no response from students and will try to work frantically, leading to over teaching.

In order to avoid an open-loop situation, it is important to 'kick start' the learning process through motivating and helping students to learn. Once the closed-loop is re-established, teachers begin to receive good responses and feedback from students. Teaching becomes less tedious and professionally more fulfilling. Students begin to recognise their own small achievements which help to further strengthen motivation. In control engineering terms, the education loop is in a 'tracking control mode'. The teaching function must always be a human one. Teachers are more flexible and efficient compared with computers, when delivering a large amount of information, in digestible form, in a short period of time.

Programming a computer to deliver digestible material to replace a teacher is very time consuming and costly. Hence the use of technology as an adjunct to human teachers is more efficient and practical than replacing human teachers with technology. Since learning is a slow process, computers can be used to help in the learning/tutoring role just like human tutors are employed to help teachers, hence assuring that the feedback mechanism is in place, motivation is high and therefore teaching becomes more rewarding and productive.

REFERENCES

Bichelmeyer, B. A., Kiggins, E.A., 1998, "Using Web-based Conferencing in Post-secondary Instruction", *Proceedings of the Annual Conference on Distance Teaching and Learning*, Madison, WI, August 5-7, 1998.

Galusha, J. M., 1998, *Barriers to Learning in Distance Education, Interpersonal Computing and Technology*, 5(3-4), pp. 6-14.

Gilbert, S. W., 1997, *Teaching, Learning, and Technology*, Change, 217, 4 6. Guernsey, L., and Young, J. R. 1998, June 5.

Forsyth, I., 1998, *Teaching and Learning Materials and the Internet* (2nd ed.), London: Kogan Page.

Roberts, L., 1996, *A Transformation of Learning: Use of the NII for Education and Lifelong Learning*, In D. P. Ely & B. B. Minor (eds.), *Educational Media and Technology Yearbook 1995/1996*, pp. 50-66, Englewood, CO: Libraries Unlimited.

Tapscott, D., 1998, *Growing up Digital: The Rise of the Net Generation*. New York: McGraw-Hill Bock Company.

5
Interactive Learning

Advancements in technology have enhanced communications and information transmission capabilities and the use of videoconferencing has escalated as the costs of providing the technology have dropped. Point-to-point videoconferencing has expanded into multipoint videoconferencing, where three or more computers or workstations can be linked with screen and database sharing, or three or more locations can be connected between different conference facilities. This technology has been used in business, medicine and education for a number of years. One of the main benefits of vidcoconferencing is seen to be in improved communications. In business, people can communicate face-to-face without large travel costs and associated risks. In, medicine, high level resources and expertise can be delivered to places where it would normally be unavailable. In education, students can attend classes or communicate with instructors in another part of the world.

The use of videoconferencing in higher education has increased steadily in recent years. The South Eastern Universities Research Association Video Development Initiative, established in 1998, has created a video cookbook for academic and research users in the south-eastern region of the USA. Various attempts have been made simultaneously to teach students located on different campuses by videoconferencing. Guidelines have been developed based on this experience.

The Advanced Networks Systems Performance and Applications Group (ANSPAG) based at Monash University, Australia, has run pilot trials in high quality videoconferencing. They are also involved in a project to allocate bandwidth dynamically in the delivery of videoconferencing using ATM connectivity between Monash University and the University of Queensland in Australia. In Scotland the provision in universities of ATM-based Metropolitan Area Networks (MANs) with associated studios has made videoconferencing accessible to academic staff.

MANs have been provided, covering each of the four main conurbations in Scotland: AbMAN, covering the Aberdeen area; FaTMAN covering Fife and Tayside; EaSTMAN, covering Edinburgh and Stirling; and Clydenet, covering the Glasgow area. At each university there is a videoconferencing studio, typically seating about 30 participants. Each studio contains a codec and a Multipoint Control Unit.

A codec is a piece of equipment which decodes the received transmission signal and provides picture and sound. A visualiser is provided to allow documents and slides to be projected between sites. The system is run on the back of a fibre network provided by Scottish Telecom. The overall network runs at 155MB and the videoconference stream is carried via ATM at an average bandwidth of around 8MB, bursting up to a maximum of around 80MB under dynamic video conditions.

The codecs interfacing to analogue audio and video inputs and outputs at each conference suite are of a proprietary manufacture from K-NET, who specialise in ATM solutions for voice video and data communications. Connections are provided dynamically throughout a conference via virtual circuits which are set up and torn down as inter-site connections demand, thus limiting the overhead on the network. The central Scottish videoconferencing network is administered by an Operations Centre within the Computing Services Department at the University of Edinburgh. The group manages all aspects of the network, including maintenance, control systems and quality standard of registered sites.

A web-based booking system allows conferences to be set up across the network. ISDN connection to other networks is also provided. Each MAN has a multi-point conference (MPC) bridge to connect multi-site conferences across the Scottish network. The Operations Centre also has an ISDN MCU with several bridges to connect the proprietary network to the ISDN world at speeds between 128KB and 384KB for IDSN2 and ISDN6 respectively.

Videoconferences originated by M-BONE tools and audio only connections can also be bridged into the Scottish network. Thus, although the Scottish MANs Video Conference Network is local to Scotland the video conferencing operation is extended worldwide through the ISDN connections and bridging facilities. In most of the studios seating is arranged in a horseshoe, with moveable desks. This allows flexible use for meetings, tutorials or lectures.

Good overall office lighting levels are provided, so that it is easy for students to take notes. Under its use of MANs initiative the Scottish Higher Education Funding Council has funded a number of projects to investigate the use of the MANs in higher education. The SUMSMAN project (Scottish Universities Mathematics and Statistics across the Metropolitan Area Networks) has worked in the subject area of Mathematics and Statistics.

From a technical perspective videoconferencing falls into two categories: desktop and studio-based. The former assumes inherently the use of personal computers, unlike the latter, in which integration with data communication is a relatively new experience. Some projects have developed tools and methodologies appropriate to desktop use and significant strides have been made towards rendering it accessible to students and academic staff.

The Scottish MANs and their associated studios however provide a ready-made facility which is immediately usable among students. The SUMSMAN project therefore has concentrated on studio-based videoconferencing and we restrict our comments to this field. There are many different ways of using videoconferencing studios and this case study includes examples of:

a) project management and dissemination meetings
b) lecture courses;
c) keynote lectures;
d) small groups/focus groups; and
e) orals and interviews.

Evaluation of videoconferencing in an educational environment is one area that has been dominated by subjective methods because of a lack of realistic alternatives. The educational influence of video channel quality factors are not clearly known, although they have important resource implications. The continual push for higher video quality may result in systems that distract rather then benefit the learner. Subjective methods show that students feel they would benefit from increased video channel quality, but objective tests indicate that the video channel does not influence outcomes. However, subjective evaluations have been shown to be unreliable, as for example perceived video channel quality is influenced by audio quality and the task at hand.

Discourse content analysis has been used many times to shed light on traditional teaching and learning. There a exists a new interesting scheme by Hentry to investigate computer-mediated conferencing (CMC). The scheme outlined below focuses on evaluating videoconferencing to support remote tutoring of small groups, as this is seen as an effective use for videoconferencing. The scheme could also be modified to suit other similar environments. The proposed method of discourse content analysis involves using subject expertise to compare recordings of students' dialogue before and after changes are made to the learning environment.

To a large extent the quality of a tutorial environment is dictated by the opportunities students have to expose and negotiate their conceptualisations, and therefore, if the quality of dialogue is seen to improve in a marked fashion after changes are made, then the learning environment will have improved. The advantages of this method include: data can be gathered in a fully representative educational context; data gathering can be transparent to the participants; the method does not rely on subjective introspection by the participants: and there is no requirement to test the student before and after the intervention.

Continuous measurement ensures that any gradual longitudinal improvement can be accounted for, as the students will inevitably become accustomed to the environment and subject matter over time. To make the scheme work in practice, it is also important that data is gathered during tutor-less periods within tutorials, as the tutor will invariably bias outcomes. In order to assess the educational quality of a tutorial a mix of approaches may provide the fullest insight.

Henri identified content analysis as a useful means to assess the written dialogue in CMC, and this method appears to draw out many indicators of educational quality. The analysis of CMC messages is said to be proving a gold mine of information concerning the psycho-social dynamics at work among students, the learning strategies adopted, and the acquisition of knowledge and skills. It can allow the educator to recognise the strengths and weaknesses of learners, and to offer adequate pedagogical support. Henri's content analysis categories comprise of:

i) *Participative*: compilation of the number of messages or statements transmitted by one person or group.

ii) *Social*: statement or part statement not related to the formal content of the subject matter.

iii) *Interactive*: chain of connected messages.

iv) *Cognitive skills and processing*: statement exhibiting knowledge and skills related to the learning process.

v) *Metacognitive knowledge and skills*: statement relating to general knowledge and skills and showing awareness, self-control and self-regulation of learning.

This scheme is capable of identifying many useful attributes which would constitute quality within a videoconference environment, although it is apparent that several aspects could not be identified outside the wordy, and often explicit, nature of CMC. In verbal conversations, utterances are said to 'radically under specify the speakers' beliefs and intentions. With CMC, there is no communication outside text, and the participants use of text often reflects their knowledge, cognitive skills and learning approach.

With videoconferencing, the iterations of dialogue are likely to be more brief, they are spontaneous and therefore less considered, and they are often incomplete due to interruptions. Although these may all appear as negative attributes of videoconferencing, the spontaneity allows participants to receive immediate feedback on their contributions. Issues can be resolved immediately and the conversation promptly steered without the asynchronous lag of CMC. The immediacy of videoconferencing enables participants to encourage one another mid-flow, which can spur the speaker on to new depths.

For these reasons, Henri's analysis scheme cannot be applied without modification as a measure of quality for a videoconference environment. The ability of the communications media to relay psycho-social support, such as encouragement, must be identified as an attribute of quality, and it must be recognised that cognitive processes may not always be identifiable. Ober *et al*. incorporated an analysis of affective issues in addition to cognitive issues with their 'Reciprocal Category Scheme'. This captures the 'climate factor' of the learning environment with such categories as 'warms', 'accepts' and corrects'. Due to the difficulty with identifying the cognitive process categories of Henri's scheme within a videoconferencing (VC) environment, it is worth considering a tutorial dialogue analysis scheme of Powell and also another scheme of Ober *et al.* called 'Equivalent Talk Categories'. Both these schemes share similarities with Henri's scheme but the categories are less theoretical and more readily applied in practice.

Taking a phenomenographic stance, classroom dialogue is represented in categories related to surface indications, and therefore does not require the content coder to deduce the most appropriate abstract category. Powell's categories are: giving an opinion, giving information, arguing, asking for information, clarifying, formulating problems and group process. Ober *et al.*'s categories include: presenting information, questioning, responding, reacting and structuring. In a similar manner to Henri, the categories are grouped into restricted or expanded thinking. The proposed scheme borrows, aspects from these other discourse content analysis schemes. Rather than being swamped with theoretical issues of how to measure the learning that takes place, it also takes a phenomenographic stance and seeks to identify aspects which a teacher/subject expert would identify as contributing towards the educational quality of a tutorial.

The scheme is not intended to provide an absolute measure of quality, or to identify processes and strategies of learning, but rather to serve as a relative benchmark for identifying changes—if present—in the quality of learning enabling opportunities before and after changes in test conditions are made. If it were possible to give an appropriate weight to each category of learning opportunity, and to quantify the size of each content item occurring within each category, then it would be possible to quantify the quality of a tutorial in absolute terms.

Powell and Henri make no explicit definition of quality. Ober *et al.*, loosely attribute quality with a mixture of interaction types. In addition, the relative importance of each component of quality will vary according to circumstance, and therefore at this stage it may have to be sufficient just to identify the occurrence of each learning opportunity and not seek to determine its size or relative importance. There is also an element of subjectivity when assigning content into categories. These are, of course, some of the reasons why content analysis has not become the evaluators' panacea.

A unit of analysis in a content analysis scheme determines how the overall content is to be broker down into manageable items for subsequent allocation into relevant categories. This choice affects how accurately the coded data will reflect the true content of the original discourse. Time division sampling has often been applied. Howell-Richardson and Mellar used what might seem a more appropriate sampling system for analysing CMC, that of the speech act outlined by Searle. This allows the underlying structure and intention of each aspect of discourse to be identified, but is difficult to apply and still relies on the subjective interpretation of experts to identify which elements constitute quality in a learning environment.

A pragmatic solution that will be adopted for the unit of analysis is to use a subject content expert to identify surface items which have the capability of enabling learning in the speaker or listener. This would appear to be more accurate than choosing an arbitrary time interval and recording the discourse type occurring within each interval, as some students can articulate their ideas faster than others. Although being partly subjective, educationalists have used such informed opinions in marking student, work throughout the years. It is thought that this element of subjectivity within an objective framework is likely to yield results which are more reliable than the subjectivity of student introspection, or the results of objective decontextualised experimentation. The new scheme, therefore, estimates the quality of the tutorial environment by identifying the number of learning enablers that occur within the students' discourse. Two types identified are:

i) direct learning enablers; and
ii) indirect learning enablers.

The enabler categories will be slightly broader, to take into account dialogue that is capable of facilitating learning in others, and not just demonstrating the knowledge of the speaker. A speaker who presents subject content will be articulating and reinforcing their knowledge, and the listener will be given the opportunity to reinforce or challenge their own knowledge. Framing an appropriate question demonstrates implicit knowledge, and others can benefit from hearing a question articulated that they may have wished to ask. Some reiteration may prove little about the cognitive ability of the speaker, but it may prompt others to learn by highlighting a point which they had missed earlier.

A direct learning enabler will therefore be any aspects of tutorial dialogue that:

i) presents subject content information;
ii) requests subject content information;
iii) interacts with the presentation or request.

However, these learning enablers are only pointers to what might encourage learning, because their final outcome cannot be identified. An indirect learning enabler will be an encouragement, or social interaction, or opportunity to participate, etc. As a secondary issue, other useful pointers may emerge on:

i) the process of learning in groups;
ii) participation within a tutorial group;
iii) other factors enabling or discouraging individual learning; and
iv) the ability to refine the content coding scheme.

An important feature of CMC is its potential for creating learning environments that promote collaboration and interaction between learners. Consequently, it has been applied in education especially when collaborative interaction has been an instructional priority. This interaction priority is closely related to the knowledge production activities of academics who create, transform, communicate, store and retrieve knowledge. The demands of this 'knowledge work' can, to a large extent, be met by both time- and location-independent collaborative CMC-interactions with colleagues and peer students sharing common goals and interests. Although CMC has been used mostly in distance studies at the college and university level in connection with both undergraduate and postgraduate courses there are experiences concerning its use in on-campus settings too.

Argumentation a process of presenting reasons to support one's opinions and conclusions. For two important reasons, its role in an academic context is fundamental.

i) a major characteristic of academic discussions is an aspiration to present well-considered reasons in order to convince the audience of the justification of the presenter's standpoint.
ii) argumentation is a fundamental tool for proving the validity of scientific knowledge.

In addition, argumentation may also help people cope with the demands of the new information society in which the supply of information is increasing all the time and its means of production are constantly developing. In order to manage this information flood one has to be able to select which information is relevant and then make critical assessments between the numerous alternatives.

Effective selection and choice presuppose developed skills in argumentation and critical thinking. Consequently, the teaching of argumentation skills is an important mechanism for achieving the objectives of higher education studies: to educate people who are able to supply, select and assess knowledge independently. Despite the fact that CMC has been found to be well suited to higher education, academic argumentation has received only limited attention in the CMC literature.

On the other hand, there are a large number of descriptive studies relating to students' experiences and perceptions of CMC as a learning environment. However, fewer studies have focused on the learning effects of CMC by evaluating students' outputs after engaging in CMC studies.

Argumentation is an element in the process of critiquing knowledge and developing one's own opinions. Critical thinking is based on reasoning that aims at reflective evaluation and careful grounding of issues under examination. Reasoning and critical thinking are closely related to the process of argumentation in which other peoples' standpoints and opinions are critically examined and one's own conclusions drawn on the basis of reasons presented for their support.

The concept of argumentation skills is based on the Toulminian argumentation theory in which an argument is divided into separate components: a claim, grounds, a warrant, a backing, a qualifier and a rebuttal. Persons possessing weak argumentation skills most often present only a few grounds in order to support their claims or opinions.

Possibilities of computer-based instruction in the field of teaching argumentation have already been recognised. Keith et al., developed a programme that used an apprenticeship approach for practising argumentation. The essential characteristics of this approach are that students do the activity, that there are valued tasks for students, and that there is a skilled mentor who coaches students in the activities relating to argumentation.

The computer-based instruction has several features appropriate for teaching argumentation: when using computers it is easy to disseminate learning materials, teaching is flexible in terms of the pace and location of learning, and activities enable students' self-reflection on their own performance. The potential of CMC in practising argumentation, is largely based on the possibility it offers for creating effective interactions between learners. This feature is most beneficial in practising informal argumentation in which arguments are presented in order to assure the audience of the correctness of one's standpoint. CMC has already been applied in fostering informal argumentation and critical thinking.

Clark organised an electronic debate through electronic mail between two classes at the elementary school level. In a college-level experiment carried out by Charlton critical thinking skills were practised through discussions at electronic bulletin boards, and Pugh reported on a higher education course in which argumentation was practised through electronic conferencing. Steinberg stresses that the key feature of CMC in respect of practising argumentation and critical thinking is the focused discussion of alternative points of view between participants.

CMC has been characterised as a democratic medium enabling participation of all the members on an equal basis. Equality, it is alleged, is promoted because the learning environment is free from some of the features typical of face-to-face settings that may inhibit the discussion, for example, gender, age, ethnicity, occupational status or performance skills. In addition, socially shy persons and those who need time to construct their ideas can, it is claimed, participate in CMC discussions on a democratic basis. Equal and democratic opportunities are important aspects for argumentation as they enable the discussants to concentrate on matters of fact free from many factors that may make it difficult to exchange opinions together.

Studying through CMC consists of text-based contributions to the topics under consideration. As Henri puts it, written text demands exactness, careful consideration, and explicit expression of thoughts. These criteria play a fundamental role in argumentative dialogues and debates because the goal of the activities is to assess the strengths and weaknesses of others' contributions. In addition, when using CMC there is an opportunity to reread one's own and other people's texts before any revisions of ideas are carried out. However, CMC may also produce interaction which does not, necessarily, always act as an advantage when practising argumentation. Tella, for example, found that texts presented during computer conferencing were not always exact and well considered, instead they included a lot of fragmentary and disconnected sentences usually met in colloquial use of language. These features of language do not belong to academic argumentative discussions in which, rather, the content and style of contributions should be carefully considered and formulated.

The asynchronous nature of CMC interaction makes it possible to participate without restrictions of time and place. To have enough time is important, for example, in a debate when a person wants to construct valid reasons in order to support his opinions with special care. In addition, when people can log on at any time they want they can make use of resource materials, books, newspapers, notes, etc., in preparing their contributions to discussions. By the same token, the asynchronous mode of interaction may also be a disadvantage, since it is possible that one gets feedback to his contribution too late or, as in the worst case, the contribution may never be commented on.

Perhaps the most unique feature of CMC is the possibility for group communication and many-to-many discussions. Through this kind of interaction participants may make use of each other's ideas and thoughts. This is important in argumentative discussions in which the main purpose is to find out many relevant points of view and, thus, create alternative approaches to issues examined.

QUALITY AND INTERACTIVITY

Quality is not synonymous with excellence, but rather indicates the management of a continuous process aimed at bridging the gap between the expected effect and the actual effect. Achieving such a result demands frequent interaction between all of the components in the process. Interaction is imperative if the quality of the process is to be raised: interaction with materials, between students and their tutors/teachers, and among all the participants. Dealing with the issue of quality in distance education is undoubtedly an exacting task. The reasons are many, the prime one being that an agreement has still to be reached on what is generally meant by quality when referring to an education process and all that this involves.

The great number of elements at play means that there is no codified recipe that will permit a univocal specification of quality factors in distance education. To clarify the discussion that follows, it is worth recalling some of the key concepts related to the various types of distance education systems, with special reference to so-called second and third generation systems. Second generation systems or multimedia systems sprang to light in recent decades and are based on widespread distribution of instruction through various media; printed matter, television programmes, audio or video tapes, education software, etc.

Personal interaction is limited to one-to-one exchange between teachers/tutors and the students, while communication among participants is only sporadic. This is hardly surprising, seeing that these systems were created mainly to solve problems linked to the coverage of wide geographical areas and/or large user communities, hurdles that can only be overcome through effective methods for mass distribution of learning material in this context, learning can only be achieved as an individual process, based on the participant's interaction with educational material. More recently, the increasingly widespread use of network technologies has made it possible to define new models for distance education that can add value to the social component of the learning process and provide strong interaction opportunities for all participants in the educational effort.

Known as third generation distance education systems, these models are also referred to, as online education. They permit the creation of a full-fledged learning community where individuals can overcome their isolation and draw benefits from interacting with the group. The method in question has yielded extremely positive results in adult education, a context in which the sharing of personal experience in the subject area may indeed play a significant role in collective betterment. The difference, then, between traditional (first and second generation) distance education and online (third generation) education lies in their different ways of organising the learning process: The former is an extensive process addressing a large community, while the latter is an intensive process targeting fewer people but involving strong interaction among them. This means that where the goal is to reach a mass usership, the second generation approach remains the most effective.

Successful analysis of distance education systems must take account of four key dimensions:

i) pedagogy,
ii) educational engineering,
iii) economics, and
iv) technology.

Pedagogical approaches involve a series of tools, procedures, and sequences, the combination of which is of special interest to educational engineers, who aim to develop distance education systems that are increasingly responsive to individual learning needs. Any teaching service should allow the beneficiaries to co-produce the service together with the supplier. Where quality in an education effort is concerned, end users must be encouraged as much as possible to take an active part in setting the objectives and defining the contents, as well as in capitalising on their professional experience so that the learning process may be enriched. The logical consequence would seem to be that of hinging the learning process on strong interaction between all the participants involved. This is a point made by Herman and Herman, who, when dealing with the subject of quality in training, highlight the importance of involving all the potential beneficiaries of the process, be they direct or indirect. All this would appear to suggest a strict link between quality and the capability to manage a learning process based on the active participation of all its beneficiaries.

Analysing distance education processes using methods similar to those applied in industry. These have been drawn from control systems theory and offer a coherent set of strategies for reaching a prefixed objective. In this sense, it is possible to identify two types of distance education system: opening and closed-ring systems.

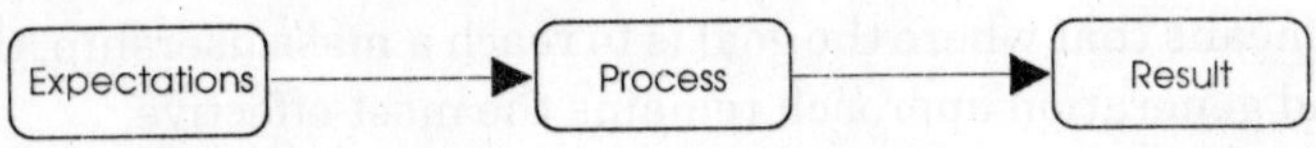

Figure: 1. Open-ring system

Open-ring systems are based on evaluation of the correctness of the system's input and of the soundness of the system's overall structure. This definition covers first and second generation systems, where the main focus is on the learning material to be studied individually (input) and the logistic support offered by the course provider (system structure).

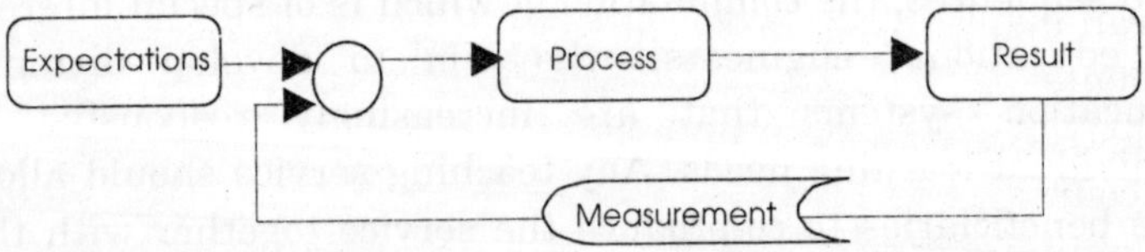

Figure 2: Closed-ring system

The benchmark for distance education that Keegan provides is represented by closed-ring systems, i.e., those that have a capacity for timely self-regulation while in progress, thanks to the measurement of what is expected of the learning process and what is actually obtained. The key to this sort of systematic realignment is constant monitoring aimed at formative evaluation of both the users and the whole process.

The third generation systems are based on intense-interaction among all the components of the process, giving the tutors and, the training provider the opportunity for in-progress monitoring of the process. In this way, they can perform any necessary adjustments to bring the course more closely in line with the stated objectives; in other words, with the expected effect. The latest applications of second generation distance education do feature some retroaction in a sort of closed-ring system, albeit to a somewhat limited degree. The strong interaction among system components that is a typical feature of third generation distance education in particular does indeed create the retroaction ring essential for matching the actual effect with the expected effect.

In 1989, Moore proposed a quality analysis model based on three types of distance interaction:

i) interaction between participant and learning material;
ii) interaction between participant and tutors/experts; and
iii) interaction among participants.

Interaction between participant and learning material: Quality of the learning material has an enormous effect on the overall quality of an online course, so the material offered to students should not only deal with topic contents in a well-structured way but also be pleasant to use. In addition, the course kit provided to participants should contain, a guide explaining the programme of course modules. This serves to introduce participants to the course, helps them interpret the assignments set at various stages, and assists in associating the learning material to the modules included in the course.

Interaction between participants and their tutors. It is the most dynamic and crucial aspect of the online course. The tutor should be seen as an advisor, leader, facilitator, and sometimes as an expert in the topic contents. There are three fundamental moments in participant/tutor interaction:

i) The initial approach, aimed at breaking the ice between the students and those responsible for leading and assisting them throughout the course. This preliminary "didactic conversation" usually takes the form of a "learning contract" where the programme is discussed, the contents, objectives and methods are brought into sharper focus, and the students' expectations are clarified. The outcome of this process is that the participants' sense of isolation is reduced, and this helps considerably in steering the process toward what was earlier defined as the desired effect, both for the course managers and for students.

ii) The act of distance tutoring, which involves a much wider spectrum of functions than face-to face tutoring. In a way, the tutor's presence online must be made apparent, as indeed must that of the participants. When using information and communication technology (ICT) and strategies typical of distance interaction, tutors need to make manifest both their presence and their readiness to help the students; this can be done by answering queries promptly, making suggestions and offering support throughout the entire learning process. Where the technology is available, tutor assistance may be reinforced by' periodic "face-to-face" videoconferences.

iii) Reflection about the process underway is a need that many participants demonstrate, especially adult learners. They feel the need to understand not only the contents being studied, but also the reason behind certain methodological choices in the management of the course. This meta-communicative space, which in courses based on computer conferencing takes the form of a permanent conference for tutors and participants, has the undoubted advantage of bridging the gap between course providers and recipients.

Interaction among participants. The previous section highlighted the importance of tutor/participant interaction in the form of two-way communication, which has a strong impact on the quality of online courses. Further and perhaps even greater impulse comes from the possibility to integrate vertical tutor/participant communication with a more horizontal form of interaction between peers. This is in fact the *raison d'etre* of third generation distance education, although it must be pointed out that a more restricted and sporadic form of inter-participant communication was in fact introduced in second generation courses.

Horizontal communication is wide in scope. At one end of the scale, there is simple free interaction, introduced largely to strengthen social ties between participants: this may cover topics like hobbies, gossip, professional problems, and so on. Then there are discussion groups set up to examine some of the issues touched upon in the course. At the other extreme, we have fully-fledged computer conferencing systems structured to suit the specific aims of the course. One of the factors that has an impact on peer interaction, and therefore on the quality of the course as a whole, is group size.

The more the communication is directed toward socialisation and sharing of ideas and experiences, the larger the discussion group may be. Conversely, the more the communication is directed toward collaborative study the more limited group numbers need to be. In either case, the tutors must be capable of guaranteeing that the whole mechanism for participant interaction runs smoothly. In this light, distance education systems, especially those based on ICT should not be restricted to the kind of individualised instruction typical of correspondence courses. Instead, they should be used for managing highly interactive groups, where greater emphasis is placed on the social aspect of learning to the benefit of the entire learning process.

One of the key ingredients for raising the quality of an online, course is strong interaction between the players in the process; organised in full-fledged virtual classes, the participants must obviously respect schedules and deadlines if a collaborative working strategy is to be successful. However, strong interaction may in some cases actually hinder flexibility in course participation. Those participants who for personal or professional reasons are unable to interpose themselves in the collaborative learning mechanism find it very difficult to exploit the full potential of interpersonal communication.

ICT has the potential to raise the quality level of distance education processes. In addition to this there are many other factors to consider when seeking to improve quality. Beginning with the clear definition of learning goals and subsequently for the learning activities to be undertaken in order to reach those objectives. Only when this has been carried out can we move on to choosing the most suitable medium, i.e., the one that will contribute toward the achievement of a good quality level in the distance education process. We should not lose sight of the fact that the choice often depends more on economic than on methodological considerations.

To analyse the technology/interactivity/quality relationship, we first need to clarify some of the aspects that characterise the direct relationships between

i) technology and interactivity, and
ii) interactivity and quality.

Technology-interactivity relationship: Technological tools are of tow types: those that do not foresee any kind of interactivity at all with the user, and those that, at least potentially, guarantee it to some degree or other. Tools in the former category provide what is known as one-way communication. Digital technology is mainly used here as a means for wide-scale dissemination of course material to participants, though without permitting any kind of interactivity. Tools in the latter category do allow interactivity, although this cannot be said to be an intrinsic characteristic of the technology, but rather of the way that technology is used.

When talking about interactivity, we should refer not so much to interaction with learning material that someone his made available on the network or on CD-ROM, but rather to human-machine interaction governed by software, or, better still, personal interaction mediated by network technology. Even when using the technology's potential to the fullest, there is no guarantee about the quality the interaction will bring to the learning process.

Interactivity-quality relationship: The development of new technology, especially over the past decade, has led to the production of multimedia material of high quality, at least in aesthetic terms. Looking at these products from the communication viewpoint, we can identify two extremes. At one end, there are products with a low level of interactivity, which tend to reproduce the traditional lecture format. At the other end, we have the so-called adaptive products, which are based on more or less sophisticated schemes of dialogue with the user. These seek to tailor the user's learning path to his knowledge requirements, learning style, and so on.

There is another type of interactivity, namely direct interactivity between individuals, where the technology does not "drive" but acts as a passive mediator. This is the case with computer networks. While interactivity is no guarantee of quality, social interaction with peers or with one's trainers plays a key role in the learning process, both from the psychosocial and psycho-affective viewpoints. In this sense, ICT services can make an enormous contribution. Despite this, there is still a general trend in distance education toward one-way schemes.

In other words, the participants are offered a multiplicity of material based on different technologies: lessons that are videotaped or distributed online using real-video technology, audio cassettes, and printed learning material, guides, etc., that are sent by post or delivered via computer network. This kind of technology-supported distance learning not only undervalues the potential of that technology, but also it is based on the assumption that frontal-type teaching is the standard to which distance learning should conform. This may well prove satisfactory for transmissive teaching, but less so when discussion, sharing of experience, or ongoing readjustment of the learning process is called for. No matter how sophisticated and interactive a multimedia package designed for individual use may be, it will never allow the learner to obtain the quality of instruction that can be achieved by direct interaction with experts/specialists in the field or with other course participants.

One way of gauging the quality of a multimedia product is to measure the number of different paths it envisages for the interaction with the end user. Clearly, no matter how well it has been designed, such a package can only cover a fraction of the possible directions that this dialogue may follow. On this point, Laurillard shows that stand-alone multimedia packages designed for individual use will no longer be capable of meeting the needs of remote learners because they are unable to support discursive interaction with the end user; as we have seen, this is the key element in raising the quality of distance courses.

Furthermore, efforts to produce multimedia material of the very highest standards do not in themselves guarantee overall improver-bent in learning quality. In fact, investment in the design and production of material could shift resources away from student support, which would be counterproductive, especially where interaction and discussion among all the participants are central to achieving the learning objective. By contrast, those who seek to meet learners' needs by fostering interaction in full-fledged cooperative communities are trying not so much to replicate traditional one-way teaching, but rather to create the conditions for a highly stimulating and fruitful learning process.

As a result of advances in telecommunication and microprocess technologies, distance education methods exist that are de-massifying delivery. The future task for education at a distance is to design and direct personalised information to specific target audiences. The industrialised form of distance education, with its mass-consumption ideology and approach, will become less dominant in the future. Economy of scale means that courses must attract as many potential beneficiaries as possible in order to offset the costs of investing in the production of high-quality learning material.

So the material must be adaptable to a wide spectrum of possible users and have a long shelf life. By contrast, courses based on the third generation model, which feature a high degree of interactivity, entail virtual classes of necessarily limited size and the presence of tutors for the entire length of the learning process. This means shifting funds away from the production of *ad hoc* learning material in order to cover tutoring and experts' fees. The problem, however, is not just one of reallocating funds; the cost per student of third generation courses is usually higher than that of second generation courses.

To problem of measurement of return on investment (ROI) in education is still open to question, especially because the issue can be approached from many different viewpoints. Some see the question from the standpoint of schooling, others from that of company training, and so on. Some consider that ROI should be measured in the long-term, ruling out any short-term evaluation. Phillip considers ROI to be the fifth in the list of item that Kirkpatrick proposes for evaluating course success. The items include:

i) *Reaction and planned action*: It means gauging the participants' satisfaction and studying how they intend to apply what has been learned during the course. However important satisfaction levels may be, they are no guarantee that the knowledge and/or skills that the course was designed to impart have actually be learned.

ii) *Learning*: It reveals what the participant has learned from the Course, which can be measured in a variety of ways such as using tests, practical activities, role plays, simulations, evaluations, etc. Nevertheless, positive outcomes at this point still do not guarantee that the course participants are actually capable of applying correctly what they have learned.

iii) *Job applications*: There is a variety of follow-up to determine whether participants apply what they have learned on the job. These are usually based on observation of the frequency and way in which the newly acquired knowledge and skills are applied. Even if the evaluation yields positive results, there is still no guarantee that the organisation to which the course participant belongs will benefit from an equally positive impact.

iv) *Business results*: The benefit gained by the organisation can be seen from different angles: in economic terms; from the viewpoint of customer satisfaction with the service offered; in terms of production costs; and so on. In this case, it is worth remembering that customer satisfaction with the quality of a product or service provided does not nècessarily lead to a positive impact on the provider. For instance, the production cost may have been excessive and the outlay may be impossible, or at least difficult, to redeem; or the organisation may not be ready to take the innovation on board.

v) *Return on investment (ROI)*: Analysis of this aspect clearly cannot be done without careful evaluation at the previous four levels. This means that to estimate ROI, we must first evaluate how the knowledge and skills acquired in the training course (level 2) are applied in the workplace (level 3), resulting in a positive impact on participant's organisation (level 4). This kind of approach is in line with the quality testing adopted by the American Society for Training and Development. Unless

> these measures are carried out, it is extremely difficult to claim that the results really are the fruit of the training course in question, and that they actually represent the ROI. In reality, evaluation in the training field rarely goes beyond the fourth level. The reason is that, apart from being difficult and complicated-ROI is also a long and expensive process because it relies on study and analysis being carried out at the previous four levels. So ROI analysis itself may end up adding to overall course costs, which in turn affects the ROI estimate.

Evaluation of the cost/benefit ratio in distance education has always been an arduous task. There are at least two kinds of organisations interested in cost-benefit analysis for distance education: public institutions that provide open and distance courses, and the private sector. In the public sector, costs analysis is usually based on comparison with traditional training, which is carried out with the aid of fairly well-defined parameters.

By contrast, the comparison used in the private sector is with the cost of hiring a classroom trainer for a fixed period. Although difficult to perform, cost analysis proves to be more objective than benefits analysis in both cases, and is therefore easier to determine. Indeed, calculating the benefits of distance education is always a subjective matter, especially where there is no reference to immediate economic benefits. It is no coincidence that, as a number of studies have demonstrated, when different definitions of benefit are applied to the same course, different ROI estimates are obtained. What is more, the weight of ROI varies according to the context in which it is measured. There is a distinct difference between companies, who need to get a return on their investment in the short to medium term, and the public education system, where investment in teaching staff has an initial impact on direct users and a long-term effect on the country's society and economy.

Distance education may prove to be more or less expensive than traditional courses, depending on how course planning, development, and delivery are approached. The common belief that distance education cost onsite < education cost is not always true; there way be cases where distance education turns out to be more costly than onsite courses. There are several ways of quantifying costs, ranging from cost per unit to the total cost of a course. The various cost items themselves may also vary in several ways. To provide an example, the cost of the course may be derived by dividing the total cost either by the number of participants who enrolled or by the number of participants who actually completed the course. Then again, the total cost itself may relate to a specific period or to a longer spell of time equivalent to the average life of the course, which would make it possible to take its depreciation into account.

Fixed costs include all expenses that are independent of the number of students enrolled, while variable costs are those that vary in response to this factor. This applies both to the use of infrastructure and personnel involved. The production of a TV programme or of multimedia courseware, for instance, represents a fixed cost, as it is totally independent of the number of eventual beneficiaries. By contrast, the payment of fees for online tutors is considered to be a variable cost, in that the number of tutors and their degree of involvement are factors related to the number of students enrolled. A further costs classification may be direct and indirect costs, i.e., those that are related to the production of given material or the delivery of a certain service and those which are incurred in any case by the educational institution and have no direct correspondence with the production of given material or the delivery of a given service.

Direct costs include the production of purposely-designed educational material regarding a given content area or the hiring of an expert to work within the learning network. Indirect costs may include the purchase of a computer conferencing system to be adopted in the course in question but which will also be used for other online events.

Let us look for parallels between face-to-face education, traditional distance education (first and second generation), and online education (third generation). The intention is to show that when it comes to costs analysis, third generation distance education has many aspects in common with face-to-face teaching.

In a study by Rumble, in 1997, compared the costs incurred for traditional students and distance education students. He expresses the total cost (TC) as the sum of the fixed costs (F) (including the semi-fixed costs) plus the variable cost per unit (V) times the number of units (N):

$$TC = F + VN$$

Fixed costs for face-to-face education are slightly lower than distance education costs. The reason is straightforward: In distance education, the economic impact of generating purposely-designed material is quite significant, while this is not normally the case with face-to-face education. The greater the attendance, the greater the number of teachers involved, thus the system's variable costs rise.

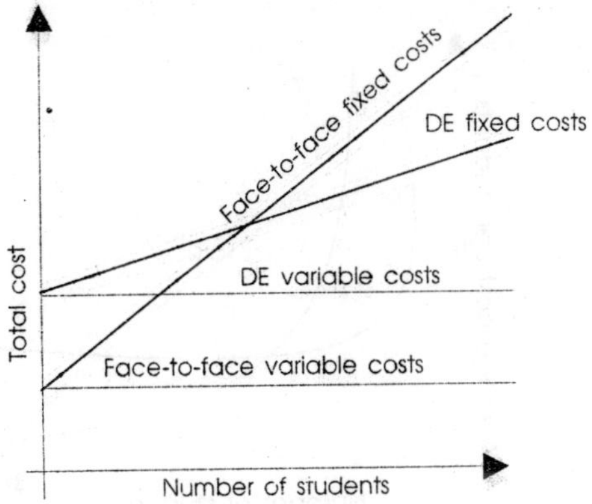

Figure 3: Fixed and variable costs in face-to-face teaching and traditional distance education

Variable costs may be incurred in distance education as well. However, the cost vs. attendance ratio does not rise at the same rate as that for a face-to-face teaching situation. Discussing the average cost per student in distance education, Rumble notes that this value tends to diminish quite markedly as the number of students in the course grows, and can be expressed as:

$$AC = TC/N$$

The average cost per distance student falls gradually and the curve flattens out when the number of students in the course grows significantly; from there on, it stays parallel to the face-to-face curve, although at a considerably lower level. The gradual introduction of communication technology in distance education and the development of innovative third generation approaches makes it imperative to revise the studies carried out by Rumble. In particular, when calculating the cost of third generation distance education systems, we need to reintroduce some items that were previously typical of face-to-face teaching. In practice, this has radically affected the economy of scale idea that has always underpinned large-scale distance education systems.

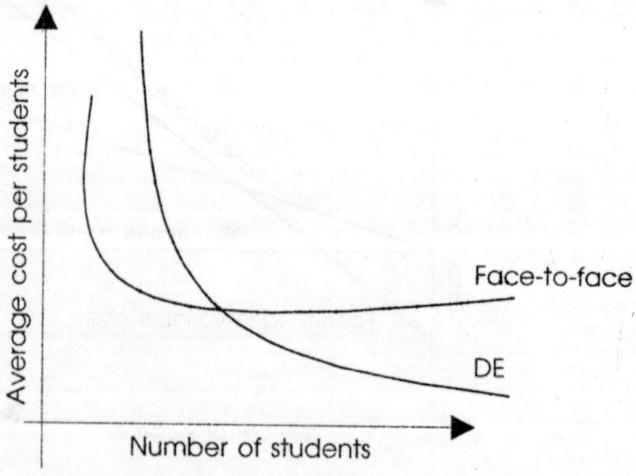

Figure 4: Average cost per student in face-to-face teaching and traditional distance education

The curve traced by the new courses closely resembles the cost graph typical of face-to-face education: low material production costs; high variable costs related to the presence of tutors. Tutor costs remain high irrespective of whether the strategy implemented is based on synchronous communication or asynchronous communication, though in the latter case they are somewhat higher, on average.

In the case of per capita costs we can find that the curve for online courses is more similar to face-to-face teaching than to traditional distance education. This means lower initial costs, but higher costs along the way resulting from online tutoring.

Defining and assessing the benefits of any education effort is a difficult task, irrespective of whether it is conducted face-to-face or at a distance. One way of tackling the problem is to make assumptions on the basis of the three fundamental needs that education systems generally seek to address:

i) professionalisation;
ii) socialisation; and
iii) individualisation.

We can classify the benefits of education efforts into expected, intangible, and unforeseen benefits.

i) *Expected benefits*: In defining these, special attention must be paid to the context in which the learning will be set. Let us fake teacher training, for instance: Suppose we are launching a typical course in the educational use of computer network technology.

   The expected benefits include:

   a) familiarisation with ICT services;
   b) familiarisation with collaborative working methods;
   c) acquisition of skills in planning and managing innovative courses based on educational use of network technology; and
   d) transfer of some of these skills to school students.

The main benefit to be gained lies in cultural growth of the participants, which flows down from them to the students and beyond. For this very reason, the benefits should be seen in the long rather than the short term. However, when we shift the focus to the business world, we see that benefits are usually gauged in terms of profit, improved image, etc.

ii) *Intangible benefits*: The benefits gained from online training are not necessarily tangible ones, like economic return. In fact, this category covers:

   a) increased work satisfaction;
   b) improved company image;
   c) improved group work within the organisation; better customer services;
   d) fewer customer complaints; and
   e) less conflict inside the organisation and with the outside.

iii) *Unforeseen benefits*: These represent the paradox of training, in that they occasional outnumber the expected benefits. In a way, unforeseen benefits do not fall entirely into one of the two above mentioned categories; there may be unexpected tangible benefits, just as there may be intangible benefits that are unforeseen.

In distance education, costs are not affected by distances, but rather by the number of tutors involved, which varies in relation to the size of the learner population.

Interaction is imperative if the quality of the process is to be raised: interaction with materials, between students and their tutors/teachers, as well as between all the participants. Information technology and, more importantly, computer communication technology can play a vital role in fostering this interaction, even if use of these means is not in itself a guarantee of higher quality. As is usually the case, a fundamental role is played by course designers and coordinators, who have the means to steer the process toward the predefined goals. However, raising interactivity in the process either involves investing in multimedia products which are very complex and expensive, or entails increasing the amount of online tutoring.

REFERENCES

Anderson, A H, Newlands, A, Mullin, J, Heming, A. M., Doherty-Sneddon, G and Van der Velden, J., 1996, "Impact of Video-mediated Communication on Simulated Service Encounters", *Interacting With Computers*, 8, 2, pp.193-206.

Anderson, D. T., Garrison, D.R., 1995, "Transactional Issues in Distance Education: The Impact of Design in Audioconferencing", *American Journal of Distance Education*, 9, 2, pp. 27-45.

Bauer, J. W., and Rezabek, L. L., 1993, *Effects of Two-way Visual Contact on Verbal Interaction during Face-to-Face and Teleconferenced Instruction*, In *Art, Science, and Visual Literacy: Selected Readings from the Annual Conference of the International Visual Literacy Association*, 24th, Pittsburgh, PA, September 30-October 4, 1992.

Berge Z. L., 1999, "Interaction in Post-secondary Web-based Learning", *Educational Technology*, 39(1), pp. 5-11.

Comeaux, P., 1995, "The Impact of an Interactive Distance Learning Network on Classroom Communication", *Communication Education*, 41(4), pp. 353-361.

Garrison, D. R., 1990, "An Analysis and Evaluation of Audio Teleconferencing to Facilitate Education at a Distance", *The American journal of Distance Education*, 4, pp. 13-24.

Heamshaw, D., 1998, "Capitalising on the Strengths and Availability of Desktop Videoconferencing, *Active Learning*, 7, pp. 52-9.

Henri, F., 1992, "Computer Conferencing and Content Analysis", In Kaye, A.R (ed.), *Collaborative Learning through Computer Conferencing*, Springer-Verlag, pp.117-36

Howell-Richardson, C., Mellar, H., 1996, "A Methodology for the Analysis of Patterns of Participation within Computer Communications Courses", *Instructional Science*, 24, 1, pp. 47-69.

Jansen, D. G., and Lewis, W. B., 1996, "Creating High-levels of Interaction in Distance Education Courses", *ATEA Journal*, 24(1), pp.8-9.

Johnson, D. W., 1981, "Student-Student Interaction: The Neglected Variable in Education", *Educational Researcher*, 10(1), pp. 5-10.

Kearsley, G., 1995, "The Nature and Value of Interaction in Distance Learning, In M. Koble (ed.), *The American Centre for the Study of Distance Education Invitational Research Conferencing Distance Education: Toward Excellence in Distance Education*, University Park, PA: Penn State University.

McHenry, L., and Bozik, M., 1995, "Communicating at a Distance: A Study of Interaction in a Distance Education Classroom", *Communication Education*, 44(4), pp. 362-371.

Yucha, C. 8., 1996, Interactive Distance Education: Improvisation helps Bridge the Gap, *Journal of Biocommunication*, 23(1), pp. 2-5.

Zhang, S., and Fulford, C., 1994, "Are Interaction Time and Psychological Interactivity the Something in the Distance Learning Television Classroom?" *Educational Technology*, 34(6), pp. 58-64.

6

Web-based Learning

Learning is viewed as a constructive process occurring during one's participation in and contribution to the practices of the community. This view translates into practices such as enriching the classroom culture with tools that mediate knowledge building and social exchanges among peers as participants in discourse communities. Online technologies are one type of tool enabling global connectivity that can support constructivist classroom practices. With these technology tools, discourse communities are expanded to encompass interactions and collaborative exchange projects among peers from diversified cultural backgrounds. They literally bring reality to the Vygotskian notion that to make schooling significant, one must go beyond the classroom walls, beyond empty verbalisms. These expanded communities open opportunities for learners to interact with multiple perspectives that challenge their existing knowledge constructions and impose cognitive conflicts requiring negotiation.

With the new online tools and their potential to enrich learning experiences beyond the capabilities of a traditional setting come new challenges for educators and educational researchers. There seems to be a link between the technologies and authentic learning and collaborative learning in general; between technologies and student-centred, constructivist practices; and discussions in the literature examine those capabilities. However, educators are aware of the void in the literature of empirical reports testing the related hypotheses. Thus, there is an urgency to develop and implement research designs that accommodate the nuances of learning atypical of nontechnology, teacher-directed environments, as well as to explore alternative instructional paradigms that optimise the potential benefits of online technologies for learning.

The internet is the world most powerful computer network connecting personal computers, sophisticated mainframes, and high speed supercomputers around the globe. Because a myriad of computers and programmes are part of the internet, incompatibility problems can result because information is created using different computers and software.

In 1989, a group of scientists at the European Laboratory for Particle Physics (CERN) in Geneva, Switzerland began developing an internet tool that would link information produced by ail of the CERN researchers. The tool provided a way to link textual information on different computers and created by different scientists. The object was to overcome issues of incompatibility and utilise a new way of linking made possible by computers, called "hypertext". Rather than presenting information in a linear or hierarchical fashion, hypertext permits information to be linked in a web-like structure. Nodes of information can be linked to other nodes of information in multiple ways. As a result, users can dynamically criss-cross the information web using pieces in the order most convenient to them.

The CERN project resulted in an innovative front-end to the internet, now referred to as the World-Wide Web (WWW). The WWW provides users with a uniform and convenient means of accessing the vast resources of the internet. In 1993, the National Centre for Supercomputing Applications (NCSA) at the University of Illinois pushed the CERN scientists' idea further by creating a software tool called Mosaic.

Mosaic is an easy to use graphical user interface that permits text, graphics, sound and video to be hyperlinked. Mosaic was the first of the internet tools that are now referred to as "web browsers". Other well-known browsers include Netscape and Microsoft's internet explorer. Web browsers permit users to connect to the internet and facilitate accessing information located on another remote computer. The web browser links to the remote computer just long enough so that the information you need can be sent to your computer for you to view.

Documents created to be viewed by a browser are formatted using Hypertext Markup Language (HTML). HTML solves incompatibility problems by using standardised tags which indicate such things as whether a piece of text should be plain, bold, italic, or linked to another piece of text. Pages of information on a computer formatted with HTML and accessible to someone with a web browser, are referred to as 'home pages' or 'web pages'.

The WWW have made the internet a more user-friendly environment. The ability to integrate graphics, text, and sound into a single tool means that novice users do not have to struggle with such a steep learning curve. In addition, organisations and individuals can create home pages independently and link to other home pages on their own computers or to pages created by others on different computer systems. For educators, the WWW provides an exciting new opportunity for distance teaching and learning.

The WWW can be used by the distance educator to build a classroom home page. The home page can cover information about the class including the syllabus, exercises, literature references, and instructor's biography. The instructor can also provide links to information on the WWW that would be useful to students in the class. Other links can access library catalogues or each student's individual home page. In addition, the home page can link students to a discussion list or listserv that set up for student communication. It is also a relatively simple matter to use the homepage to create forms that students can fill out and that will end up being sent to you as an e-mail message.

Distance educators who are ready to develop a web presence, should avoid the following pitfalls:

i) Rushing in without a master plan. Don't get so caught up in learning HTML and developing the home page that the purpose for developing your presence on the WWW is lost. Spend less time struggling with HTML, developing amusing graphics or playing with possible background and more time considering the purpose and content of the home page. Before you start your home page:

ii) Think about your reason for developing a web presence. Will your home page be a stand alone course or will you be using it in conjunction with other technologies such as video or audio? Sound instructional design principles apply to home pages just as with any other materials prepared for a course.

iii) Become familiar with new software tools for developing home pages. Computer software tools such as HotMetal and HotDog mean that anyone familiar with using word processing software can develop a good looking and functional home page. Reviews of other such computer software tools are available on the WWW and many of them can be downloaded for a free trial.

iv) Utilise information that already has been developed for your course. If you already have your notes and syllabi in word processed form, make use of tools such as HotDog to format them for distribution on the WWW.

v) Look at what is already available. Hundreds of home pages have already been developed for courses. Some of these home pages allow students to complete an entire course from the WWW and others are developed in conjunction with lectures delivered on-campus or by video or audio. A great place to check out what others have done is The World Lecture Hall. The World Lecture Hall contains links to pages created by faculty worldwide who are using the web to deliver class materials.

vi) Laying out home pages poorly and inconsistently. To avoid ugly and confusing home pages, consider the following:

vii) Consulting sites on the WWW which provide information on home page layout and style. Two popular sites are the *Web Style Manual* and *Guide to Web Style*.

viii) Utilising a consistent format for each of your pages. Based on suggestions made by the above mentioned style manuals, develop a consistent format for each web page. While coloured or patterned backgrounds can be used on homepages, plain grey or white backgrounds make text easier to read.

ix) Keeping page lengths short. Your main index should jump to a lot of shorter pages. In cases where page information is long, index internally so that the student can jump to specific information as needed.

x) Maximising links to internal information and minimising links to external information. The purpose of your home page is to provide information on a specific subject area. Only provide external links to home pages that provide useful related information for your students.

xi) Using unnecessarily large graphics or including sound/video clips. Consider that while graphics can add appeal to a home page, a large number of internet users are still accessing the internet using a 14.4K modem. Graphic images which are 20K to 40K are acceptable for people with 14.4K modems. Pages which take too long to download frustrate students and may force them to beat a hasty retreat. If your home page requires extensive use of graphics to demonstrate points, warn your students. If you plan to use sound or video clips, you will need to be sure that all of your distant students have access to computers that have sound and video cards installed in them.

xii) Letting the home page become out-of-date. The home page should be an ongoing part of course development. Make sure that you add or change information as necessary. Periodically verify whether other home pages to which you are linking still exist.

The home page should help your students to find necessary course information, learn the material, and get involved in thinking about the course material. Properly designed home pages will encourage thought, discussion and active participation by your distant students. The following elements can be included in your class home page:

i) *Course and instructor information*: Include such items as course topics to be covered, your office hours, textbook information, course objectives, and grading policies.

ii) *Class communication*: Provide access to your e-mail, link to discussion groups that you have set up for student-to-student communication, and create forms that your students can use to report problems or provide biographical information about themselves.

iii) *Assignments and tests*: Distribute assignments and tests, provide for online completion or submission, and give solutions, hints, or samples of what you expect.

iv) *Material covered in the classroom*: Make lecture notes and handouts available either as web pages or as downloadable files.

v) *Demonstrations, animation, video, audio*: This is more complex than other suggestions and will require that your students have access to computers with sound and video cards.

vi) *Reference material*: List materials in print and electronic form that supplement the textbook. To avoid copyright problems, electronic articles should either be written by you or in the public domain.

Jones and Paolucci propose the use of an Instructional Systems Design (ISD) approach for addressing questions about web-based learning and instruction as a framework for evaluating the impact of educational technologies. The ISD approach follows a process of instructional development starting with a needs assessment, proceeding on and continuing with instructional goals and objectives, instructional strategies to facilitate targeted types of learning, and formative and summative evaluations of the instructional product and learning environment, with an iterative relationship specified among all the components.

Earlier ISD models prescribed a linear application of the components aligned with an objectivist, instructional transmission model of information flow from the teacher as the authority, to students, the consumers. Recent attention to learner-centred environments has led to a rethinking of ISD, in terms of recursive, nonlinear models. The models encompass the essential components of the ISD process, but offer a more flexible, adaptive instructional design paradigm in their applications. For example, objectives are critical to the design of instruction in learner-centred (LC) environments, but all the objectives are not necessarily explicitly identified at the "front end" of the instructional design process.

The design process results in an instructional sequence allowing for student-generated objectives likely to emerge in an LC environment enriched with social interactions among peers and mediation tools. Performance objectives in LC environments, for example are written at the individual and collective levels; instructional goals include social dimensions of learning- strategy designs are mediated with technology tools to foster multiple perspectives and opportunities for conferencing and collaboration; evaluations focus on analysis of a social context of learning, interactivity, dialogic processes, communication and language acts as units of analysis, and learning outcomes.

The design is more in line with LC principles that post the importance of the individual's experiential knowledge in learning and knowledge construction in a social context, as part of a community. We employ an adaptive ISD approach to draw on the sociocultural theory and constructivist perspectives in conceptualising the design and assessment of LC sites. These domains, along with previous research on technology-mediated environments, are foundations to the model presented here.

The three domains of the framework are background, design, and impact domain. In each domain are subcategories of theoretical constructs/variables to consider in both the design of the environment and the research design of studies investigating process and product outcomes of the technology-mediated environment.

i) *Background domain*: The three core background dimensions are:

   a) pedagogical and theoretical philosophies of the instructor,
   b) Students' perceptions of learning strategies and practices, and
   c) Instructional goals are significant to measuring the impact of a technology-mediated environment are the participants' current positions regarding their views and beliefs about learning, instruction, and assessment

   Longitudinal studies of effective practices and patterns of change with increased integration of technologies into instruction and learning are needed, and can offer resourceful input to theory development and instructional design practices.

   According to Reeves and Reeves there are ten dimensions of interactive learning with the World Wide Web. Each dimension is placed on a continuum, with a contrasting descriptor at each end. For example, pedagogical philosophy, is defined in a range from an instructivist to a constructivist perspective; teacher's role from didactic to facilitative; structural flexibility from fixed to open; and collaborative learning strategies described in terms of their degree of integration within the context.

ii) *Design domain*: The design domain consists of variables descriptive of features of instruction and learning in technology strategies as an advance organiser to facilitate learners connecting prior knowledge to new schemes or concept maps to visually demonstrate relationships among concepts, and physical tools as levers or pulleys. Bonk and Dennen and Rowley, Lujan, and Dolence present a ten-level continuum for qualitatively describing degree of web integration in a course. Examples include student use of the web for exploring preexisting resources, instructor use of the web as a repository of course information, and students' different geographical sites participating in an online course. Degree of integration is defined by three subcategories:

   a) the role of the web tools throughout the course
   b) qualitative description of how the web tools are used; and
   c) course requirements regarding student use of the tools in meeting course objectives.

   Structure refers to standards, requirements, and assessment rubrics associated with use of the technologies.

iii) *Impact domain*: This domain identifies hypothesised influences of technology-mediated environments on cognitive and socio-cultural-based constructs, including participants' performances, their pedagogical and learning beliefs and perceptions of technology-mediated learning, and social dimensions of learning. Cognitive and social processes and outcomes are described in the model by four dimensions:

a) learning assessments,
b) communication/interaction,
c) student engagement, and
d) collaborative/distributed learning.

Socio-cultural theories emphasise the importance of the collective in a person's learning development. Constructivist thought acknowledges the contributions of the individual's experiences to the collective, and the link between the two is shown in Cobb and Yackel's emergent framework. In line with these theories, learning assessment in the model is specified for measurement at both the individual and group level. A single utterance is a communication act—a language act—that produces the flow of dialogic processes. The dialogic processes become a primary unit in studying learners' developments in technology-mediated environments as learners create, construct, negotiate, and use tools in seeking knowledge in the multiple learning spaces.

There are a few dimensions of the communication/interaction component that are considered in the framework:

a) *Message flow*: relates the communication path, including the source and the continuing chain of the discourse, as conversational turns are taken.
b) *Message function*: refers to the purpose of the communication act. Rueda identified 21 perceived message functions, which were collapsed into the three main function classes: reporting information, requesting information, and other. The framework offers an organisational framework, especially for categorising qualitative data.

c) *Multiple voices*: defines a collection of all the forms of social speech or rhetorical modes one uses in the course of ongoing dialogue. It can be represented by the different languages one uses in communications with different people and in varied contexts. For example, electronic interactions in web-based and traditional (on-site) classes show different characteristics and patterns in terms of level of detail and use of elaborations.

d) *Inter-subjectivity*: describes a shared collective reality among individuals that can foster collaborative processes of negotiating meaning, designing, constructing new knowledge, and assimilating multiple perspectives.

Collaboration/distributed learning component of the framework represents the collection of processes of group dialogue to include negotiating knowledge, sharing and co-constructing knowledge, and appropriating ideas and knowledge. From these processes is constructed an analysis of the learning process in social contexts of learning, where knowledge and the exchange of knowledge are treated as a function of the collective, a community of learners. The student engagement component refers to students' active participation in learning developments. In fact, the dialogic and collaboration process constructs are indicators of student engagement. Collaboration activities help learners feel part of a community of learners, which is conducive to helping them to become engaged in the learning processes of knowledge construction and co-construction.

INTERACTIVITY IN WEB-BASED LEARNING

Interactivity is two-way communications among two or more persons. The purpose of interaction is to promote explanation and challenging perspectives among two or more learners. The interaction itself is categorised within a learning context with the purpose of task/instructional completion or social relationship building, with a mixture of both types of interaction being common. Moore classifies interaction as engagement in learning through:

i) interaction between participants and learning materials,
ii) interaction between participants and tutors/experts, and
iii) interaction among participants.

Northrup and Rasmussen take a similar approach in classifying interaction as

i) student to student,
ii) student to instructor,
iii) student to instructional materials, and
iv) student to management.

The notion of adding management/feedback as one of the interaction strategies arose due to the need to close the communications loop on areas of instructional content, but also on general social communications. Until students receive a reply in some form verifying that what they sent was accurate, they typically are uncomfortable.

This chapter provides a framework of interacticn attributes that can be used to select strategies and tactics to facilitate interaction on the web. The framework encompasses five interaction attributes, including:

i) interaction with content,
ii) collaboration,
iii) conversation,
iv) intra-personal interaction, and
v) performance support.

Interactions should involve complex activity by learners to include engaging and reflecting, annotating, questioning, answering, pacing, elaborating, discussing, inquiring, problem-solving, linking, constructing, analysing, evaluating, and synthesising.

The levels of interactivity include:

i) interaction between participants and learning materials,
ii) interaction between participants and instructors/ experts,
iii) interaction among participants, and
iv) management/feedback communications

Although content and social interaction are interwoven into highly interactive web-based courses, each will be discussed independently to further explain the role of both forms of interaction in a web-based course.

Content interaction: It is based on the theory of learning that is most appropriate to achieve educational outcomes within the course itself. In many web-based courses, multiple layers of learning outcomes exist, thus suggesting that multiple strategies may be incorporated into the course. Some courses may include an intensive case study, while maintaining a weekly schedule of online lectures and discussion sessions. Other courses may adhere more loosely to a semester-long simulation with its outcome being an explanation of findings and events.

It is difficult to prescribe one best fit for content interaction, given the wide range of possibilities available on the World Wide Web. It is important, however, to ground the design of the learning environment in solid theory and pedagogy, as distance learning has been criticised for having very little, if any, theoretical context. Hannafin, Land, and Oliver discuss grounded design as a context for dealing with the range of design decisions that best facilitate learning outcomes. Grounded design is defined as the systematic implementation of processes and procedures that are rooted in established theory and research in human learning.

Social interaction: It is a key element in online learning. Given that the nature of online learning is anytime anywhere, the potential for isolation and frustration exist. The social interaction of the course must, at least initially, be designed into the course. Through collaboration and communication, the opportunity for learning more about peers and connecting with them in non-task specific conversation is more likely to occur.

Although social interaction may have very little to do with a course, it is still valued as the primary vehicle for student communications in a web-based learning environment. Non-task/content specific social interaction may include conversation in a chat room, inquiries about used textbook purchases, or questions about using a new version of a piece of software.

When collaborative teams of students work toward project completion, there is still the need for relationship building in the learning community. Relationship building is a necessary component of collaboration and communication and the perceptions of the efficacy of this type of social interaction can impact the learning outcomes of the course. By the very nature of social interaction, learners are directly able to foster content interaction.

The overuse or misuse of interaction strategies can lead to boredom, overload, and frustration. It lessens the likelihood that students will be able to surmise what is important, and once again, frustration may occur when students perceive interaction as online busywork.

The more interactive the web-based course becomes, the more complex it is to use. For novice distance learners, complexity may very well lead to more frustration and isolation. Future web-based tools hopefully will promote collaboration and interaction online in a much easier-to-use format. For now, designers of web-based courses should weigh the frequency and the quality of interactions required that best facilitate the learning outcomes to be achieved, where frequency does not always equal quality.

The attributes of web-based instruction should be filtered through the philosophy and pedagogy that is presumed appropriate for the course, preferably adhering to the grounded design approach suggested by Hannafin. Oftentimes, lists of strategies and tactics are provided as design suggestions for web-based courses. When suggested out of context, it is difficult to surmise how the online experience may be structured. For example, in a list that suggests threaded discussions be used, there is still little detail as to how they are to be used within the learning experience itself.

In a more behaviourist notion, threaded discussion may be used to elicit responses to given questions. In a situated learning environment, threaded discussions may be used to discuss influences on the environment with a scientist in an attempt to determine why native plants are not surviving.

Instructional content is the central component of a web-based course, as this is where new knowledge, skills, and abilities are presented. Whether students learn declarative knowledge or participate in a large-scale simulation, the way in which knowledge is shared sets the stage for all interactivity within the web-based course. When given a choice, instructors many times will select land design instructional methods and techniques that are consistent with their theoretical and philosophical views.

Instruction is presented either through an instructor-centred approach or through a more student-centred approach. There are times when one style of instruction is better than the other. When the outcomes of instruction are to analyse, synthesise, or evaluate, or when ill-defined authentic problems are the focus, a more student-centred approach would best facilitate the learning outcomes.

An instructor-centred approach would work well for instruction that is procedural, declarative, or well-defined in role and definition. Much of what exists online as web-based courses appears to have a strong instructor-centred influence. In much of the instruction, information is presented, examples are provided, practice exists, and in many cases, feedback is available through mentors and instructors.

Student-centred learning is appropriate for outcomes of instruction that are focused on analysis, synthesis, and evaluation. Student-centred learning provides interactive, complementary activities that enable individuals to address unique learning interests and needs, study multiple levels of complexity, and deeper, understanding.

Using open-ended strategies for learning, such as situated, learning, learners will actively construct meaning to determine how to proceed. This student-centred approach fosters a greater responsibility for learning and requires students to be more self-regulated in their approaches to learning. In some cases, scaffolding is provided that will facilitate self-regulation, thus providing strategies that students can use to create unique approaches to complex problems.

Collaborative online learning environments is an obvious strategy for promoting interactivity. Many of the same factors that exist for campus-based students in collaborative groups parallel collaboration on the web. Topics such as group size, group role definition, group assignment and shared grading all are issues as well on the web. A collaborative group's members should be committed to the "group goal" and to maximising each other's learning. Johnson and Johnson suggest very strongly that groups do not become collaborative just because someone assigns them together as a group. An effective collaborative group requires positive interdependence, group and individual accountability, promotive interaction, and interpersonal skill.

Quality can be obtained through highly interactive courses. Occasionally, however, a strong collaboration component in the course may hinder some students' participation. If, for whatever reason, some students are unable to participate in collaborative, group building exercises, those students may be left to communicate with only the instructor or mentor.

Many students complain about getting too much information online, not being able to follow concurrent threads in a threaded discussion, and not being about to keep up with multiple conversations occurring in chat sessions. Despite some of the negative student comments, much can be said about conversation and e-discussion. Written communication seems to be more reflective, as students have more time to compose their thoughts and articulate in the manner intended online.

Strategies for successful online conversation are given below:

i) Building group coherence by getting to know one another online. This form of social interaction will go far in establishing a comfortable environment and in establishing the community of learners.
ii) Sharing information by assigning collaborative groups to become resident experts in specific areas-then, requiring the collaborative group to share its knowledge with others online.
iii) Processing ideas by elaborating on discussions, sharing cases, and asking questions of one another through listservs.
iv) Online tutoring as a tool for asking peers questions in preparation for an upcoming test.
v) Refining communication skills by framing arguments and leading e-discussions.
vi) Providing feedback to students through peer critique and instructor critique online.

Monitoring is essential for survival in a web-based environment, even more so than in a traditional environment. This element of web-based design is not included, yet it is essential that work independently and can self regulate their own learning. Many cognitive strategies can be embedded within a web-based course, along with tips and ideas for time management and independent learning.

Performance support can be defined as an electronic system that provides integrated access to information, advice, learning experiences, and tools to help someone perform a task with the minimum of support by other people. A review of the literature on EPSS suggests a series of goals and benefits of performance support, in prompting day-one performance. The basic premise of this just-in-time tool is to generate performance and learning at the moment of need, while assisting in building the knowledge infrastructure for work that will be done in the future. Karat suggests four benefits of performance support:

i) enhanced productivity,
ii) reduced training costs,
iii) increased worker autonomy, and
iv) increased quality due to uniform work practices.

EPSS provides cognitive training wheels that can be progressively removed, as the performer no longer requires guidance and assistance. Supporting performance for the technical and even motivational components of the course is important and must be considered when a web-based course is designed and presented. In addition to supporting entire programmes at a distance, performance support can also provide in course assistance.

PEER-TO-PEER INTERACTIVE COMMUNICATION

It is the multi-way interaction between individual learners and the faculty member and commonly between learners and the learning group. This features is most often implemented with text chat; more sophisticated communication options are implemented with voice communications. May allow selective interaction between learners and/or instructor, but control of the conversation is shared equally among all participants. Web based delivery is attempting to address all three Learning

Formats, with varying degrees of maturity and success. Successful distance education programmes seek to combine all three forms of learning in programmes of study.

There are several functional categories of software tool suites covered in this web site:

i) *Authoring tools*: These are multimedia creation tools. Typically used on an individual computer workstation by a multimedia professional to create media that can either stand-alone or be added as a module into a management system. Examples include Macromedia's director and authorware software.

ii) *Course Management Systems (CMS)*: A software product that generally incorporates an educational delivery system for a topic typically called a course in traditional academic educational institutions and most often facilitated via asynchronous-based formats and provides integrated tools for measuring outcomes and reporting progress for individual or groups of students. CMS systems are currently most popular for educational institutions that are inclined to think of online development as course-centric. Examples include Blackboard's Course info product and WebCT. Generally consists of functions including Content manager, asynchronous collaboration tool, and learning record-keeper. May include integrated but limited authoring tools.

iii) *BEWARE*: 'CMS' is sometimes used in industry trade journals to indicate Content Management Systems', a term applied to systems that organise, retrieve and present modularly packaged content. Such a reference is typically used for web-based portals or as the predecessor to LCMS systems.

iv) *Educational delivery systems*: Software product or suite that facilitates the delivery of content or interaction by the web, but is not necessarily intended to comprehensively measure performance over time or handle course administrative tasks. May also be called a real-time virtual classroom or advanced collaboration tool.

v) *Learning Management Systems (LMS)*: Software product that provides learners an integrated view of all their active coursework and assignments in a syllabus that spans multiple courses and that provides comprehensive assessment and goals tracking spanning multiple courses. LMS systems are most often found in large corporate training departments and corporate universities. They tend to be relatively expensive compared to CMS systems and require significant customisation, but return a great deal of power to both the corporation and the users engaged in multiple learning projects.

vi) *Learning Content Management Systems (LCMS)*: A relatively new category with basic characteristics of a standard Learning Management System (LMS), but enhanced with strong, integrated authoring tools and the capabilities of a knowledge management system.

Development of web-based courses can be very demanding, and often quite different from developing other kinds of media. Most self pace web based training includes the following features:

i) *Copiers*: Outline and overview to tell learners what the learning is about, what the learning goals are, how long it will take and what instructors expect of them.

ii) *Body content*: Must read area where you put your introduction and explanations, procedures and instructions. But remember, most users don't like to read a lot of copy on the screen so keep it short, simple and to the point

iii) *Demonstration or practice*: Demo, practice the lesson or simulate an environment, where possible.

iii) *A self checking quiz*: It gives trainees immediate answers and scores is part of the value added of WBT.

iv) *Help desk.* Provide an e-mail address or phone number on your WBT pages so learners know where to get help.

SYSTEMATIC CHANGE IN EDUCATION

The new sciences of chaos, complexity, and dynamical systems offer important new insights and ideas which can effectively be integrated into work in systemic change. Systemic change has its foundations in systems theories, both hard systems, having their roots in engineering and hard sciences, and soft-social systems, wherein the designer has much less control over the result. A large number of systems has been identified, including mechanical, cybernetic, positive feedback, creodic, reproductive, demographic, ecological, evolutionary, human, and social.

The three primary characteristics of systems are preservation of identity, organisation, and goal-directedness. Systemic preservation of identity is not just constancy, it is constancy and change. Organisations in the sense of organised complexity—a living being is an example of organised complexity—do not lend themselves easily to broad analysis.

Goal-directed or purposeful forms of behaviour can, in principle, be explained in wholly non-teleological terms. While Bertalanffy distinguishes between static structures, clock-works, control mechanisms, open systems, lower organisms, animals, man, sociocultural systems, and symbolic systems, he nevertheless terms the general systems theory a theory of wholeness. While in the past, science tried to explain observable phenomena by reducing them to an interplay of elementary units investigatable independently of each other, conceptions appear in contemporary science that are concerned with what is somewhat vaguely termed 'wholeness,' in short, 'systems' of various orders are not understandable by investigation of their respective parts in isolation.

One of the more well-known applications of systems approaches within education is to the design and creation of instruction. While this area has provided a jumping-off point for considering systems in education, Banathy and Reigeluth have been largely responsible for translating many of the fundamental ideas from instructional design to Educational Systems Design or ESD. Policy authors have also used the term systemic to refer to broad-scale change. However, there are major differences in the ways in which ESD theorists and policy theorists use this term.

The most important difference is the source of innovation—for ESD theorists and practitioners, the source is stakeholders, whereas for policy theorists, the source is typically policy makers. For the most part, ESD theorists are heavily systems theory oriented, while policy systems theorists do not typically rely on systems theories to any recognisable, degree. Systemic change has been defined by Jenlink, Reigeluth, Carr, and Nelson as an approach to change that:

i) recognises the interrelationships and interdependencies among the parts of the educational system with the consequence that desired changes in one part of the system are accompanied by changes in other parts that are necessary to reach an idealised vision of the whole; and
ii) recognises the interrelationships and interdependencies between the educational system and its community, including parents, employers, social service agencies, religious organisations, and much more, with the consequence that all stakeholders are given active ownership of the change effort.

Systemic change is a process based on systems theory and systems design principles. Each of these areas contributes certain necessary characteristics to our understanding of systems change. Systems theory focuses on the importance of global perspectives, multiple components, interdependencies, embeddedness and interconnections in any system.

Systems design creates a new entity by applying future-oriented design, methodology to the ongoing design of human learning environments. Understanding a system's natural tendency to resist change implicates school culture as necessary for broad systemic change. Here, critical theory becomes important in the consideration of systemic change efforts by calling into question the processes in which changing schools engage.

Systemic change is a continuous process based primarily on soft systems thinking. It embraces particular values, such as community, moral conversation, and democracy. One of the cornerstone values of systemic change and systems thinking is the fundamental value of stakeholder participation and indigenous knowledge. This value realigns power distributions within the enterprise of educational reform, wherein expertism has in the past reigned supreme. Squarely at the intersection of critical theory and systems theory lies critical systems theory, which recognises the overlap in fundamental values underlying both social systems theory and critical theory, while extending them both to consider traditions not typically part of the discourse in either field.

System theories are substantially different theories which have a great deal in common. While there is a shared history in the hard disciplines, hard systems theories spring primarily from engineering rather than the physical sciences. Von Bertalanffy's work to the contrary, the actualisation of many of the general systems theories in application has been in areas outside of physics and hard sciences, which are the primary parents of the new sciences of chaos, complexity, and dynamical systems. The new sciences do draw heavily from systems theories, but they also draw from a variety of other sources for their inspiration, including physics, quantum mechanics, and pure mathematics.

However, there are parallels in current systems literature particularly. Excellent examples are mentions of chaos and complexity applications to the systemic notion of Metapatterns in the tradition of Bateson and made popular by Volk. In Volk's systemic text, he identifies the usefulness of chaos and complexity to systems thinking:

"Linked ups and downs in complex systems can be difficult to predict. If the LIPS and downs cannot be unambiguously sorted out, how much more difficult the complexities of global climate change, the vagaries of politics and economics, the dynamo of love. And yet try we must. Computers can help. They let us assemble intricate systems of interacting variables. Even a rather simple system to formulate—just beyond the binary with three (or more) components twisted together in positive and negative nonlinear relations can produce the famously complicated behaviour called deterministic chaos.... Complexity theorists study how nets of such units can create a mixture of properties, arrows up and down. They seek to understand the big arrows of stability and change as a holarchy of component arrows in so-called complex adaptive systems language, culture, economic organisms, ecosystems and the biosphere".

Education is a complex adaptive system to which the underlying concepts of chaos and complexity can be applied. This confluence of systems new sciences, and change theory is one of the most promising theoretical extensions of the past decade, because it opens up whole new areas of understanding. Both systems theories and the new sciences rest fundamentally on the challenge to the Cartesian dualism and the existence of absolute knowledge. These theorists reject the machine metaphor—a clockworks—of the world which eventually became more than mere metaphor and came to represent the real thing—our physical and social world. They reject the idea that traditional science, which seeks to find ultimate truth, is a viable enterprise.

If the world is presumed to follow such mechanistic, deterministic patterns, there is little scope for individual and group action to change it. But one of the core principles of chaos theory, demonstrated in many physical as well as social realism, is that small causes can have large effects. Thus, in systemic change, as in systems theory, more broadly, there is a clear connection to chaos, complexity, and the new sciences. As Uphoff writes of this correspondence: "...what goes under the term of chaos/ chosen more for its shock value than its denotative accuracy, is quite consistent with the systems perspective". In fact, quite the contrary of the suggestion that systems theory has become the new sciences, Uphoff eloquently argues that chaos, which is currently residing under the larger rubric of complexity sciences, should more properly be termed, "nonlinear dynamics", or "dynamical systems".

The following paragraphs examines the metaphorical applications of some of the important concepts of the new sciences as they apply to system behaviour.

Concept of perturbation is perhaps metaphorically best associated with the conscious creation of dissatisfaction. School reformers have come to realise that dissatisfaction is necessary for movement. While a community is complacent, little will change. Since the system tends to perpetuate itself and has, in essence, become a rigid, closed educational system, the old change model of unfreeze-refreeze comes to have much stronger implications. The creation of dissatisfaction is antithetical to the most fundamental motivations for entering educational reform.

It is natural for any system, whether it be human or chemical, to attempt to quell a disturbance when it first appears. But if the disturbance survives those first attempts at suppression and remains lodged within the system, an iterative process begins. The disturbance increases as different parts of the system get hold of it. It becomes so amplified that it cannot be ignored. However, without this sort of substantial unrest in any rigid or closed system, the status quo will merely perpetuate itself, despite waves of reform attempts. In chaos terms, we seek to create a far-from-equilibrium state.

Work on the conscious creation of positive dissatisfaction may be far more generative, though it can be more difficult to establish. Creating negative dissatisfaction requires little more than effectively publicising lower standardised test scores. Creating positive dissatisfaction involves showing the positive aspects as well as the negative aspects of the current system and helping communities to understand how, through design methods, they can create an even better school.

In self-organisation, control of the whole is derived from the interactions of the whole. Kelly describes the problem of control over distributed systems. He uses the example of bees in a hive to define distributed systems, but generalises the point to various social systems, including organisations, the internet, and learning systems. When everything is connected to everything in a distributed network, everything happens at once. When everything happens at once, wide and fast-moving problems simply route around any central authority. Therefore, overall governance must arise from the most humble interdependent acts done locally in parallel, and not from a central command. A mob can steer itself, and in the territory of rapid, massive, and heterogeneous change, only a mob an steer. To get something from nothing, control must rest at the bottom within simplicity. This understanding of self-organisation accounts for the system's inherent autonomy, balanced by its interaction with its environment.

Understanding self-organisation assists systemic change agents in letting go of expert models of solution-generation and moving toward distributed systems of control and design. This fundamental understanding of systemic behaviour central to the new sciences is also the foundation for one of the critical components of systemic change.

Primarily through increasing bureaucratisation, we see rigid structures in many social systems, such as health care, social services, and of course education. The rigid structures in schooling can cross many levels of the system and would include such artifactual examples as the physical structure of the room, building, desk, or physical plant. These physical rigid structures we can touch. But there are many structures which are more abstract, but still prevalent in our own consciousness. Perhaps most difficult to alter are those rigid structures which are subconscious and not easy to identify, such as unquestioned perceptions.

Possibly the most critical of these are the general public's perception(s) of the purpose of public schooling, the professional educators' perceptions of the identity of a teacher and, most centrally, all stakeholders' perceptions about how change occurs in the system. There is a generally accepted notion that change of education comes from experts-top-down mandates and is solution oriented. This deep-rooted belief is extremely difficult to address because it is a prevalent social construct. We are a people who seek solutions, not continuous processes. Redesigning physical buildings pales by comparison to changing people's fundamental, unquestioned perceptions and beliefs about how change happens. This is partially because it is an unrecognised cognitive construct, but it is also because these ideas are more often than not related to people's identities in the system that we are involved in changing. Dissipating the rigid structures of unseen perceptions is perhaps one of the most fundamental challenges facing educational reformers today.

Transformative change, involving basic restructuring, does not happen in a system at or near equilibrium. A system at-or-near equilibrium is a stable and closed system; indeed, it is ore worn out in terms of energy matter exchange. The very stability of such a system is a forerunner to its own demise. Conversation and the creation of positive forms of dissatisfaction may be key strategies to dissipation of this class of rigid structures.

Sensitivity to initial conditions speaks to the inherently unpredictable nature of any open system. Slight imprecision in initial measurements of a system can make prediction over the long term very difficult or impossible. It has become colloquialised as the idea that a butterfly stirring the air today in Beijing can transform storm systems next month in New York. The power of the concept of sensitivity to initial conditions is that it contributes to our understanding of the limitations of prediction.

Previously, scientific theories have been measured based on their ability to accurately predict future behaviours. However, sensitivity to initial conditions calls this dualistic perspective into question. No measurement of any physical, biological, or social state is infinitely precise; there is always some uncertainty. If the underlying dynamics governing the evolution of the measured state is chaotic, the initial uncertainty will inevitably grow so large that long-range prediction becomes impossible.

Understanding very clearly the initial conditions is an important undertaking in the reform process, as is a clear understanding of the context into which an innovation is being placed. Since the butterfly effect is about unpredictability, it is not as though we might choose which wings to blow upon and thereby effect substantive change. It is instead a condition which we must recognise and deal with as we attempt to change schools.

Entropy is the inescapable loss of energy in the universe. This fundamentally simple concept has created a huge stir in the scientific community, which to that point had thought of time as reversible in theory. But if the laws of entropy are true, then in fact, time is not reversible, it is a one-way, rather dismal future that sees the clock of the universe winding down to eventual death. We see entropy in many systems, and it may be most clearly, and commonly analogised as the dissipation of a drop of ink in a dish of water.

This concept, founded on the second law of thermodynamics, contributed fundamentally to our understanding of chaos. The guiding principle of thermodynamics is the second law of thermodynamics, which expresses the fact that a macroscopic system, left to its own devices, will evolve to a state that maximises the entropy of the universe. One can think of the entropy in the thermodynamics as a quality that determines a system's capacity to evolve irreversibly in time.

We may also think of entropy as measuring the degree of randomness or disorder in a system. In physical entities, such as people or grapes, entropy is dealt with in the short term through the building of boundaries—rigid structures of the physical type. A constant sloughing of skin is the result of having a boundary of near-death between life and environment. On the other hand, most open system functions require a large dissipation of energy to maintain their functions.

In social systems, however, entropy can be used to convert energies that serve to perturb the system so that it overcomes the rigid structures which currently keep it from self-organisation. Entropy is the energy exchange that is key to substantive change in any social organisation.

Bifurcations occur when a powerful systemic event creates a positive feedback. It is so powerful, that it shatters the preexisting organisation. This shattering creates a singular moment, a bifurcation point, after which it is impossible to predict the path which the system's future will take. Self-organising systems driven to change by this amplification process are given opportunities for creative reordering. If amplifications have increased to the level where the system is at maximum instability, the system encounters a future that is wide open. No one can predict which evolutionary path it will take. Particularly given the unpredictability of any open, social system via the initial conditions' ripple effect, it is risky to approach a bifurcation point.

Objectors to such radical approaches may criticise the application of new-science ideas to educational change. The current educational system was designed to sort people for industrial era work and integrate them into a monolithic industrial social culture. It does that job rather well. But society needs different things today from its schools. The schools are in the process of being and becoming, an interplay between society and school, wherein each affects and is affected by the other.

As a system reaches its attractors, entropy diminishes, naturally. While plotting system behaviour using only one or two dimensions reveals apparently chaotic behaviour, plotting behaviour in three dimensions reveals pattern in the chaos. While, in fact, the system does not return at regular intervals to precisely the same place or behaviour, it does hover around certain attractors or values for a given variable. This behaviour is revealed through phase space diagramming.

In phase space diagramming, the system's behaviour over time and space is diagrammed, such as the swinging of a pendulum is charted, illustrated as it moves toward its attractor over time. Metaphorically, understanding the behaviour of the system in relation to its attractors—that it never exceeds them—can be useful if we can identify the attractors and effects of initial conditions upon system behaviour in relation to those attractors. The idea of exploring the direct connections that can be made between attractors and mathematical mapping of systemic behaviour through phase space diagramming is an important new possible avenue within educational systems change. This sort of direct connection might lead to understanding the educational system as a dynamic social web.

If phase space diagramming and mathematical models of chaos reflect system tendencies, then it may be possible to mathematically plot points in order to graphically represent the behaviour of a given system. A first step in this work is looking at similar ongoing explorations in less deterministic systems, such as turbulent flow in the physical sciences. The physical sciences are continually searching for increasingly enigmatic systems to explain with mathematical phase-space modelling.

REFERENCES

Berge Z. L., 1999, "Interaction in Post-secondary Web-based Learning", *Educational Technology*, 39(1), pp. 5-11.

Brown, J. S., Duguid, P., 2000, *Learning-in Theory and in Practice*, In J. S. Brown, P. Duguid (eds.), *The Social Life of Information*, Cambridge, MA: Harvard Business School Press.

Bichelmeyer, B. A., Kiggins, E.A., 1998, "Using Web-based Conferencing in Post-secondary Instruction", *Proceedings of the Annual Conference on Distance Teaching and Learning*, Madison, WI, August 5-7, 1998, *ERIC Document*.

Duhaney, D., 2000, Technology and the Educational Process: Transforming Classroom Activities, *International Journal of Instructional Media*, 27(1), pp.67-72.

Forsyth, I., 1998, *Teaching and Learning Materials and the Internet* (2nd ed.), London: Kogan Page.

Bengu G. and W. Swart, A., "Computer-Aided Total Quality Approach to Manufacturing Education in Engineering", *IEEE Transactions on Education*, 39:3, pp. 415-427, 1996.

Galusha, J. M., 1998, *Barriers to Learning in Distance Education, Interpersonal Computing and Technology*, 5(3-4), pp. 6-14.

Paterson K. G., "Student Perceptions of Internet-Based Learning Tools in Environment Engineering Education", *Journal of Engineering Education*, 88:3, pp. 295-304, 1999.

Maddox, C. C., 1997, *The World Wide Web and School Culture: Are they Compatible*?, in D. L. Johnson, C. D. Maddux, and L. Lieu, (eds.), *Using Technology in the Classroom*, New York: The Haworth Press.

Phye, G., 2000, "Engaging Technology and Learning Opportunities: Technology Assessment Tools", *Paper presented at the Annual Meeting of the American Educational Research Association*, New Orleans.

Pisapia, J., Coukos, E., Knutson, K., 2000, "The Impact of Computer on Teacher Capacity, Attitudes, and Behaviours in Elementary Schools", *Paper presented at the Annual Meeting of the American Educational Research Association*, New Orleans.

7

Online Learning and Teaching

Online learning as a form of distance education is expanding at a tremendous rate. This new format requires more time for preparation and maintenance than either past forms of distance education or traditional on-campus teaching. This causes additional stress for instructors, especially if they are put into action without proper training and support. The assistance and advice of faculty development specialists are crucial for the success of novice distance educators.

Since the 1980s, the number of universities offering distance education courses and programmes has increased exponentially. The two primary conditions that have enabled distance education to prosper are the advancement and proliferation of technology and the increase in numbers of the non-traditional student population. While many universities have chosen correspondence and video-based methods of delivery in the past, and many still use these technologies, the current major growth area within distance education has been with those programmes that offer courses wholly or primarily online. Many universities are currently competing in the rapidly expanding online distance education market.

For higher education institutions, online learning provides access to a potentially vast new student population. For students, the attractions are convenience and flexibility. Students can schedule schooling around their everyday lives without being constrained by the rigidity of regular class hours and the necessity of being in a physical classroom. Faculty members, on the other hand, are apt to feel concern and anxiety about engaging in this most-talked-about but never-experienced online teaching. Integrating unfamiliar technology into one's instructional strategies can be stressful at first.

Even good instructors who have experience using the internet for social and/or professional reasons can suffer from unexpected barriers to successful implementation, such as technology problems, student dropout, work overload, and overwhelming amounts of administrative housekeeping. One of the top requirements for the success of distance education is the availability of quality faculty support. Post-secondary institutions commonly employ faculty development specialists to assist faculty members in their online course development. The number of these positions is growing at a fast pace.

Developing an online course is a complicated and time-consuming process, with many new and unique elements for instructors. Without the help of support services, developing and implementing successful online course can be an uphill battle. This chapter provides some guiding concepts and related principles for supporting instructors as they develop online courses.

The demands that developing and teaching online courses pose to instructors are unique and novel. The faculty development specialists must accommodate the increased support needs of faculty. Instructors are likely to approach the project with a fair amount of anxiety, which is justifiable. In order to make the development process efficient and faculty-friendly, faculty development specialists must keep in mind the aspects of the course development process that facilitate success.

Some major concepts for online course development are as follows:

i) *Organisation*: The development of an online course is complex and involve, not only the selection of content and pedagogy, but also the integration of technology, which requires clear and purposeful organisation of the development programme, and the implementation efforts that will follow. The faculty development specialist must also take the lead in developing a realistic time-line for the process, and in the case of larger development projects, in mobilising project teams that are usually formed from a variety of campus support professionals.

ii) *Communication*: Frequent and clear communication is necessary to coordinate the various development activities that constitute the overall development programme. In particular, each project team member needs to be kept abreast of the progress of the others. In addition, the faculty development specialist must take the responsibility of communicating individually with all of the team members, and ensuring that their input informs the development process.

iii) *Collaboration*: The instructor, who may very well feel overwhelmed early on in the project, must be encouraged to take an active role in the development process. Therefore, the instructor's teaching style, course goals, instructional objectives, and particular wishes should drive the development process, rather than making technology choices first and then trying to fit instructional strategies to these. By working collaboratively with the instructor, the faculty development specialist can ensure that the design will take full advantage of his/her knowledge and expertise.

iv) *Enculturation*: One of the most disturbing aspects of embarking upon an online distance education project for many instructors is the feeling of isolation and/or distance from traditional educational communities of practice. One of the most enduring contributions that a faculty development specialist can make is to provide opportunities for an instructor to place him/herself within both the local and international communities of distance educators.

Some other important aspects which should be remembered during the process of online courses development are described below:

i) *Start the design and development process early*: Starting the development of the course as early as possible is critical, since the time-line for the development of online courses is generally far longer than it is for traditional courses.

ii) *Research the minimum hardware / software available to students*: The online students possess an incredible variety of computer hardware and software. An older system could restrict a student's speed and access to class material, and act as a hindrance to communications with the instructor. For instance, a course website that uses frames or Java applets will not be accessible to a student with a computer browser that is version 2.0 or earlier. Connection speed and amount of RAM memory will also influence the format in which material can be delivered. Digital images, audio, and videoclips take much more storage space and download time than text-based materials, and may potentially even be prohibited by student technology limitations.

iii) *Identify and arrange for necessary administrative and technical support, both for students and instructors.* Servers can go down at a critical moment Students' accounts might not be properly set-up. An international student might have a hard time purchasing required text books online. Students' levels of computer competency also will vary, and frustration with the technology itself may be enough for some students that they will consider dropping the course.

iv) *Develop a plan for evaluating student learning and assessing course quality*. Student course evaluations are commonly the primary methods used to measure the quality of post-secondary courses, and they are taken seriously by institutions when considering promotion, award, and tenure. Many colleges and universities have standard course evaluation forms, although there are some institutions that give instructors the freedom to develop their own evaluation instruments, or adapt standard instruments.

v) *Look for models and colleagues*: For a novice instructor, stepping into the world of online education is like beginning the exploration of an unknown wilderness. Knowing the common elements that cause instructors to have a less-than-ideal online education experience is extremely important for faculty development specialists. Activities between the mentoring pairs may involve peer observation of teaching, trouble-shooting, information sharing, and/or informal conversations about the emotional/psychological aspects of online teaching. These formalised relationships are often more significant when they span disciplines, because they give both instructors the opportunity to establish general professional connections outside their own departments.

vi) *Publicise course offerings in both traditional and online venues*. Nothing is more dispiriting to an instructor who has spent a great deal of time developing an online course than finding out that it has attracted only a minimal number of students. With an on-campus course, if the enrolment for a given course is not reached, not much is lost, since the instructor has usually only created a syllabus and ordered books by that point. But with an online course, hundreds of hours could potentially have already gone into the course website by the first week of classes. Especially since many online courses are elective courses, or courses designed outside of a specific degree programme's requirements, just relying on a listing on the university website and in the schedule of classes may not be enough. Faculty development specialists should assist instructors in attracting students to their courses by pointing them to relevant newsgroups, mailing lists, search engines, and directories.

vii) *Arrange for necessary copyright permissions*. The fear of copyright-related legal problems can be a powerful disincentive for online distance education course development efforts, so faculty development specialists should guide their instructors to up-to-date resources on "fair use" and related issues.

viii) *Focus on the management of instructor-student communication*. For many students, the flexibility of working at one's own pace has often resulted in course requirements being put off for a day that never comes, as other, more immediately pressing, obligations take their time, eventually resulting in their dropping the course. Internet technology has the capability of lessening the isolation of distance education students. Instructors need to be given guidance in managing student communications, so that students feel like the instructor is aware of them and their concerns, yet the instructor has time for work other than answering e-mail and conference postings.

ix) *Facilitate faculty in their efforts to become self-supporting*. Most instructional support systems will quickly find themselves overwhelmed if their people receive "handholding" for the faculty through every small step of the development process. Instructors will also want to work on their course website in the evenings and weekends, when support is not available. Therefore, it is best for everyone involved if instructors are trained to be self-sufficient as early as possible in the development process.

x) *Arrange for usability testing with potential and past students of the course*. A website that is not easily used will not be used by most students. If a student is unable to quickly access a site and find what he or she is looking

> for, whether it is the syllabus, the schedule, the discussion group, or other website elements, then the technology is standing in the way of the learning, rather than enhancing it. This is a situation which cannot be allowed to occur.

David Kember developed a comprehensive model of student retention/attrition in distance and open education that is certainly applicable to student access in web-based course and degree study. Validated at four distance institutions in Asia, Australia, and Europe, the model was derived from both extensive qualitative and quantitative research. Working, part-time adult students succeed on a course-by-course basis. In other words, once they have completed each course, they reassess their situation and educational goals in a cost-benefit analysis to determine whether to continue to enrol.

A primary component of Kember's model for student persistence is academic integration. Students become integrated into the course academically when they take a deep approach to learning, they are intrinsically motivated, and they receive a positive course evaluation. Similarly, those students who valued the importance of online learning and developed effective learning strategies succeeded in the online study environment. The goal of many online courses is the creation of a learning community, one where students and the instructor collaboratively share responsibility for the creation of joint knowledge as they jointly share responsibility in addressing learning tasks.

Students who thrive in this environment tend to be more introverted in face-to-face situations, those who reflect deeply, are self-directed in their learning and are intrinsically motivated. Learners need to see the value of such learning properties engendered by this environment as collaboration, constructivism, interactivity, reflection, self-direction, individualisation, and experiential learning. In the web-based course, a number of new communication elements confront the learner and must be addressed: asynchronicity, multiple conversations, interactivity, information overload, and pacing. Other online characteristics, such as social norms, instructor relationship, student role, and the academic atmosphere, are largely carried over from other school experiences.

Students take these factors into consideration in developing learning approaches to work effectively online. Some are directly related to the technology, such as means of processing online information, deciding when and how to contribute, expressing oneself through written communication, dealing with multiple conversations and a deluge of messages, and determining interactivity. Other learning strategies come from prior study patterns in school and work settings: setting goals, individualising assignments, managing time, establishing attitudes, and seeking and using feedback.

Another study of online learning discovered similar patterns while noting that effective students kept their pace "in sync" with the conference and that reflection was a critical learning strategy. Peer behaviour—such things as providing positive feedback, participating online, responding directly, and exchanging short, focused messages—needed to be added to the conventional taxonomy of learning strategies. Students are supported in their individual course study by effective course design. Such design engenders "deep learning", characterised by enjoyment of the academic task, a holistic approach to the content, making the task applicable to one's own situation, and seeking the meaning inherent in assignments and activities. Poor course design conversely can foster shallow assessment procedures, restrict student freedom over activities and topics, and cause students to be extrinsically motivated. Faculty members have praised the internet communications environment for the ease by which it enjoins collaboration, interactively, self-direction, experiential learning, individualisation, and reflection—all characteristics of effective learning—but these elements need to be explicitly designed into web-based courses.

Pedagogical aspects must be intentionally facilitated. Kember states that tutor-student interaction should be devoted to:

i) diagnosing students' conceptions of the subject by demanding meaningful responses to questions;
ii) clearing up misconceptions by posing alternative conceptions; and
iii) giving deep, challenging feedback.

He recommends peer tutoring as another important feature of effective distance instruction. Web-based conferencing is a wonderful environment for such instruction because of the topical interactions by students and the instructor, leading to deep learning.

To prepare students for learning online in their degree programme, Boise State University's (BSU's) Instructional and Performance Technology (IPT) programme offers an initial course that intentionally fosters student abilities to work with online distance technology while engendering study skills and explaining the importance of the required online participation. The syllabus explains the importance of participation—frequency, quantity, and quality of contribution—and the instructor works intentionally to maintain a strong online presence and respond with positive feedback. This has been a strong factor in lowering attrition rates in their courses. Several virtual degree-granting institutions have specific faculty development training for teaching effectively online, such as University of Phoenix's programme.

Adult students who succeeded online were either technologically adept themselves; or had someone in their immediate support system who could readily assist them. Technical problems were found to be an obstacle for students taking web-based courses with the SLN. The most common practice is to have a help desk available to students for assistance with technical problems. Most programmes have a technician on call at all times by phone, fax, and pager, and then a technical support area online where support personnel can reply through e-mail or chat mode to more advanced questions. Beyond just providing technical support, virtual institutions are using their help desks to route urgent administrative or academic requests to the appropriate office for timely attention.

Redesigning a course for web-based delivery can be quite involved, requiring a steep learning curve, especially where there is limited institutional support for this activity. When a regular teacher decides to accommodate some distance students as well as the classroom ones, she or he finds there is twice as much work if taught like two different sections of the course. Course developers and instructors are often part-time, adjunct faculty and may be doing this in addition to their other full-time jobs. To attend to all of the web conference areas can be demanding, especially when there are 15 to 25 students enrolled in a course.

Some educators claim that the time involved in delivering an online course can be up to three times as much as a face-to-face one, but this need not be the case it teachers and students budget their online time. Due to the emphasis placed on student participation, teachers need to shift roles to facilitating and managing peer-learning, instead of lecturing or inserting themselves as often into the discussion as they might in the classroom. One approach for handling the increased workload is to provide a teaching assistant for each online course or have instructors co-teach the course with another faculty member. This allows for somewhat larger enrolments and improved instructional quality.

There are institutions who have adopted an independent study model of web-based education that demands more investment in up-front course development, but can accommodate greater numbers of students without continual faculty involvement during delivery. For example, Brigham Young University's Independent Study programme allows students to start their courses on any date with a year to complete; they also provide automatic grading of web-based, multiple-choice assignments with immediate feedback. These courses are supplemented by related websites, multimedia resources on CD-ROM, and have optional online discussions with peers.

The institutional dimensions of academic student support are similar to those faced by lower-tech delivery systems, but the college or university offering web-based courses needs to mount these services online. The provision of a web-based programme was a chief reason distance students chose the institution, and it is the means by which students interact in their courses. They expect that other communications with the campus about academic and administrative matters will be online as well. These fuller academic supports go beyond single-course interaction, and therefore require programmatic responses. They include:

i) online counselling for educational adjustments and advising for degree planning;
ii) assessment for prior learning;
iii) student discussion areas;
iv) online career centres; and
v) access to academic resources via the internet to support their degree programme study.

Social integration through a positive family and social support environment that encouraged enrolment was crucial for success. Students who lacked these environmental supports attributed their failure to external factors such as insufficient time, distractions, and circumstances that arose over which they had little control.

Readiness is the major component of successful online learning. Readiness includes personal factors such as a compatible learning style, proficient computer skills, an interest in the content of the course, mastery of prerequisites, and good reading, writing, and keyboard skills. It also include, such environmental factors as having a quiet, roomy study area, a social network of family friends, and work associates that value the student's educational pursuits, a lifestyle with existence within it for distance study, and technical/ institutional assistance in place for obstacles that might arise.

Institutions are obliged to present realistic and accurate information about course demands, but their marketing efforts sometimes overshadow this voice. Kember recommends effective counselling as the primary means of accomplishing this. This role, assumed by full-time counsellors, tutors and support staff means being supportive, encouraging, and pastoral to some extent. Such counselling sets forth realistic expectations about online study demands for working adult students who have been away from college and/or never juggled their education with other roles they must play. The counsellor suggests, needs to let students know that it is those who take direct responsibility and control of their college experience that prove to be most successful. This counselling can also address the readiness factors listed above and assist students with time management, organising their situation for a successful educational role and activities, and garnishing support from spouse, children, and their employer.

Web-based courses generally have an important advantage over independent study, because the online class has a fixed schedule with a dedicated professor assigned to the course. Rapport develops through supportive online interactions, and an astute online faculty member will pay attention to students who seem to be falling behind in their web-courses and give them private notices of encouragement and support, i.e., assuming the counselling role. Suny Empire State College's Centre for Distance Learning provides an example of such counselling support. Once admitted, each student is assigned an advisor who mentors them throughout their individualised degree programme. With that advisor, they take a required independent study in their first enrolment that addresses many of the readiness issues outlined above, as well as allows them to assess their academic abilities and career aims.

For many years distance programmes have accepted most standard forms of prior learning credit as it related to the student's degree programme, such as accredited college transcripts, CLEP test scores, and ACE, PONSI, and DANTES recommended credit equivalents. However, individualised credit by evaluation (CBE) was restricted to in-person settings. No longer will this be the case, however. SUNY-ESC's Centre for Distance Learning has begun individualised CBE in common areas, done at a distance through e-mail, the phone, and mail and such an web-based environment is being designed. Other virtual supports are social in nature, such as announcement areas, student bulletin boards, and topical conversation areas; these integrate students with their peers, create an online Community of scholars, and create institutional affiliation. The British Open University (BOU) Students' Association maintains several hundred such conferences covering the gamut of topics to bring together its student body. It operates a bulletin board for events and activities of student interest.

A majority of adult distance students pursue further education for career advancement or change. These individuals are returning to college as necessity learners—where education is essential for them to keep or obtain a job—or as rainy day planners—where education provides a safety net to give them options if opportunities come up or something goes awry in their current position. Therefore, an important student service on the virtual college site would be a career centre. Such a centre could have such features as information about jobs and employment; career testing and counselling; networking about jobs with other students, university personnel, and alumni; as well as links to online job search services.

The library is a key component, of quality education, and academic institutions have a responsibility to provide external students with resources, facilities and services equivalent to their internal peers. The virtual institution must provide an online bookstore for students to order course guides, textbooks, and major instructional resources for their online course. Other resources could include lab kits, calculators, CD-ROMs, computer software, audio and videocassettes, and so forth. Such facilities will allow students to purchase materials by courses as separate components, paying for their purchases online by credit card. Increasingly these institutions will compete with local bookstores, conventional bookstores that sell textbooks online like Barnes and Noble, or online bookstores like Amazon. Distance students are expected to use libraries like their campus counterparts; fortunately many of these services are going online as well.

Reference librarians are available on the web or by toll-free call to answer specific research questions, as are online interlibrary loan services. Distance libraries allow online students to search databases that may only have citations and abstracts, and then allow them to retrieve the documents from their own collections for modest photocopying and mailing fees. For book check-outs, these institutions have an online circulation desk that allows for longer periods to compensate for postal mail exchanges.

Libraries employ user identification and password procedures to ensure that only genuine students of the institution can use online subscription services for which it pays fees. The WGU has established an electronic reserve, putting an electronic version of an article or a chapter of a book on a password-protected website for a limited period of time. Often, distance students can, purchase access to a local academic library in their community or region for a nominal fee and use interlibrary loan services at their local library for books.

High quality academic resources are being made available through the World Wide Web, but sometimes it is difficult for distance students to judge the academic quality of these sites.

Institutions like the University of California at Riverside, have created an online service, Infomine that recommends 15,000 university level web links by academic area. The WWW Virtual Library provides a similar service. SUNY ESC has also developed a website to help students refresh or develop academic skills.

Most distance programmes and institutions seem to be shifting to the latter while trying to develop access possibilities for students to these resources so they are not disadvantaged from their campus counterparts. Distance educators should integrate information gathering and evaluation skills into the distance curricula as it has on campus. Additionally, libraries must get students familiar with their services and raise their expectations to use what online information resources are currently available. In concentrating on the individual course interactions, institutions have often neglected the fuller academic resource supports necessary to mount full-service web-based degree programmes.

Although distance educators think it would be a good idea to create greater institutional affiliation by bringing together distance students online and provide the services outlined in this section, few have fully developed these web-based environments to make these interchanges possible. One of these difficulties is reliable dial-up Internet service when the campus acts as an Internet Service Provider (ISP). For on-campus students this internet connection may be supplemental to on-campus services; to the distance student it is a continuous, absolute necessity for academic and administrative support. Some supports are strictly operational, providing students with efficient institutional services through web-based communication and information technologies. These services include:

i) online information about the institution, its degrees, programmes, and services;
ii) online admissions for expedited matriculation;

iii) an online enrolment system where students and fees;
iv) a virtual support can enter to resolve technical, administrative and academic issues;
v) financial aid services for information, application, and dispersal of funds; and
v) online records system where students can view their academic progress, request transcripts, and so forth.

For students to be successful in web-based university learning they must be enabled to accomplish this learning in the academic interaction of the individual course. To progress through their online degree programme, they must have the academic and administrative services of a virtual institution.

ONLINE LECTURES

The computers have revolutionised the teaching and learning process. Sutherland and Johnson demonstrated that it was possible to draw interactively on a cathode-ray tube (CRT) and Schwartz and Taylor showed the educational value of simulating a rocket travelling at a speed significantly close to that of light. Their visual demonstration showed roadside telephone poles not only bending backwards down the road, but the L-shaped crosspieces rotated. Their simulation enabled students to "focus on the phenomena without being burdened by the constant onslaught of mathematical symbols".

General purpose systems upon which courseware was produced were far from being simply keyboard-orientated, designed only for text-based drill and practice. The IBM 1500 Instructional System with its conventional television CRT refreshed from disk, a light pen for interaction, and a separate image projector, allowed for text and graphics to be displayed and manipulated. The PLATO system adopted a plasma panel display; it had the ability to cverlay a projected image with computer generated material, and had an audio capability.

In the long term the classroom would be more capital intensive and that it would become less labour intensive. While this might be so in the classroom, it certainly does not apply to the preparation time. For example, Oliver and Brooks reported a preparation time of four hours for each one hour of classroom activity; most of the teaching was talk and chalk but was supplemented by online demonstrations. Clarke refers to a CD-ROM based programme that replaced 20 lectures, twelve hours of practicals and 10 hours of workshops. He estimated that the project took five person-years to complete.

From an institutional point of view it would be unwise to commit wholeheartedly to teaching by computer because of the enormous fall in research income and output that would necessarily be incurred. While in principle courseware can be shared among institutions, the time required to appraise a number of pieces of courseware will be very much greater than appraising the course textbook, particularly if the courseware is organised in a spaghetti-like web. If lecturers do not prepare for a live presentation, their ability to answer the difficult questions from students will be weakened. Furthermore, if lecturers cease to determine the content of their courses, they lose their professional claim. But perhaps the most important reason for lecturers determining content is that it leads to university courses that are unique and provides students with choice.

The lecturers cannot be expected to have the knowledge or capacity to engineer a good user interface, which enables students to concentrate on what they are learning rather than on how to manipulate the system. Producing courseware with some of today's authoring systems requires that knowledge and even programming skills. Courseware often places an over-reliance on hierarchically arranged structures that effectively hide information and allow the act of exploration to become an educationally purposeless activity. Information is often updated in a computer-efficient manner; the resultant movement leaving students cued to the wrong place on the screen. Having to think about relocating their focus of attention interferes with what they are learning. There is a temptation for the lecturer-developer to include multiple paths along which students can travel by pointing-and-clicking, leaving the students in danger of losing the focus of their learning objective. Indeed what is actually required is support for a personal discovery of insight, not the chance discovery of already publicly known facts. Widely available development environments actually leave authors open to more bewildering design considerations than did previous generations of authoring systems.

Students achieve successful learning outcomes by attending lectures, reading textbooks, and then personally consolidating the material. If information technology is to be exploited then one of its main contributions should be to speed up the learning process. This can be simply achieved by removing the tedious impediments to learning such as note-taking errors and repetitious clerical activity, and ensuring that concepts are explicitly described and illustrated. If lecturers are to be encouraged to exploit information technology then preparation time ought to be of the same order as for 'talk and chalk' lectures and problem classes and achieve the same level of quality as they do without IT. But exploiting the computer should provide an upgrade path to higher quality in the learning experience. The authorware must allow lecturers to concentrate on their specialities and not on the design of the navigational interface.

While the lecture theatre is not the place where most of the learning takes place, its prominence in the learning process has stood the test of time. Students overwhelmingly demand the retention of live lectures. Lectures offer a framework that identifies the scope of the material. They lubricate the learning process that takes place later during private study when the material is consolidated.

A conventional lecture presentation, a situation familiar to university lecturers, provides in one place on the screen the integration of text, diagrams, animation, illustrative pictures and video material, all sequenced and synchronised with a spoken narrative into a linear presentation. This compares favourably with the live-lecture situation in which projector foils, 35mm slides, video and audio are all controlled by different pieces of equipment and displayed possibly in different parts of the lecture theatre. The metaphor used for both the creation and presentation of each lecture is that of an electronic book whose content can be roamed in much the same way as with a real book even down to experiencing the same page turning cues that are inherent in real books. Students may have the whole lecture played in sequence; they may truly browse to any slide and have it 'played' through, or see/hear a fragment of the sequence. Thus students can passively experience the lecture, or navigate nonlinearly around it. Links to external material such as supportive technical papers held locally or on the World Wide Web can be incorporated together with additional notes below the slides.

A visual programming method is used throughout to specify both the content of the slides and the dynamics of the presentation. This method is based upon a schematic drawing paradigm. It might be useful to regard this as a fifth authoring paradigm alongside those of structure, time-line, flowchart and script as identified by Hardman and Bulterman. While there is some resemblance to the flowcharts approach, the flow lines are absent, the sequence is determined instead by the relative position of symbols, and the flowchart is placed on the slide rather than have the slide content accessible through the flowcharts. In some ways the emphasis is on fitting the dialogue to the picture rather than fitting a picture to the dialogue; though of course a presentation should be prepared using an iterative process and the system allows for this.

The central software uses the Book Emulator as its user-interface mechanism and they are connected together through two way UNIX pipes. The whole system runs on a Silicon Graphics Indy. Drawing Board requires porting from Sun Microsystems hardware.

The Book Emulator presents a book-like user interface to information enabling that information to be truly browsed by flicking through the pages of an electronic book. The page turn is animated, indicating directional travel, and the splayed page images down the sides of the book change size according to the user's position within the information space.

Two mouse buttons provide for forward and backward travel, while the third button enables selection. A number of central services are provided through the utensils located above the book including word and symbol searching, proper bookmarks, inter-book hyperlinking, and an import gateway for external links to arbitrary fragments of information. A Book Emulator has a schematic drawing capability based upon symbols that are interconnected by lines and annotated with text. When a symbol is selected it is attached to the mouse cursor and can be relocated on that page, moved to any other page within the book, or moved to any other book that is also open on the screen. A grouping facility automatically groups lines, text and other symbols that are contained within a symbol.

The last item or group selected is remembered through the 'glue-pot' and its content is available in any other book on the screen that has a glue-pot. The utensils located above the book provide for the moving and copying of complete diagrams and, of course, when attached to the mouse cursor these may be dragged to any other page within the book or to any other book. Symbols, text, lines, groups, whole drawings may be deleted by selecting and tacking outside the confines of the book. Symbols and fonts are usually selected from library books containing such collections. Two function keys are provided to speed up drawing. If either is pressed when nothing is attached to the cursor, then what is in the glue-pot is attached to the cursor. This enables the fast repetition of a symbol in a drawing without the need for a large movement of the mouse cursor up to the glue-pot.

If a symbol is attached to the cursor then pressing the function key causes it to be changed to a related symbol if one exists. In this way, for example, having selected a transistor symbol, the different orientations of the transistor are quickly available to the user. The two function keys cause the changes to go opposite ways around the 'ring' of related symbols. If a string of text is selected, then the appearance of the string is changed when the function keys are pressed. User-authored links to external fragments such as audio, pictures, movies and other books are available through special symbols which act as anchors. Their manipulation is identical to any other symbol, so may be moved within and between books, be grouped, and be changed with the two function keys.

The central system provides for up to two library books to be open at any one time including a library book maintained by the user for collecting often used symbols, text strings, or privately created symbols. Up to 20 slides per book can be created. Through this interface the lecturer can create paper-based booklets of slides for students (one slide per page with room for personal notes, or two slides per page). In addition another booklet can be created, this time with the slide followed by a blank story-board table all on the same page. The lecturer can also create a set of slides, one per page, for transfer on to view-foils or 35mm slides.

Two electronic hardcopies are available. One creates a HTML file suitable for a Netscape type viewer, while the other creates a HTML compatible file that has additional tokens. This enhanced HTML file is automatically passed through a separate converter that creates a book version of the electronic slides. One of these additional tokens forces information to begin on a new page and another enables dynamic instructions to be passed through. These dynamic instructions are required for animation and the sequential spoken narrative; facilities that are not available through viewers such as Netscape.

Creation of online slides exploits the schematic paste-up facilities of the Book Emulator. It is arguably no slower than any other method of slide creation including those written by hand. Lecturers need go no further than this to have benefited from using the system and, like other systems, slides can be edited. The minimum requirement for changing online slides into online lectures is to provide a spoken narrative and the sequencing of that narrative is visually programmed with the same schematic paste-up facilities as are used to create the slide content. The audio fragments are usually of thirty to sixty seconds duration and are captured on to the local file-server using a separate audio capture tool.

With a single command, the speech fragments are imported into the Book Emulator's in-tray, that is located above the book. From there, their link symbols (anchors) are extracted and placed in position on the slide. They are sequenced according to a left-to-right, top-to-bottom rule that has a degree of tolerance which enables the correct sequence to be interpreted without the need for exact alignment. By default the command that sends the anchor to the in-tray assumes that an audio file contains speech and chooses one of the speech symbols (the speech bubble). Using the function keys this symbol can be changed by the user to identify it as music. As well as showing the whole slide all the time, some lecturers like to reveal material gradually as they progress through the slide.

The slide must be partitioned with rule-off symbols. Then any speech fragment between rule-offs is sequenced after the revelation or identification has taken place. In this way the lecturer can specify what is to be revealed and what has to be said after that revelation. It is important to 'top and tail' a lecture; that is to begin by defining the scope of the lecture, describing the benefits that will accrue from understanding the information, and reminding the students what they should know as preparation for what is to come. At the end they need to repeat that information, emphasising how the new knowledge can be used.

In consequence, it may be useful for the lecturer to show briefly some of the key slides and this can be incorporated in the sequence with the 'show slide' specification symbol. Colour pictures and movies can be incorporated in a slide by placing them appropriately in the sequence of specification hyperlinks. These links are imported into the Book Emulator through the in-tray using the same command as for the speech fragments. Colour pictures and movies can be used to illustrate aspects of a lecture as well as be central to a lecture. While the revelation/indication mechanism works particularly well for slides containing textual bullet points, it is not satisfactory if a diagram is to be described in which, for example, flow of data needs to be animated or the diagram needs to be built up as the narration progresses.

In these circumstances it is necessary for an animation book to be included in which the individual frames of the animation can be specified. This book is the same as that fronting the OHP programme. The content of each animation frame is pasted up in the same way as all the other slides and the same specification facilities are also available; but in going from one frame to the next, there is only a short delay imposed, thus enabling animation to be shown in steps.

The central software generates different HTML files for the World Wide Web browser and the Book Emulator versions of the online lectures. For the Book Emulator some additional tokens have been defined to accommodate the notion of pages, enabling each slide to start on a new page. In addition the necessary animation instructions are also passed through so that a lecture can be played. For the World Wide Web version no such dynamics are possible but each fragment of the sequence is made available through a point-and-click button interface as they are in the Book Emulator.

The online lecture generator goes through each slide visually removing the lecture specification material, leaving only the slide content. The cleaned-up slides are then bitmap dumped, resized appropriately without loss of detail, and is being prepared for the World Wide Web are coloured according to the 'colourway' specification. Such colouring ensures that the slide, background, and button highlights are all colour coordinated. Below each slide the fragments of the lecture sequence are accessible through buttons. These buttons are titled: narrative, picture, movie, document, www link, music, or textbook. Below the fragment access buttons, additional notes may be included. These notes are created with an editor and are converted into HTML. HTML tokens may also be used provided they are recognised by the HTML-to-Book Emulator converter.

Among other facilities, words or phrases can be made bold, in-line images may be incorporated, and further hot references may be included. In the Book Emulator version where the lectures are dynamic, the student can go to the front of the book and select the button that causes the whole lecture to be played through with all the covering-up, revealing, animation, overlaid pictures/movies correctly sequenced with the spoken narrative. The speech can be paused and resumed by pressing the space bar and when resumed it plays the last few seconds again before carrying on. This enables users to orientate themselves before the next part of the information is conveyed.

Pressing the backspace key causes a bigger jump backwards in the speech. The complete lecture can be stopped, and then can be resumed by selecting the button at the front of the book; it continues from the start of the slide at which it was stopped. Alternatively the student can browse to a particular slide and select it and see it dynamically presented. In either the complete lecture case or the single slide case, the last fragment heard or seen is indicated by greying the appropriate access button below the slide.

By the end of the slide, all the access buttons have been greyed and are then restored when the sequence ends. This process indicates which of the access buttons will return the user directly to a specific fragment. The access button is not greyed while the fragment is heard or seen and then restored when it has finished, because this would attract eye movement away from the slide and its animation. The Book Emulator allows the student to make personal annotations either directly on to a book or through electronic Post-Its like that used to specify the 'additional notes'. Furthermore, links between individual slides both in and between books can be installed by creating a link to the current slide on display using one of the utensils. The resulting anchor is then selected from the in-tray and taken to the slide where the link is to be made, placing it where it is most appropriate.

All material directly used in a lecture is copied to the same directory, i.e., all documents, pictures and movies are copied in their original form. It is these copies that are displayed when the fragment access buttons are selected. So colour pictures can be seen in their original full size. However, the colour pictures used when playing a slide in the Book Emulator version are scaled to fit exactly the slide area below the running header and these are also created in the directory and in the same format as their originals. To fit, it may be necessary to change the aspect ratio from that of the original. But if the picture is too thin, it is only scaled to fit exactly in either the vertical or horizontal direction, and is then centred in the other direction; the original aspect ratio is thus retained.

If the picture is smaller than the slide area, it is centred in the slide and no scaling is applied during the playing of a slide colour pictures and movies are overlaid on to the slide area so that they are placed where the eyes are focused; it is not necessary for the user to search visually around the screen for the picture or movie. Audio files are converted to a single channel and compressed before copying. A delay of one second is imposed between the playing of one fragment and the playing of the next when the sequence is translated into the online lecture. Pauses play a role in supporting either the linking together of topics or their dissociation. When parts of slides are revealed or highlighted, there is a short pause after the last speech fragment and before the next revelation, followed by a long pause between the revelation and the next speech fragment. This timing provides the supportive cue that the information on the same slide is related and not dissociated.

When going from one slide to the next, there is a long delay after the last speech bite has finished and before the page is turned; once the page is turned there is a short delay before the speech bite is played. This ensures that the correct dissociation between slides is surreptitiously cued to the user. Preliminary investigation suggests that the long pause is at least twice as long as the short pause, with the long pause being between two and three seconds. Revelation in the online lecture is presented by clearing the slide and then gradually pasting back the slide. Highlighting is achieved by greying the whole slide except the indicated section. By default the revelation mechanism is generated when rule-offs exist, but can be overruled by the special 'grey and highlight' symbol placed somewhere on the slide so as to specify highlighting.

Revelation or highlighting takes place in sequence with the audio narrative so that a visual change does not take place as the narrative is played. Bligh notes that there is some evidence which suggests that people watching television will "tend to ignore auditory information when auditory and visual information are present". Thus if a concept were described in parallel with a visual example it is likely that students would concentrate on the illustration, particularly if it were striking, and ignore the underlying concept. So by adopting a sequential policy it encourages the explicit description of concepts before an appropriate illustrative piece of animation or movie clip is shown; this can then be followed by a restatement of the concept.

It is technically difficult to ensure synchronisation between audio and visual information with a general purpose computer and to expect lecturers to try to achieve synchronisation would increase the difficulty in producing the lecture. However, when the slide has a 'parallel audio' specification the strong sequential approach is diminished. The duration of each picture being displayed is determined by the playing time of the audio fragment and each picture is displayed for an equal amount of time unless a 'wait' specification follows immediately after the picture specification. In this way the music and the picture display times do not have to be accurately specified by the lecturer. If there is a fragment of music to be played in parallel with a series of pictures, followed by a second fragment of music with another set of pictures, then the second music fragment is not started until the last of the slides for the first fragment have been displayed. In other words audio fragments are always played sequentially and never in parallel. When the display of pictures is signalled by selecting the appropriate button below the slide, they are displayed in their original size for ninety seconds and then removed from the screen.

Online lectures are similar writing a book: both published, albeit in different forms. They are therefore available for scrutiny by peers. Thus more care is taken in preparing the material, and this must lead to higher quality. Koumi offers some useful guidance for creating educational videos that are attractive to the target audience and this has been interpreted elsewhere specifically for online lectures. The lecturer is advised to script the narrative, breaking it down into speech bites of perhaps one to four sentences such that it contains an atomic piece of information with perhaps some qualification. The lecturer is then advised to record the speech bites away from any background noise such as the cooling fan of a desktop computer. In practice this means recording on audio tape at home.

Prior to recording, the narrative needs rehearsal and must be spoken with at least the same flamboyance as that conveyed in a live lecture. Preferably they should be even more flamboyant to counteract the lack of any body language such as gesticulations that would naturally arise at a live presentation. The whole process is clearly very time consuming and in the author's view is likely to discourage the take-up of online lectures. However, it does ensure that the slide can be talked through in an orderly way, that all that needs to be said is captured, and it does provide the cement that is necessary to make the slides properly understood. In this way the additional spoken narrative improves the quality of the 'electronic slides'. While a similar tedious process may be experienced when incorporating movie clips, the majority of lectures require no such sophistication.

View-foil versions of electronic slides are almost guaranteed to be readable from anywhere in the lecture theatre. Their editing is straightforward and thus a course can be easily kept up to date. Furthermore, in principle, fragments of material can be shared with other members of staff and tailored by them for their specific student needs. However, it should be noted that a change in voice, even the same lecturer's voice after several months, can be wrongly inferred as a change in topic, or that it is a conflicting view compared with the previous statement. So editing the spoken narrative requires some care. Editing of course amounts to throwing away fragments and recording and inserting replacements. In practice, the author has adopted the inclusion of the scripted narrative as the 'additional notes' that appear in the online lecture below the fragment access buttons. This enables students to speed read and also to not have to listen to the author's voice.

Students want live lectures. But unless the institution is prepared to equip lecture theatres with projectors with high resolution and high light output, the resultant presentation would need to be undertaken in a dimly lit lecture theatre with students straining to read the fuzzy lettering on the screen. Using the conventional overhead projection view-foil overcomes these problems. Yet the integration of animation, pictures and movies is a strong motivator to provide the online lecture in a form that would enable it to be presented live by the lecturer while signalling step changes just as weather forecasters do on television.

Work is proceeding to provide a third version of the online lecture which will be created in the form of a HTML file with embedded Java tokens. This will enable the lecturer to single step forwards and backwards at both the fragment and slide levels without the spoken narrative, as well as be able to play the whole lecture through with the lecturer listening with the students. While the lecture paradigm may be regarded as a straitjacket, it also offers a completely choreographed show with no new skills to learn except that required for a slide projector type control. Unfortunately it appears that the user-interface particularly with regard to timing, cannot be as well controlled as it can be within the Book Emulator and so association/dissociation may well be hindered in the continuous play version.

ONLINE TEACHER TRAINING

Information technology revolution has considerably influenced the development of Distance Education (DE) systems. This first generation of DE systems was superseded in the 1950s by the so-called multimedia or second generation DE systems, which incorporated various media, like printed material, television programmes, audio recordings and, in some cases, educational software. Teacher-student interaction remained virtually unaltered from the first generation, even if supported by the telephone, face-to-face tutorials and, more recently, fax and e-mail links. Thus first and second generation DE systems were based primarily on production and distribution of learning material for the learning community.

Communication with the student only played a marginal role, while communication between students was virtually non-existent. From this perspective, DE seemed merely to be conceived to bridge geographical distances, a problem that can be solved by effective presentation and distribution methods. Hence education was no longer seen as a social activity centred on student-teacher interaction but rather as an almost totally individual pursuit. The distinctive element of these virtual classes was that they were spread over a wide geographical area; the socio-cognitive potential inherent in traditional classes was totally lacking. The driving force behind the development of third generation DE systems is the redefinition of learning as a social activity, albeit performed at a distance with the inevitable mediation of technology.

In DE terminology, third generation systems are also known as online education, a definition that gives a clear idea of how extensively the computer network is used in the learning process; participants interact in a fully-fledged learning community, which helps them overcome their isolation and enhances their contribution to the group. This approach is particularly suited to adult education, where swapping personal experience about the topic being studied can play an essential role in collective development.

Through frequent inter-student and student-tutor exchange, tutors have the opportunity to monitor both the overall progress of the course and knowledge acquisition by each individual participant, more or less in real time. This allows a sort of running evaluation of the students and the course itself, permitting tutors to modify, reinforce and model educational processes. In this way, tutors can meet the learning and cognitive requirements of each participant, requirements that can be gleaned on a daily basis from network discussions. Traditional DE courses are considerably more rigid given that the learning material has been designed and structured for individual use within a specific timeframe.

Moreover, with interpersonal communication confined to sporadic exchanges between tutor and students, it becomes extremely difficult to introduce new learning material and topics, or to modify parts of the course. Therefore, there is little scope for any modification that may be needed to adjust the course to the participants' different learning styles, or cultural or professional background, and so forth.

The online education creating virtual classrooms where a group of participants may 'meet up' to discuss particular aspects of the course. This lays the ground for groups to work in parallel, or for continuing a discussion on units of the course already covered without interfering with the schedule set down by the tutors. Anyone interested can stay in the virtual classroom while the others carry on with the work at hand. The technology generally used for managing online education comes under the category of computer conferencing, which creates fully-fledged distributed learning environments that overcome the hurdles of time and space.

Computer conferencing opens up a whole new range of possibilities for managing and participating in the educational process, benefits that neither traditional DE approaches nor conventional face-to-face courses can offer. While the face-to-face approach favours many-to-many interaction the necessary physical attendance by all participants poses time and space constraints. Conversely, traditional distance learning overcomes space/time hurdles but is none the less biased towards two types of interaction: one-to-many (teacher/students) or one-to-one (student-teacher). In practice, theoretical and practical models that address one or the other of these domains cannot, when considered individually, cover all the learning and interpersonal communication needs that distinguish online education.

Computer-mediated communication (CMC) not only offer asynchronous, many-to-many communication but also make full use of interaction via the written word. This is actually a fairly informal style of communication, which reproduces spoken language in written form. Peer interaction produces a number of benefits for the learning process, especially when conducted in written form. Formulating one's ideas and setting them down in writing is a major cognitive skill, as is considering and responding to the ideas of others. In addition, active participation helps to enrich the learning environment, allowing each participant to consider the topic under discussion, or a difficult situation, from different viewpoints, namely those of the other participants.

Computer conferencing has the capacity to promote and support collaborative learning activities. In fact, the computer conferencing environment favours a kind of learning based on collaboration between all the actors in the learning process—learners, tutors and experts. Using this approach, each member of the learning group can help define what is being learnt; this is a key activity in that it brings to the fore a variety of viewpoints and highlights the range of opinions about a single event or topic. It does not matter if this leads to disagreement, because the disparity of opinion itself stresses the very complexity of many knowledge domains.

In collaborative learning environments, the learner, when called upon to address and solve a problem, is able to identify and take full account of all the various points of view. The ability to take full account of the point of view of others when addressing a problem or situation is undoubtedly a key factor in much inservice training. Traditional distance learning courses have often neglected this factor, making little use of the knowledge, ability and experience that each learner brings with him, an asset that can be shared where the participants are connected up in a network. When the extraordinary information resources available on the network are added, the difference between conventional distance learning and online education becomes even clearer. Up to this point the network has only been considered as a vehicle for interpersonal communication, but it is also an incredible source of information, material and knowledge.

Students and teachers may well be free to set off in search of information and knowledge, but if they are to make sensible and profitable use of the network for educational purposes they require some preparation. First they need to acquire specific skills in utilising the network, identifying the most suitable and authoritative information sources, and learning how best to exploit the information collected, otherwise they run the risk of wasting considerable time and energy for little return.

A the project, known as POLARIS, been developed to examine the educational potential that telematics can offer in-service teacher training. The two partners involved are the Italian Research Council's Institute for Educational Technology (ITD) and the Technical Education Board (Division II) of the Italian Education Ministry (MPI). The main aim of the project is to define a special model for in-service teacher training based on intensive use of telematic resources, along the lines of the online education approach, otherwise known as third generation distance learning. Actually, the model is not confined to the training stage, but also includes follow-up online support for trainees. This will bring about a more effective transfer of knowledge learnt in the course to the classroom context.

Through a series of pilot activities the project aims to:

i) define the proposed model in methodological terms (online education + online support and counselling) and ascertain its effectiveness by delivering a series of courses based on that model;

ii) design a teaching package based on online education for 'online tutors' (a role of vital importance in any online course), and ascertain its effectiveness in a pilot course;

iii) outline the criteria for engineering the model to allow autonomous management by MPIs of both tutor training, and the design and implementation of further online courses.

POLARIS will not adopt the 'cascade' approach to tutor training, i.e., training an initial group of tutors who then go on to teach other trainees in the same methodological/ disciplinary context and so on. The tutors in POLARIS follow a particular method for designing and running their online education courses, which have contents that may vary and are not necessarily linked to their particular area of competence.

The first year of the POLARIS project was divided into three main phases:

i) creation of a communication infrastructure for conducting online training courses;
ii) distance training of a group of 10 tutors in methods for planning and managing online training courses;
iii) distance training of 10 groups of teachers on the subject of network-based education.

Communication Structure

Development of a communication infrastructure to permit experimental delivery of the early online training courses involved: design and construction of a computer conferencing environment hosted on and managed by an ITD server; and identifying an Internet Service Provider for each of the course participants to enable them to have access to the network at local telephone rates. Communication between participants was handled by a computer conferencing, system called POLARIS FC.

Developed using first-class software, this system features a simple graphic interface and offers the user a series of advanced interpersonal communication functions such as e-mail, bulletin boards, file transfer and real-time chatting. POLARIS FC users have direct access to the information that interests them most and are not disturbed by all sorts of messages, a common problem with e-mail. POLARIS FC resembles bulletin board systems (BBS) in that communication is organised into themes, or conferences. Messages are not sent to a single mailbox but are arranged by the users and the moderator in specific niches.

Online Tutor Training

Online tutor course drew on the British Open University's

Teaching and Learning Online (TLO) course, although extensive modification was required in order to tune it to the Italian context and adapt it for use with upper secondary school teachers. The course centred on the special features of third generation DE systems and was designed for 10 educators with previous experience in face-to-face tutoring.

The prime objective was to train these tutors in the design and running of online courses in order to create a pool of tutors to be used in later phases of POLARIS for coordinating online training activities on methodological/subject themes. A secondary objective in this phase was to raise the participants' awareness of the potential limits and problems involved in running distance courses based on intensive use of network technology. The tutors were trained over a three-month period by ITD researchers; after a two-day face-to-face induction meeting, the remainder of the course was entirely online.

The main goals set for participants in the online tutor course were to:

i) develop skills in initiating and moderating online discussions and group work relying on asynchronous text-based communication;
ii) gain familiarity with the most widely used internet services;
iii) know how to combine telematic resources with other media and methods when engaged in network training activities;
iv) be able to identify the pros and cons of using computer conferencing and network resources in training courses, both in general terms and in the particular contexts in which the participants may be called upon to operate as tutors.

The course was divided into four stages of varying duration, each comprising a series of modules that lasted from two to five weeks. Areas covered in the various stages included: familiarisation with network services relevant to course activity; learning the methods and strategies which were proposed for correct use of CMC in distance learning; development by individual course participants of original projects in which the knowledge acquired during the course could be put into practice. Each course stage contained strong operational and communication elements: individual work such as reading, planning, etc., alternated with interaction with other participants. The participants who received a positive assessment were those who took an active part in group discussion, handed in a weekly report to their tutor about their progress in the course, undertook the tasks linked to the various stages, and who developed a mini-project on the application of CMC to inservice teacher training.

Evaluation of the course was carried out by ITD in conjunction with an assessment panel appointed by the Ministry of Education's Directorate of Technical Education. Both qualitative and quantitative evaluation were performed. The former was based on observation and classification of the messages exchanged by the course participants, as well as on analysis of the tasks completed at the end of each stage. The latter focused on communication flow and dynamics using socio-metric analysis techniques.

In the third phase of POLARIS the main aim was to put a group of newly-trained tutors to the test by calling on them to design and conduct an online training course. In this way it was possible to evaluate the progress that each individual tutor had made and assess the educational effectiveness of the online tutor course they had taken. To these ends, four of the 10 newly-trained tutors were involved in the design, creation and running of an online course for groups of teachers located throughout Italy. The subject was the use of network communication resources in education and the course was called T&D. In this first actual experience of online education, the tutors were supported by ITD researchers, who offered their expertise in content matters and helped the tutors learn the ropes.

The T&D course was designed entirely online as the tutoring staff and the experts were spread throughout the country, the former located in Genoa, Rome, Modena and Verbania, and the three experts in Genoa and Palermo. The T&D course involved 50 upper-secondary school teachers from all over Italy. The themes covered were familiarity with the major educational applications of telematics and criteria for designing and conducting network-based education activities. The teachers came from 10 different technical schools and were divided into learning groups. The members of each group all belonged to the same class advisory panel. This was dictated by the need to launch small online learning projects of an interdisciplinary nature as a follow-up to the training course.

The goals in the T&D course were:

i) becoming acquainted with the major network tools and services;
ii) using the internet to support educational activities;
iii) design and management of network-based educational activities.

The course was divided into two levels of difficulty to account for variation in the teachers' degree of familiarity with network services.

The first level was of medium-low complexity, ensuring that all participants would attain the minimum required objectives.

The second was aimed at more experienced participants and was organised into a series of specialised workshops so that the various aspects of the course could be examined in greater depth.

The criteria of evaluation was adopted for evaluating the online tutor course were applied to assessment of both the T&D course and its participants. Evaluation was two-tiered: evaluation of the teacher training process, and evaluation of the teachers' ability to transfer knowledge acquired in the online course to the classroom. At the end of the courses, the participants were asked to evaluate their own participation by completing a questionnaire.

The participants identified as more negative were:

i) the workload that was involved in the online training course;

ii) the bulk of messages generated in the various conferences;

iii) the need to work mainly from home;

iv) having to attend a face-to-face meeting halfway through the course;

v) the lack of breathing space between the various stages to allow everyone to reflect and fall back into line with the group.

Participation in POLARIS was considered favourably by most of those involved, even though some parts of the model require revision and improvement.

COLLABORATIVE COURSE DEVELOPMENT

It is an informal context defined as that informal education that goes on student-to-student gathering in hallways and libraries between classes and informally digest and share their learning experiences. Sometimes called community in the distance education/e-learning literature, this format also embraces one-on-one interaction with mentors/instructors and faculty. Traditional faculty office hours fall into this format.

Learning experiences using small group collaborative formats often address development of practical application of abstract ideas. Small study groups working on a team project learn not only cooperative teamwork skills, but the interpersonal structures and goal setting strategies needed for career-oriented work.

Small group collaborative activity may utilise asynchronous tools common to directed study such as e-mail, threaded discussion groups, listserves as well as use of synchronous tools common to instructor led events such as telephone and text chat. Successful incorporation of small group collaborative learning activities both increase the learner's satisfaction with the learning process and can decrease the time required from an instructor in administering and structuring a course or programme.

i) *Awareness*: means a learner is aware of when other members are present online.

iii) *Shared objects capabilities*: Shared objects capabilities enable instructors and learners to view learning content simultaneously.

Collaborative online course development is a model that broadens instructor participation in projects such as work isolation, production of supplemental resources and activities for their classroom or completion of online courses that are limited by their personal technical knowledge and/or available technical support. Collaborative online course development brings together a group of staff with expertise in course content, instructional design, multimedia, graphic arts, and HTML formatting to create a course. The development team creates a centralised community of support to address the large, learning curve for educators starting online course development. The team also lends itself to an active model of faculty professional development, providing faculty with an opportunity to examine the instructional design of their courses while adapting them to an online environment.

The initial changes to facilitate online course development and delivery was the implementation of a collaborative course development model. The workflow process chart outlines the staff roles for adapting existing print-based courses to an online format. The chart represents a linear progression for each step in the process, but also includes spaces for consultations between development staff. The final step for piloting and evaluation is an important one that should be considered part of course development.

Without a means of evaluating a newly developed course with an appropriate student audience, course developers have no real information about the effectiveness of their work In the Learn Online project, we are exploring ways to maximise the benefit of course evaluations, including inserting an opportunity for quick feedback about assignment directions or scope on the assignment page or at the end of each module, as well as an online, end-of-course evaluation form. Moving to a collaborative design model provided instructors with resources to which they had little or no access prior to the project.

The transition requires instructors and development team members to understand their roles in the development process. The role of the instructor is to provide content and to make decisions about how the course is developed online. The role of the development team is to provide development expertise in their respective areas and to guide the instructor. Instructors need to be able to articulate to the other team members their instructional goals and the purpose of the learning and evaluation—activities within the course.

Faculty professional development practices and current course development contract terms influences the shape of the collaborative course development model. Faculty professional development for instructors developing online courses must include:

i) training to use the course software;

ii) education to effectively adapt and design instructional activities for an online environment; and

iii) orientation to the group-design process.

The real challenge for instructors is learning how to implement and adapt learning activities that use the functionality of the courseware to facilitate student learning, communication, and resource sharing. In the collaborative course development model, one of the ways in which these professional development needs are being addressed is through an information web of support staff, including an instructional designer, curriculum specialist, web services librarians, an educational technology facilitator, and other technical staff. This core group of online learning experts contributes a variety of strengths to the course development process.

The model for online professional development is moving away from the short, one-topic training session—although there will always be a need for a concentrated acquisition of knowledge and skills—to an active learning model in which the instructors learn while they are developing online courses. One example of instructional design for an online course is an adaptation of three common correspondence learning activity, which is reading the module and answering review questions.

The self-test feature in many courseware programmes provides a more attractive way for students to check their understanding than flipping to the last page of the module. Instructors can include explanations in the self-test, which the students receive when they select either the right or the wrong answers. By including explanations at a point of learning, instructors can enhance the benefit of this relatively rote learning activity. Another common learning activity used in online courses is exploring relevant websites. In one study, students were overwhelmed by the amount of information available online, and reported spending much more time than anticipated at recommended websites.

A directed paraphrase exercise can be applied to an exploration of online information in which students are asked to summarise in their own words the essential ideas or concepts from the site for a pre-determined audience. This is a skill often used in the fields of public health, law, and social work, in which information synthesis and sharing is often accompanied by advocacy. Collaborative relationship between the instructor and instructional designer provides a peer-mentorship role, fulfilling the need for just-in-time instructional development. The building of this relationship takes time and the instructor's willingness to revise existing course materials and activities. The peer-mentor relationship provides instructors with feedback on their courses at their point of learning; their need to produce the course drives the need to learn about online course design and delivery.

This relationship also provides the opportunity to discuss what course materials should be developed online and the ones that may be better suited to print, video, or other formats. Given the cost of multimedia development, the limitations of the hardware, and the ability of our current Students to successfully access more sophisticated multimedia, such as streaming video, using development time to justify the choice of format for content, learning, and evaluation activities reduces overall development costs.

Incorporation of the work flow process into the current academic calendar year is one important challenges of collaborative course development. One way to meet this challenge is through a revision of instructor course development contracts to include specific terms that facilitate the collaborative course development process. Specific terms include the responsibilities of each member of the course development team, a definition of what constitutes an online course, a description of the course deliverables, and the time frame for each stage of development. A collaborative development process can take more time than one done by an individual instructor particularly if the course involves the development of multimedia elements, such as video clips or simulations.

The need for an instructor's involvement sometimes exceeded the specified term in the course development contract. Course development tends to occur during the summer, making for intense periods of development work for the design team prior to the fall semester. Delays in any part of the work flow process impact the ability of the other team members to complete course development according to original timelines. Deviations from the original contract should be renegotiated and documented so everyone involved in course development understands the consequences of delays for the production of the course.

One of the most important factors for course development decision-making is determining the most appropriate delivery mod, for the students. A well constructed online course is only useful if one's students can access it without having to overcome significant technical, cost, and scheduling barriers, Many instructors are introduced to online teaching by retaining their current delivery mode and supplementing it with some online course activities, such as e-mail communication, web links to online resources, online course syllabi, bulletin board discussions, and by developing one assignment or course module online.

This incremental approach is strengthened by including an evaluation tool to gather student feedback about the benefits and barriers of online course activities. Another way to incrementally incorporate online course development is to build it into courses across a programme of study. Introductory courses can be structured to include introductory online computer skills, such as communicating or submitting assignments by e-mail. Later courses can incorporate discussions or even group projects, once students' online communication skills have been developed. Deciding what computer and internet skills one wants students to have by the end of the programme provides a framework to incorporate online activities into existing or new courses.

REFERENCES

Auter, P. I., Hanna, M. S., 1996, "The Challenge of Developing Online Courses", *Paper presented at the Annual Meeting of the Speech Communication Association*, San Diego, CA, November 23-26, 1996.

Banathy, B. H., *Instructional Systems*, Belmont, CA: Fearon Publications, 1968.

Bichelmeyer, B. A., Kiggins, E.A., "Using Web-based Conferencing in Post-secondary Instruction", *Proceedings of the Annual Conference on Distance Teaching and Learning*, Madison, WI, August 5-7, 1998.

Gilbert, S. W., *Teaching, Learning, and Technology*, Change, 217, 4 6. Guernsey, L., and Young, J. R. 1998, June 5, 1997.

Kirby, E., "Building Interaction in Online and Distance Education Courses", *Paper presented at the Society for Information Technology and Teacher Education International Conference,* 10th, San Antonio, TX, February, 1999.

Regan, K., and Tuchman, S., "The Importance of Authority and Peer Relations on the Educational Process of Onsite and Online Students: An Exploratory Investigation", *Paper presented at the International Conference on Technology and Education,* 7th, Brussels, Belgium, March 20-22, 1990.

Wilson, A., "Instructional Multimedia in the Math Classroom and Beyond", *Paper presented at the Annual Conference of the American Mathematical Association of Two-year Colleges*, Tulsa, OK, November 3-6, 1994.

8

Electronic Lectures

The rapid changes taking place in the field of higher education is the consequences of various types of computer-based information handling technologies. There are a number of scenarios that could be used to describe the future evolution of post-compulsory education in universities and colleges. For example, the benefits of economy of scale could well make the mega-universities an attractive way forward. Such an approach could involve the central distribution of a national curriculum with other universities simply playing a pastoral and tutorial role.

Another possible scenario could involve the large-scale computerisation of existing university campuses in order to accommodate the more effective and efficient use of new technologies. This approach is referred to as 'electronic campus'. A third possibility could see the widespread adoption of 'virtual universities' in which modular course material in electronic form is made available through computer networks.

The history of educational technology is littered with the high hopes and limited success of radio, film, TV, video, teaching machines, stand-alone computers and CD-ROM. If the facilities offered by computer networking and the still developing WWW are to fare better in the educational context than its predecessors, it must be closely integrated with tried and tested conventional teaching methods, and viewed neither as a panacea nor as a bolt-on extra. This point is clearly articulated for computer-assisted learning (CAL) by Tickner who suggests: "The most important factor in the successful implementation and student uptake of CAL in higher education is thorough, planned and supported integration with more traditional teaching media". It is flawed to think that if the delivery mechanism for information is correctly designed then people will team.

Using the computer as an interactive multimedia training delivery medium is an exciting possibility that has been promised for a long time. With the arrival of internet authoring tools, "streaming" and "push" technologies, and various internet plug-ins for playing multimedia, many are asking themselves if the CD-ROM, and other more traditional methods of delivering multimedia, are not now becoming obsolete.

The internet is being used now more than ever as a means of disseminating information and facilitating learning. While it once consisted uniquely of text-only web "pages", the internet now offers sound, video, and animation. It is now possible to send multimedia over the internet, it is far from practical. The reality is that piping multimedia courseware over the internet is like, as Rakow put it, "trying to shove a golf ball through a garden hose." This is because the big files—graphics, audio, and video—still take significant amounts of time to download. When employees are required to wait for information to download to their computer, a "just in time" training course can quickly become a waste of time. The internet is being used increasingly as a means of distributing information. If the information includes text and/or small graphics, it can be successfully delivered over the internet.

Company intranets are basically smaller versions of the internet, used for distributing information within a given company. Like the internet, the use of a company intranet for distributing multimedia is limited by the capacity of the server, the infrastructure, and the number of users. Depending on these factors, users may or may not have to spend considerable amounts of time waiting for multimedia files to download.

The CD-ROM remains one of the most common ways of delivering multimedia training, largely because CDs have the capacity to store large multimedia files. Depending on the speed of the PC processor, the amount of RAM, and the speed of the CD-ROM drive, users running a course from a CD-ROM will not have their training interrupted by downloading media, nor will they have media "break up" during delivery. The down side of using CD-ROM as a delivery medium is the fact that if updates need to be made to a course, a new CD must be burned and given to each user.

Multimedia courses typically run the best from a PC hard drive. That is, graphics come up quickly, and audio and video play smoothly. The only real question is one of storage space. Since one can write to a hard drive again and again, courses residing there can be updated as often as needed. In addition, if the PCs are connected to a local area network (LAN) or wide area network (WAN), course updates can be downloaded from a central location.

Most company local area networks (LANs) and wide area networks (WANs) are not equipped to store and deliver multimedia—again, because of bandwidth limitations. If a company already has, or is willing to invest in, a high-speed LAN, it is possible to deliver multimedia over a network. This is, at least for the next couple years, an expensive way to go.

There are many hybrids strategies that are in use today. One of the most common is the one in which the course is run from individual workstations and student enrolment and performance data is communicated across the network. In this scenario, audio and video run smoothly, and, for courses running from the hard drive, updates come from a central location on the server. The hybrid solution is an attractive option to many because they can get both updatability, together with the appeal of high-impact graphics, audio, and video.

One of the most common reasons companies choose interactive multimedia in the first place is because it can make training more accessible to learners than does classroom training. For example, a CD-ROM can be taken anywhere a user has access to a multimedia-capable PC with a CD-ROM drive. Likewise, a user can log in to an internet, intranet, or LAN-based course, anywhere they have access to the internet, intranet, or LAN. On the other hand, if they cannot get to the internet, an internet-based course is not going to work. Nor will a CD-ROM based course work for those with no CD drives in their computers. Of course, hardware and infrastructure can be installed, but such installations usually impact time-line, budget, or both.

COMPUTER-ASSISTED LEARNING (CAL)

Information technology (IT) in teaching and learning started out as computer-assisted learning (CAL), during 1960s. How to create and develop IT resources for teaching and learning is beyond its scope to consider how to create pages for the World Wide Web (WWW), write a piece of tutorial courseware, or set up a moderated discussion list or videoconference. Creation of resources had become a little less difficult, but it still required technical specialists to produce materials.

By the 1980s, applications were broadening out in range and variety, a change which again reflected the underlying change in technology away from centralised mainframe computers; 1981 was the year in which the personal computer was launched. The ways in which applications could be created were becoming more accessible to non-specialists, through the use of specialised but accessible programming using authoring languages.

However, the creation and use of computer-based materials in learning and teaching was still restricted to a small specialist group of enthusiastic academics. An important aspect of effective use and integration of technology is the way in which it effectively reflects and articulates a given learning model.

At the same time as technology has moved forward, the dominant models of learning have changed from behaviourist, through objectivist, to constructivist. In the constructivist model the learner, in acts of understanding, constructs knowledge.

It is constructive to consider the use of IT in terms of the way it can affect conventional teaching situations. It is essential that practitioners build their use of IT upon the foundation of good teaching methods which have already been established.

Many new academics will have basic familiarity with IT, but this will vary according to discipline. If the range of skills is not great, then it will be worthwhile spending a small amount of time acquiring those IT skills that seem most relevant. Familiarity will provide a confident starting point from which it is possible to imagine potential gains, such as ways in which using IT in teaching could make the learning better for the students, or could enable more effective use of time. It is possible to use IT in teaching and learning in a whole range of ways:

i) accessing electronic journals;
ii) computer-generated presentations to accompany lectures;
iii) electronic publication of lecture notes;
iv) research using the web or CD-ROM;
v) running electronic discussion groups with your learners;
vi) setting computer-based bibliographic searches;
vii) setting worked examples making use of tools such as spreadsheets or databases;
viii) using computer-based learning programmes;
ix) using e-mail communications for class management;
x) using real current databases to retrieve information;

xi) videoconferencing with other students overseas; and

xii) word-processed lecture notes.

Let us consider the ways in which learning resources may be tailored to accommodate differing teaching methods and learning styles. One particularly useful way to view the learner's experience of technology is from the perspective of the levels of interactivity that it enables.

IT may be concerned solely with content (presenting information in text or graphics). Such uses are often the first things that are generated by technology, for example, word-processed lecture notes, producing computer-generated slides and presentations, creating reference materials which are accessible via the web or from CD-ROM. These types of uses have advantages such as being easy to maintain and update from year to year, and may not add significantly to the ordinary workload and are by now relatively commonplace.

Constructed interactions are a key component of classic computer-assisted learning that provides a learning environment which offers the learner structured introductions and interactions as a means of explaining and enabling understanding of particular sets of knowledge and the underlying concepts. It should be noted that producing such applications to high quality is time consuming and expensive.

A more sophisticated and complex worldview is provided for the learner when information is presented and accessed via a mathematical or graphical modelling programme, simulations or role play. Ready-made programmes have an advantage in that they are less prone to crashing. Small-scale simulations are sometimes integrated into CAL programmes or tutorials that guide learners through a set of learning pathways and offer a more constrained version of such interactions. In either case the necessary groundwork can be time-consuming.

Computers and networks must be powerful enough to let the programmes run satisfactorily, and they may require on hand technical support, or demonstrators to assist learners if they encounter problems while using the programmes. Programmes that enable learners to produce new resources by using computer-based tools can provide the next layer of interactivity. Simple examples include learners working individually to produce their own hypertext for the World Wide Web.

For example, music students at the University of Southampton have produced pages which describe and discuss the products of their research into composers. In such instances, the programme acts as an integrator, providing the framework within which to assemble, organise and reflect upon content knowledge through the use of real-world IT skills. In face-to-face formats this is often in the form of tutorial or seminar discussions.

With a computer as a facilitator the dialogue can be introduced in a number of different ways. At its most closed form this is as feedback or pre-programmed discussion of an interactive tutorial system. Such programmes require considerable skills to assemble, and require a large number of development hours for a very small number of teaching hours. However, the more recent alternative, and less development-intense form of interactivity, has been achieved through the use of computer-mediated communications. Here the learner communicates with the tutor, or other learners, either via some form of e-mail, structured bulletin board discussion, or through a live 'chat room' style discussion. Such applications are sometimes introduced to keep in contact with learners who are on placement, or work experience, but are also relevant in traditional university teaching, offering an additional means of achieving small group teaching. Tutors who work in an online environment may need to acquire moderating skills if they are to make the best use of this resource.

Another automated closed style of discussion is enabled by electronic access to frequently asked questions (FAQs) in the style of an 'Answer Garden'. Answers are planted to be picked as needed, and new answers are added to the garden as they are needed to grow organisational knowledge. A closed discussion is again less open than unconstrained participation in a wider (internet) electronic discussion group. However, all are predominantly at the highly interactive end of the gradient, providing the learner with the opportunity to process, reflect upon, and interact with information rather than try to simply 'learn' presented knowledge.

Information technology in teaching and learning is most valuable when it is integrated with other approaches and when it is used to mediate learning. The need to evaluate the impact of information technology interventions has been emphasised, as has the importance of creating/using materials that will promote deep learning. Higher education is bound to go for the unavoidable shift from the culture of print to a culture of digital technology, which affects not only teaching, learning and research; but the whole of university life. IT has arrived with a big bang. We have to find but its implications for our universities and colleges.

The very nature of teaching, learning and research has to depend also on electronic data, over and above the print material. Conduct of research now requires cooperative resource sharing and networking of local, national and global resources. Universities and colleges shall have to share the resources and change their nature of dependirg exclusively on their own limited resources. Cost containment through regional approach is the only solution. Our universities have to develop new paradigms of teaching, learning, research and management of learning resources.

Inter-university structures and organisations will have to emerge in various regions for resource sharing with the help of IT and inter-university committees for resource sharing, within about 500 km. IT has influenced in depth all components of higher education and research. University administration in India has to go for IT on regional basis. INFLIBNET, as inverted pyramid was bound to fail because it was a design of national structure without regional foundation in a large country like India, although INFLIBNET has now become a part of the University Grants Commission. Out of the regional networking only DELNET has shown worthwhile growth and success. CALIBNET, BOMNET and efforts in South India are suffering from serious teething troubles during their infancy. A faculty member and a researcher have a different *modus operandi* for learning and research in their areas. In addition to the print material they generally have:

i) an e-mail address of the library or the department, if not a personal one;

ii) connection with on line-e-print archive, dealing with ongoing research in their respective areas, with access to World Wide Web and other databases on the Internet. Users can get daily listing of research titles and the abstracts; hepth archive, Rossetti archive, GSS guide are some such services;

iii) access to data transmission lines, terminal and laser printers;

iv) access to desktop machine and data libraries;

v) access to electronic library as a gateway to global knowledge;

vi) access to global reference room via internet; and

vii) a access to electronic journals and books.

In teaching techniques, there is a lesser emphasis today on the erudition and intellectual impact, as such, and more emphasis on the very process of search for objective knowledge with a spirit of inquiry by the learner. The Gutenburg revolution, five centuries ago, shifted oral method of teaching to self study by individual student.

Now, IT and multimedia have changed the pattern of teaching where the learner uses technology, through critical thinking, to manipulate and query data in newer ways instead of just lecturing and/or reading activity. In this IT era, we have moved from old practice of memorising facts to discovering data and information; and synthesising them for problem solving. Learning is understanding of concepts, as against memorisation alone for examinations. It is problem solving. Learning should enable one to use what one has learned. Learning requires active involvement of the learner in learning processes as against passively observing the information. Elements of learning cover reading, thinking, analysing, deduction, meditation, writing work and discussion, etc.

Learning requires discovery of relevant information through navigational techniques out of various sources-print and non-print material. Hypertest and hyper media assist in linking the sources of learning, if proper navigation is done. Research today is understanding of ideas, activity and text, by evaluating their context or frame of reference. In research, there is greater emphasis on general theories and on novelty. It is often focused on the present or recent past.

Expressions of everyday life in a society or region have got emphasis in modern research. Technology makes research more convenient and efficient. It connects and helps in synthesising disparate bits of information. For research it is essential to use information in print as well as electronic information. Both are available in various sources crossing the boundaries of a specific library. There has to be a cooperative arrangement in providing for information needs of researchers and learners. Research today, in many areas, touches or covers almost all disciplines. Modern research requires navigational tools and filtering of information electronically and professionally, by generating tools and by developing filters. Packaging and dissemination of print and electronic information has to be done by a modem librarian.

Finding out of relevant information in the internet depends on the structure of the software, which in turn stands on the five facets, viz., queries, filters, spatial navigation, links and agents. A software works in these five stages to pinpoint a user's specific subject for providing information. These stages provide editorial services for identifying a user's need. These steps also minimise garbage or noise.

E-LECTURES

Knowledge is not information but an emergent property—knowledge is a dynamic process, a vibrant, living thing, resting on shared assumptions, beliefs, complex perceptions and the ability to 'go beyond the information given'. In higher education the aim must be to develop students' critical faculties, understanding and independence of thought, and this implies much more than simply employing an alternative medium for the distribution of teaching materials. Any teaching approach must match the needs and capabilities of a particular category of students and the course content.

The students involved in the work reported here were final year undergraduate students, who had completed two taught years on a BSc in computing and information systems and one year on industrial placement. The students were accustomed to accessing files over a Novell network, and most were familiar with the WWW, though not all had used file transfer protocol (ftp). The module involved was on Human-Computer Interaction, in which students can benefit greatly from exposure to a wide range of user interfaces. It also has a higher visual component than most other topics in computing.

In the hierarchy of the cognitive domain, lectures are appropriate for conveying 'surface' learning, in the form of knowledge, manipulation and application. This is essentially knowledge which can be made objective, formal and explicit and directly accessible. For 'deep' learning, where the student applies analysis, attempts synthesis of concepts and evaluates what has been done, largely subjective and tacit knowledge is involved and this comes through experience and dialogue, and therefore is supported best in tutorials, practicals and other forms of group work.

There are various categorisations of learning styles. Some students like to have information presented in a step-by-step, cumulative, sequential manner that develops the concept. Others learn best when they are first presented with the general concept and then the details. Some prefer to work cooperatively while others prefer independence. There is also some evidence that female students have a marked preference for face-to-face communication. Although it may not be possible to accommodate everyone's style of learning, the provision of a variety of course materials will go some way to enabling individuals to employ their own preferred learning style. Development of electronic teaching resources is relatively recent, and the rate of technological change so rapid that there is little theory and limited practical experience to build on.

One recent attempt by Mayes presents a high level model of the learning cycle which provides useful theoretical perspectives and guiding principles. Information presentation starts the conceptualisation phase. Subsequently, concepts are iteratively refined, understood and internalised by action—applying the knowledge in performing meaningful tasks, such as in practicals, assignments or projects. Mayes argues strongly that "Dialogue is fundamental to education. It is, of course, possible to learn without discussion, but the need to support deep learning through tutorial and peer-group dialogue is paramount".

The lecture is an efficient and cost-effective way of communicating knowledge, but on its own it promotes surface learning and does not provide the appropriate context for deep learning. This form of provision may also tend to promote relatively passive learning strategies focused on memorisation and inhibiting the development of decision-making skills. The most conventional forms of dialogue in higher education include one-to-one discussion, tutorials, seminars, peer group working and written feedback on assignments. Indeed, it has been claimed that appropriate assessment and feedback are the most effective differentiator between the best and worst courses.

Students need to be able to ask questions to correct misconceptions. It is important to get them working together, to share insights and identify common confusions. Presenting students with information in some form and through some medium, while a necessary step, is by no means sufficient to define an effective teaching and learning strategy. Viewed from this perspective, learning is a by-product of understanding, where understanding occurs best through performing tasks, and reflecting on them alone and with others.

The live lecture is not only highly effective for explaining concepts, but can also motivate and convey enthusiasm, and with it an appreciation of the value of the subject, set learning goals, add humour and asides, provide a developing overview of information, point to resources, keep students to at least a minimal reading and practical schedule and provide a social setting. So the lecture has many advantages, and, of course, represents no additional costs to the educational institution.

The university, in electronic form, will no longer be either the locus of learning nor the determining agent of what will be learned and when. Some of the advantages of a virtual university over a conventional one are: it overcomes the main constraints of time and space, it will support learning-on-demand with the additional benefits of continual student monitoring and rapid student feedback.

The future of the universities in the digital age will depend critically upon the more widespread provision of open learning.

Possible successful strategies for the effective use of technology in higher education will depend upon the realisation of 'community and conversational paradigms'. This approach is a valuable one since it lies deeply rooted in the underlying theory of constructivist learning environments. The logistics underlying the development and functions of a virtual university are critically dependent upon the future availability of an appropriate and all-pervasive information super highway.

There are four necessary building blocks that are needed for the realisation of a virtual university system for the provision of education on demand, namely, one or more electronic libraries; various types of virtual laboratory and studio (for the teaching of science, engineering and arts subjects); collections of online (or electronic) lectures; and mechanisms to support tele-teaching (tutoring and/or mediated face-to-face teaching). The nature and purpose of digital electronic libraries, the use of tele-teaching techniques and the realisation of virtual laboratory systems are each discussed in detail elsewhere.

There are three basic ways in which the introduction of computers into lecture theatres can be used to enhance learning:

i) by providing an environment in which various principles, ideas and techniques can be demonstrated 'live' to the audience.
ii) by providing a live window on the outside world.
iii) by providing tools that enable the quality of live lectures to be improved.

An electronic lecture is one which has been prepared using a computer-based presentation package and which is subsequently delivered in a lecture theatre by a human presenter using appropriate computer-based projection equipment. One of the major advantages of using electronic lectures is the fact that they are easy to share and distribute using computer-based communication networks. This means that they can be used as a resource to support distance and open learning. They can also be used as private, self-study resources by students—either as a substitute for, or to augment, live lectures. However, when used in this way it is important to consider how these basic resources should best be augmented using additional text, audio and graphical materials in order to maximise their usability.

A variety of different ways of implementing electronic lectures currently exist. Benest, for example, uses an 'electronic book' emulator in order to create and deliver his online lectures. On the other hand, Anderson uses Microsoft's PowerPoint within a Windows environment running on an IBM compatible personal computer (PC) system while Busbridge uses this package running in an Apple Macintosh environment. In our own work we have been exploring three different approaches. These involve:

i) the use of an in-house presentation package running on both stand-alone and networked PC systems;
ii) the use of PowerPoint; and
iii) the use of HTML and Netscape running on a distributed UNIX environment that constitutes a departmental intranet facility.

The case with which the online lecture material can be integrated with other electronic resources in order to provide a seamless environment for the support of teaching and learning activities is an attractive feature of the intranet approach. An important feature of the system that we have implemented is the automated online self-assessment testing that students can undertake as and when they feel the need.

Lectures perform a useful and important pedagogic function within the teaching/learning activities that take place within academic institutions. However there is a case for the more widespread deployment of electronic lectures. The four basic perspectives should be considered are

i) institutional infrastructures;
ii) student and staff attitudes;
iii) pedagogic issues; and
iv) resource accessibility.

Institutional infrastructures: In this perspective, many academic organisations have committed significant financial resources for the development of new lecture theatres. These lecture theatres are 'kitted out' with state-of-the-art teaching equipment such as computers, high resolution projection equipment and connections to various types of telecommunications equipment. Of course, these are the very components needed to support the delivery of electronic lectures to large groups of students. As well as financing the development of new high technology lecture theatres, many organisations are actively involved in refurbishing older teaching rooms with the types of equipment needed to present electronic lectures.

Student and staff attitudes: Most students and staffs expressed considerable support for the use of lectures as a teaching vehicle. The use of electronic methods represented a significant improvement over conventional presentation techniques. Significant improvements were achieved in terms of the overall quality of presentation, the content of the lectures themselves and the ease with which they could subsequently be accessed for the support of self-study activities.

Pedagogic issues: Lectures provide a useful narrative structure that facilitates guided navigation through a given corpus of knowledge. Such structures thus enable students to piece together the various elements of a subject in an efficient and effective way. Naturally, by following up lecture material, it is possible for students to develop rich mental models of their study domains. The use of electronic presentation packages can have a dramatic impact on the format and structure of lectures and the effects that they, in turn, have on students.

Resource accessibility: Three of the most attractive features of electronic lectures are:

i) the ease with which they can be updated and maintained;

ii) the ease with which they can be shared and/or disseminated to others; and

iii) the significant potential that they offer for the creation of self-study resources.

These resources can act as a powerful basis for the development and active promotion of both distance and open learning activities.

REFERENCES

Anderson, D. T., Garrison, D.R., 1995, "Transactional Issues in Distance Education: The Impact of Design in Audioconferencing", *American Journal of Distance Education*, 9, 2, pp. 27-45.

Albrecht, R., Bardsley, G., 1994, *Strategic Planning and Academic Planning for Distance Education*, in B. D. Willis (ed.), *Distance Education: Strategies and Tools,* (pp. 67-85). Englewood Cliffs: Educational Technology Publications.

Bichelmeyer, B. A., Kiggins, E.A., 1998, "Using Web-based Conferencing in Post-secondary Instruction", *Proceedings of the Annual Conference on Distance Teaching and Learning*, Madison, WI, August 5-7, 1998.

Burow-Flake, E., Kocher, D., Reiser, A., 2000, *Changing Students, Changing Classroom Landscapes: Meeting the Challenge in the Small Liberal Arts Institution,* in L. Lloyd (ed.), *Teaching with Technology, Rethinking Tradition,* Medford, NJ: Information Today, Inc.

Cohen, J. A., Castner, M. H., 2000, *Technology and Classroom Design: A Faculty Perspective*, in L. Lloyd (ed.), *Teaching with Technology, Rethinking Tradition*, Medford, NJ: Information Today, Inc.

Forsyth, I., 1998, *Teaching and Learning Materials and the Internet* (2nd ed.), London: Kogan Page.

Gilbert, S. W., 1997, *Teaching, Learning, and Technology*, Change, 217, 4 6. Guernsey, L., and Young, J. R. 1998, June 5.

Kelch, P. E., Karr-Kidwell, P. J., 2000, *How Computer Technology Expands Educational Options: A Rationale, Recommendations and a Pamphlet for Administrators*, ERIC Document Reproduction Service, no. 439 668.

Bibliography

Albrecht, R., Bardsley, G., 1994, *Strategic Planning and Academic Planning for Distance Education*, in B. D. Willis (ed.), *Distance Education: Strategies and Tools,* (pp. 67-85). Englewood Cliffs: Educational Technology Publications.

Anderson, A H, Newlands, A, Mullin, J, Heming, A. M., Doherty-Sneddon, G and Van der Velden, J., 1996, "Impact of Video-mediated Communication on Simulated Service Encounters", *Interacting With Computers*, 8, 2, pp.193-206.

Anderson, D. T., Garrison, D.R., 1995, "Transactional Issues in Distance Education: The Impact of Design in Audio-conferencing", *American Journal of Distance Education*, 9, 2, pp. 27-45.

Auter, P. I., Hanna, M. S., 1996, "The Challenge of Developing Online Courses", *Paper presented at the Annual Meeting of the Speech Communication Association*, San Diego, CA, November 23-26, 1996.

Banathy, B. H., 1968, *Instructional Systems*, Belmont, CA: Fearon Publications.

Bauer, J. W., and Rezabek, L. L., 1993, *Effects of Two-way Visual Contact on Verbal Interaction during Face-to-Face and Teleconferenced Instruction*, In *Art, Science, and Visual Literacy: Selected Readings from the Annual Conference of the International Visual Literacy Association*, 24th, Pittsburgh, PA, September 30-October 4, 1992.

Bengu G. and W. Swart, A., 1996, "Computer-Aided Total Quality Approach to Manufacturing Education in Engineering", *IEEE Transactions on Education*, 39:3, pp. 415-427, 1996.

Berge Z. L., 1999, "Interaction in Post-secondary Web-based Learning", *Educational Technology*, 39(1), pp. 5-11.

Betts, M., 1994, "States Bypassing Feds on Information Highways," *Computerworld*, June 20, 1994.

Bichelmeyer, B. A., Kiggins, E.A.,. 1998, "Using Web-based Conferencing in Post-secondary Instruction", *Proceedings of the Annual Conference on Distance Teaching and Learning*, Madison, WI, August 5-7, 1998.

Brown, J. S., Duguid, P., 2000, *Learning-in Theory and in Practice*, In J. S. Brown, P. Duguid (eds.), *The Social Life of Information*, Cambridge, MA: Harvard Business School Press.

Brundage, D., Keane, R., and Mackneson, R., 1993, "Application of Learning Theory to the Instruction of Adults", In Thelma Barer-Stein and James A. Draper (eds.), *The Craft of Teaching Adults*, Toronto, Ontario: Culture Concepts, pp. 131-144.

Burge, E., 1993, "Adult Distance Learning: Challenges for Contemporary Practice", In Thelma Barer-Stein and James A. Draper (eds.), *The Craft of Teaching Adults*, Toronto, Ontario: Culture Concepts, pp. 131-144.

Burow-Flake, E., Kocher, D., Reiser, A., 2000, *Changing Students, Changing Classroom Landscapes: Meeting the Challenge in the Small Liberal Arts Institution,* in L. Lloyd (ed.), *Teaching with Technology, Rethinking Tradition,* Medford, NJ: Information Today, Inc.

Cohen, J. A., Castner, M. H., 2000, *Technology and Classroom Design: A Faculty Perspective*, in L. Lloyd (ed.), *Teaching with Technology, Rethinking Tradition*, Medford, NJ: Information Today, Inc.

Comeaux, P., 1995, "The Impact of an Interactive Distance Learning Network on Classroom Communication", *Communication Education*, 41(4), pp. 353-361.

Dalton, D. W., 1990, "The Effect of Cooperative Learning Strategies on Achievement and Attitudes during Interactive Video, *Journal of Computer-Based Instruction*, 17(1).

Dick, W., and Carey, L., 1990, *The Systematic Design of Instruction* (3rd ed.), Glenview, IL: Scott, Foresman, and Company.

Duhaney, D., 2000, Technology and the Educational Process: Transforming Classroom Activities, *International Journal of Instructional Media*, 27(1), pp.67-72.

Duffy, T., Jonassen, D., (eds.), 1992, *Constructivism and the Technology of Instruction: A Conversation*, Hillsdale, N., Lawrence Erlbaum Associates.

Forsyth, I., 1998, *Teaching and Learning Materials and the Internet* (2nd ed.), London: Kogan Page.

Galbreath, J., 1995, "Compressed Digital Videoconferencing", *Educational Technology*, 35(1), pp. 31-38.

Galusha, J. M., 1998, *Barriers to Learning in Distance Education, Interpersonal Computing and Technology*, 5(3-4), pp. 6-14.

Gagne, R. M. and Briggs L. J., 1979, *Principles of Instructional Design*, Holt, Rinehart and Winston, New York.

Garrison, D. R., 1990, "An Analysis and Evaluation of Audio Teleconferencing to Facilitate Education at a Distance", *The American journal of Distance Education*, 4, pp. 13-24.

Gilbert, S. W., 1997, *Teaching, Learning, and Technology*, Change, 217, 4 6. Guernsey, L., and Young, J. R. 1998, June 5.

Graham, S.W., and Wedman, J.F., 1989, "Enhancing the Appeal of Teletraining", *Journal of Instructional Psychology*, 16(4), 183-191.

Heamshaw, D., 1998, "Capitalising on the Strengths and Availability of Desktop Videoconferencing, *Active Learning*, 7, pp. 52-9.

Hearn G. and Mandeville T., 'The Electronic Superhighway: Increased Commodification or the Democratisation of Leisure?' *Media Information* Australia no. 75, 1995.

Henri, F., 1992, "Computer Conferencing and Content Analysis", In Kaye, A.R (ed.), *Collaborative Learning through Computer Conferencing*, Springer-Verlag, pp.117.

Ho, M. S., 1996, *Learning and Teaching in Cyberspace: An Empirical Investigation of Computer-assisted Instruction for Geography*, Academic exercise, Dept. of Geography, Faculty of Arts and Social Sciences, National University of Singapore.

Howell-Richardson, C., Mellar, H., 1996, "A Methodology for the Analysis of Patterns of Participation within Computer Communications Courses", *Instructional Science*, 24, 1, pp. 47-69.

Huges, K., 1994, *Entering the World Wide Web: A Guide to Cyberspace*, Enterprise Integration Technologies.

Jansen, D. G., and Lewis, W. B., 1996, "Creating High-levels of Interaction in Distance Education Courses", *ATEA Journal*, 24(1), pp.8-9.

Johnson, D. W., 1981, "Student-Student Interaction: The Neglected Variable in Education", *Educational Researcher*, 10(1), pp. 5-10.

Jones S., 1995, 'Understanding Community in the Information Age' Cybersociety; Computer-Mediated Communication and Community, S.G. Jones (ed) Thousand Oaks CA.: Sage.

Kearsley, G., 1995, "The Nature and Value of Interaction in Distance Learning, In M. Koble (ed.), *The American Centre for the Study of Distance Education Invitational Research Conferencing Distance Education: Toward Excellence in Distance Education*, University Park, PA: Penn State University.

Kerr, E. Hiltz, S., *Computer-Based Instruction*, 17(1), 1982.

Kochmer, J., 1995, *Internet Passport: Northwestnet's Guide to Our World Online*, Bellevue, WA: NorthWestNet and Northwest Academic Computing Consortium, Inc. (http://info.nwnet.net/passport).

Kirby, E., 1999, "Building Interaction in Online and Distance Education Courses", *Paper presented at the Society for Information Technology and Teacher Education International Conference*, 10th, San Antonio, TX, February, 1999.

Lochte, R.H., *Interactive Television and Instruction*, Englewood Cliffs, NJ: Educational Technology Publications, 1993.

Maddox, C. C., 1997, *The World Wide Web and School Culture: Are they Compatible*?, in D. L. Johnson, C. D. Maddux, and L. Lieu, (eds.), *Using Technology in the Classroom*, New York: The Haworth Press.

Martin, B. L., "Using Distance Education to Teach Instructional Design to Preservice Teachers", *Educational Technology*, Vol. XXXIV, No. 3, March 1994.

McHenry, L., and Bozik, M., 1995, "Communicating at a Distance: A Study of Interaction in a Distance Education Classroom", *Communication Education*, 44(4), pp. 362-371.

Misanchuk, E R., 1992, *Preparing Instructional Text: Document Design using Desktop Publishing*, Englewood Cliffs, NJ: Educational Technology Publications.

——————., 1994, "Print Tools in Distance Education", In B. Willis (ed.), *Distance Education: Strategies and Tools*, Englewood Cliffs, NJ: Educational Technology Publications, pp.109-129.

Moore, M.G., Thompson, M.M., with Quigley, A.B., Clark, G.C., and Goff, G.G., 1990, "The Effects of Distance Learning: A Summary of the Literature", *Research Monograph* no. 2. University Park, PA: The Pennsylvania State University, American Center for the Study of Distance Education.

Morgan, A., 1991, *Research into Student Learning in Distance Education*, Victoria, Australia: University of South Australia, Underdale.

Paterson K. G. "Student Perceptions of Internet-Based Learning Tools in Environment Engineering Education", *Journal of Engineering Education*, 88:3, pp. 295-304, 1999.

Phye, G., 2000, "Engaging Technology and Learning Opportunities: Technology Assessment Tools", *Paper presented at the Annual Meeting of the American Educational Research Association*, New Orleans.

Pisapia, J., Coukos, E., Knutson, K., 2000, "The Impact of Computer on Teacher Capacity, Attitudes, and Behaviours in Elementary Schools", *Paper presented at the Annual Meeting of the American Educational Research Association*, New Orleans.

Regan, K., and Tuchman, S., 1990, "The Importance of Authority and Peer Relations on the Educational Process of Onsite and Online Students: An Exploratory Investigation", *Paper presented at the International Conference on Technology and Education,* 7th, Brussels, Belgium, March 20-22, 1990.

Roberts, L., 1996, *A Transformation of Learning: Use of the NII for Education and Lifelong Learning*, In D. P. Ely & B. B. Minor (eds.), *Educational Media and Technology Yearbook 1995/1996*, pp. 50-66, Englewood, CO: Libraries Unlimited.

Schuemer, R., 1993, *Some Psychological Aspects of Distance Education*, Hagen, Germany: Institute for Research into Distance Education.

Stenerson, F., 1998, "Systems Analysis and Design for a Successful Distance Education Programme Implementation", *Journal of Distance Learning Administration*.

Tapscott, D., 1998, *Growing up Digital: The Rise of the Net Generation*. New York: McGraw-Hill Book Company.

Verduin, J.R., Clark, T.A., 1991, *Distance Education: The Foundations of Effective Practice*, San Francisco, CA: Jossey-Bass Publishers.

Velayo, R. S., "Supplementary Classroom Instruction via Computer Conferencing", *Educational Technology*, 1994.

Whitelock D. and Scanlon E., 1996, "Motivation, Media and Motion: Reviewing a Computer Supported Collaborative Learning Experience, In *Proceedings of the European Conference on Artificial Intelligence in Education*, P. Brna, a. Paiva and J. Self (eds)., Euro AIED, Lisbon, 1996.

Williams, M., and Paprock, K., 1994, "Instructional Design in Distance Education", *The ED Journal*, 7(4), 1994.

Willis, B., 1993, *Distance Education: A Practical Guide*, Englewood Cliffs, NJ: Educational Technology Publications.

Wilson, A., 1994, "Instructional Multimedia in the Math Classroom and Beyond", *Paper presented at the Annual Conference of the American Mathematical Association of Two-year Colleges*, Tulsa, OK, November 3-6, 1994.

Yucha, C. 8., 1996, Interactive Distance Education: Improvisation helps Bridge the Gap, *Journal of Biocommunication*, 23(1), pp. 2-5.

Zhang, S., and Fulford, C., 1994, "Are Interaction Time and Psychological Interactivity the Something in the Distance Learning Television Classroom?" *Educational Technology*, 34(6), pp. 58-64.

Index